BASIC PRINCIPLES OF PROPERTY LAW

Recent Titles in Contributions in Legal Studies

Law and the Great Plains: Essays on the Legal History of the Heartland
John R. Wunder, editor

Judicial Entrepreneurship: The Role of the Judge in the Marketplace of Ideas
Wayne V. McIntosh and Cynthia L. Cates

Solving the Puzzle of Interest Group Litigation
Andrew Jay Koshner

Presidential Defiance of "Unconstitutional" Laws: Reviving the Royal Prerogative
Christopher N. May

Promises on Prior Obligations at Common Law
Kevin M. Teeven

Litigating Federalism: The States Before the U.S. Supreme Court
Eric N. Waltenburg and Bill Swinford

Law and the Arts
Susan Tiefenbrun, editor

Contract Law and Morality
Henry Mather

The Appearance of Equality: Racial Gerrymandering, Redistricting, and the Supreme Court
Christopher M. Burke

Religion, Law, and the Land
Brian Edward Brown

The Supreme Court's Retreat from Reconstruction: A Distortion of Constitutional Jurisprudence
Frank J. Scaturro

Respecting State Courts: The Inevitability of Judicial Federalism
Michael E. Solimine and James L. Walker

BASIC PRINCIPLES OF PROPERTY LAW

A Comparative Legal and Economic Introduction

Ugo Mattei

Contributions in Legal Studies, Number 93

GREENWOOD PRESS
Westport, Connecticut • London

Contents

Preface **xi**

1 **History** **1**

Avoiding Tragedies 1
Property Law: An Historically Contingent Aggregate of Formal and Informal Constraints 3
Common Law 7
Civil Law 13
Dissimilar Form and Similar Substance? 18
Notes 21

2 **Sources** **29**

Constitutional Law 29
Codes and Common Law Principles 37
Special Statutes 39
Lower Regulation 41
Machinery of Justice 44
Notes 46

3 **Economic Analysis** **51**

Efficiency as a Legal Principle 51
Efficiency as Waste Prevention 53
Property Law: Default and Mandatory Rules 54

Judicial Interpretation and Private Bargaining 55
Minimizing the Costs of Failures in Negotiation 56
Property Rights and Internalization of Social Costs 58
Collective and Decentralized Systems to Avoid Externalities 60
Property Rules and Liability Rules 62
Efficiency and Security of Property Rights 65
Clear Social Signaling in Movable and Immovable Property 66
Efficiency and the Nature of Property 68
Notes 71

4 The Object of Property Rights **75**

Taxonomy 75
Immovable Property 83
Movable Property 86
The Legal Regime of Property Rights Other Than Ownership 91
Public Law Ownership 93
Notes 94

5 Transfer of Ownership **99**

A Complex Legal Problem 99
Voluntary and Involuntary Transfers *Mortis Causa* (after Death) 100
Voluntary *Inter Vivos* Transfers of Immovables 102
Transfers of Movables 105
Involuntary Transfers of Immovable Property 109
Riparian Property Rights 117
Notes 118

6 The Power to Use Ownership **123**

Ownership as an Aggregate of Positive and
Negative Characteristics 123
Power in General 124
The Power to Fence the Land 127
The Power to Use the Subsoil 128
The Power to Use Water 130
The Power to Plant and Acquire Fruits 132
The Power over Buildings (*Superficies Solo Caedit*) 134
The Power over Borders 137
Notes 142

7 Negative Aspects of Ownership: Limits and Liabilities **147**

In General 147
The General Ban on Abuse of Property Rights 149

Rules and Standards to Limit Property Rights 149
Limits to the Power to Build 150
Limits to Property Rights Due to Incompatible Uses in General 153
Minimal Distances and Other ex Ante Rules 154
Ex Post Standards: Reasonable Use 156
Emissions 157
Incompatible Uses: Some Economic Analysis and a Theoretical Framework 158
The Relative Nature of Emissions 160
First Come, First Served: Coming to the Nuisance 161
Industrial Emissions 163
Other Limits in the Interest of Neighbors 164
General Liabilities 165
Taxes 166
Notes 168

8 Remedies **171**

General Background 172
Possessory and Proprietary Remedies 173
Forward-Looking and Backward-Looking Remedies 175
Protection of Title and Protection of Enjoyment 176
Effectiveness of Remedies 178
Property Rule 181
Damages 187
Notes 189

9 Loss of Ownership **193**

The Nature of Expropriation 193
Legal and Economic Principles 195
Informal Taking and Regulation 197
Public Use and Due Process of Law 199
Just Compensation and Due Process of Law 201
Notes 204

Index **207**

Preface

The conception of this book explains its nature. I have been asked by Professor George Fletcher of Columbia Law School to write a framework for a book on property law that could be used as a teaching tool for former communist countries in transition. The project was sponsored by the Constitutional and Legislative Policy Institute in Budapest. Such a framework had to be filled up with footnotes and insertions of actual local law (Russian, Hungarian, Romanian, etc.) by a local expert and published in local languages. It was, in other words, something that, if done by someone else, I might have regarded as an exercise in cultural imperialism, but in which I eagerly engaged because it was a wonderful occasion to travel East and to meet interesting people. Among these, at least Anita Soboleva, Zaza Namoradze, Attila Harmathi, Zita Abraham, Csilla Kollonay Lehoczky, and Asif Amirov deserve to be mentioned and thanked because, in their different capacities, they made my trips to Budapest and Moscow most pleasant.

Given the target and the nature of the project, it was crucial to be as nonpositivistic as possible (in many transitional systems there was not yet a positive local law to discuss) and to write something that could reflect the Western legal tradition as an aggregate of common law and civil law countries. Eastern European countries, though imbedded in the civil law tradition before the communist experience, are today particularly interested in the common law. I had some experience of this kind of comparative approach in teaching property, both at the Faculté Internationale de Droit Comparé, where I taught property for a few years, and at the University of Trento, where some years ago I taught a course in comparative property with Professor James Gordley.

Also, I teach seminars in comparative law and economics of property at Hastings, and property at the University of Turin (Italy). Some years ago I published, in Italian, a book on immovable property where I take a comparative approach. Quite a large portion of my scholarly interest is attracted by property law, which I have approached in such different contexts as Italy, California, England, Somalia, Congo, and France.

In this book, I discuss basic principles, taking them from the law in Italy, France, Germany, the United States, and England, although none of these systems is covered in any detail nor can I claim to be an expert on property law in any one of them. The scholarly ambition of this book is therefore modest and the footnotes are essential. It is only a first step in the direction of comparative research that seems in need of a lot of work, because the myth of the fundamental abyss between common law and civil law in the domain of property has precluded much interesting work being done. This book is, indeed, a challenge to the conventional comparative law wisdom that the domain of property law is that of fundamental differences. The idea behind it is that property law can be reduced to a relatively low number of basic principles, mostly of an economic and political nature, that lawyers in different Western legal systems describe in radically different ways. Such different descriptions can be seen, however, as variations along a few fundamental themes. The discussion of these themes, with the help of tools developed by the economic analysis of the law, is the aim of this book.

Comparative legal purists (or "preservationist" comparative law scholars) and legal formalists of a different kind will regard this approach as anathema. My focus on functional analogies has left a number of important differences in the penumbra. Also, I have selected the contents in a way that leaves aside some of the most problematic areas of comparative research, such as trust law. I did this on purpose. This is a book on basic principles of substantive law. Where the differences that really matter are in the domain of procedure and fundamental institutional setting, there was no point in discussing them here. Also, I dealt only with problems that most of the legal systems I have considered would regard as property law or at least as strictly connected to it. Consequently, those scholars that are attracted or fascinated by modern developments and hot issues will be frustrated. There is no discussion of bioethical issues (property of the embryo, DNA, etc.), no Internet and property of new technologies, and so on. Most of this book deals with traditional, classic topics.

I have also discussed the subject matter at quite a high level of abstraction, a level that makes most of my statements compatible with opposite rules of detail. At this level of detail are located most of the differences considered important by "black-letter" comparative legal scholars and formalists of different kinds. In a way, this philosophy is not different from that of any hornbook of American law, where footnotes will explain to the reader that the actual rule in Arkansas or Texas is the opposite than the one of Arizona or California. Details are for narrow practitioners only, and do not add much to our global understanding of the law. There is only one methodological difference between my approach and that of any American teaching tool (hornbook or casebook) based on "general principles of the law." This book provides a framework that was developed by thinking comparatively, and the footnotes might contain the law of different "foreign" states. The comparative legal and economic approach allows me to detect what can be seen as a basic principle of the law as a general organizational phenomenon. I do not consider as a fundamental institutional principle of law something that is entirely dependent on the peculiar structure of a given legal system and that is considered basic only because of the parochialism of the local commentators.

The thank-you list opens with the late Professor Rudolf Schlesinger. When I communicated with him about the project, he had just finished reading the autobiography of George Soros and he commented with that enthusiasm that I miss so much, "Well, I'm glad that he is funding some of our common core research! Write a good book he might fund more of it in the future!" Thanks also to my predecessor in Turin, Professor Rodolfo Sacco. He is the general editor of a treatise on Italian civil law for which I'm committed to write the volume on property law. I'm four years past the deadline and he is still supportive of my work with many insightful suggestions. My mentor, Professor Antonio Gambaro (Milano), author of a monumental work on Italian property law, taught me most of what I know in the field and certainly has infected me with an interest in the institution of property. Professor George Fletcher (Columbia) involved me in the project from which this book stems and I always enjoy his company, friendship, and scholarly conversation. Gianmaria Ajani (Torino) taught me the fundamental aspects of post-socialist law, a much needed background in the unfolding of this project. Professors James Gordley (Berkeley), Francesco Parisi (George Mason), Jane Stepleton (Camberra and Oxford), and Kenneth Reid (Edimburgh) were patient enough to read and comment upon the whole manuscript helping me enormously. So did another anonymous referee (who I would pay any money to meet), who while creating a lot of problems for me gave me the sense of possible reactions in some circles, hopefully helping me to prevent some of them. Thanks also to Elisabetta Grande (Alessandria), Mauro Bussani (Trento), Michele Graziadei (Como), Piergiuseppe Monateri (Torino), Marco Guadagni (Trieste), Radhika Rao (Hastings), Laura Nader (Berkeley), David Faigman (Hastings), Robert Cooter (Berkeley), Thomas

Ulen (Illinois), Luisa Antoniolli (Trento), Angelo Chianale (Torino), Hein Kötz (Hamburg), Melvin Eisenberg (Berkeley), Meir Dan Cohen (Berkeley), Richard Buxbaum (Berkeley), and Jeffrey Lena for comments, insights, and/or scholarly and personal company during this project. Many other colleagues involved in the *Common Core of European Private Law Project* in the *Comparative Law and Economics Forum* and in many workshops and seminars in the United States and Europe provided me with important intellectual stimulation. Mentioning all of them would make the list too long.

This project received generous financial support from the Constitutional and Legislative Policy Institute (Budapest), the T.M.R. Network on Principles of European Private Law (Prof. Rainer Shultze, Muenster), the *Associazione Rudolf Schlesinger per lo studio del diritto europeo* (Dott. Andrea Pradi, Trento), the International Center for Economic Research (Prof. Enrico Colombatto, Torino), the Department of Economics of the University of Torino (Prof. Ugo Colombino), the Department of Law of the Univerity of Trento (Prof. Diego Quaglioni), and, particularly, the University of California, Hastings College of Law (Deans Mary Kay Kane and Leo Martinez). Excellent editing, support, and research assistance was provided by Regina F. Burch, Joel M. Weinstein, Alexis Rodriguez, Brian Walsh, Arianna Pretto, Andrea Rossato, and Raffaele Caterina at Hastings, Torino, and Trento. Finally, thanks to Heather Staines, the editor at Greenwood Press, and John Beck, who produced the book for Greenwood, as well as Linda Weir and the library staff at Hastings.

CHAPTER 1

History

AVOIDING TRAGEDIES

Students in the United States and Europe are often introduced to property law by the famous story taken from the title of a paper by Professor Hardin, the so-called "tragedy of the commons."[1] This story is meant to demonstrate the necessity of individualistic property rights, although it actually conveys the more limited idea that scarce resources need regulation, rather than unrestricted freedom. Regulation over scarce resources, as the product of the relationship between individual powers and legal restrictions, defines the meaning of property law for the purpose of this book.[2]

The tragedy of the commons is a useful starting point in explaining the institutional restrictions that, when inherently connected to a tangible scarce resource, make up modern property law in the broad meaning that is the necessary starting point for comparative analysis.[3] Of course, different legal systems recognize as property law only varying fractions of these legal restrictions.[4] Nevertheless, if we strive to gather basic principles common to a variety of legal systems, we cannot be restricted by the internal taxonomy of any one of them.

Imagine that on the shores of the Balaton Lake live three communities of fishermen in a rather primitive state of development. Fishing is the only activity, and the fish in the lake currently mate enough to feed all three communities. An economist would say that an equilibrium exists because the three communities live on the income from the capital rather consuming the capital itself. Imagine now that the need for fish of one of the communities suddenly increases because, for example, a doctor has invented medicine that decreases the rate of infant death and the community experiences unexpected growth. As a consequence, its need for fish will increase (and the price of fish will increase) to a point where natural reproduction is insufficient. Indeed, due to increased demand, fishermen will invest more time fishing or will invent more efficient fishing techniques. Consequently, the fish population in the Balaton will decrease, and to meet consumption needs the three communities will compete to develop new and more disruptive techniques of fishing; for example, bombs.[5]

Unless the communities find some sort of binding agreement (say a treaty that bans fishing with bombs) the result will be tragic. Eventually the communities will kill all the fish and may starve. There may be many other reasons for the disruption of the equilibrium around the Balaton. For example, the introduction of imported consumption habits due to the development of market capitalism may cause eating fish in expensive restaurants in another community (say, Budapest) to become more fashionable. Thus, the price of the fish may increase with demand, providing more incentive to fish. A similar example of tragedy due to overuse can be seen in the destruction of whales taking place in our oceans due to the unrestricted competition among some countries still permitting whaling or, as discussed in specialized literature, the impoverishment of ocean fish.[6]

The tragedy of the commons is the distortion due to overuse because of the absence of restrictions over the consumption of scarce resources. Indeed, one community may have a strong incentive to fish extensively because it will keep for itself all the benefits of the fish it captures while facing only one-third the cost of the excessive use of the scarce resource. The remaining two-thirds of the costs are in fact met by the other two communities. Economists, lawyers, and political scientists agree that the way to avoid this tragedy is to develop techniques that, rather than allowing free exploitation of scarce resources, are able to determine a "price" that corresponds with social costs. One of these techniques in every legal system, although not the only one, is a system of private property rights.[7] In certain conditions, systems of private property develop, sometimes spontaneously, when common property becomes economically inefficient.[8]

Property law can thus be described as the formal or informal set of restrictions on the use of scarce resources that recognizes and permits the exercise of private decision making by the individual or group whose behavior is targeted.[9] Such restrictions need a minimum of hierarchical coordination. Some literature has pointed out that equally tragic consequences might develop because of the so-called "anticommons" problem.[10] While the commons might become tragic because too many individuals in the community enjoy unrestricted access to scarce resource, excessive restrictions might become tragic too. Property rights usually develop to include not only the power to access a given resource, but also that of excluding everybody else from accessing it. When such "veto power" essential to property rights in their function of granting exclusivity gets allocated to different individuals over the same set of scarce resources, problems of coordination arise. Property law needs to work out mechanisms that allow one decision over the use of resources to be recognized as final, otherwise the resource might be underexploited and decay.[11] Examples might be seen by taking a walk in the beautiful hills of Tuscany. Many old country homes are in a state of abandonment despite the tremendous potential value of them. The rules of Italian succession law do not efficiently solve the problems of coordination among co-heirs so that all of them have incentives to opportunistically use the veto power that is granted by the anticommons aspect of their property rights.

Literature on the origins of property rights shows individuals organizing themselves in complex social organizations to pursue the efficient exploitation of scarce resources and take care of basic needs of survival.[12] In a sense, the world can be considered a gigantic commons to be divided up in order to avoid the tragedy. The division of such a complex common between so many communities, and further between so many individuals within the community, is made possible through development of fundamental institutions. The most important of these are markets, property rights, and the state.[13]

Property rights can be described as formalized powers to rule over commodities. Property law is the body of law that grants such power and limits it. This body of law deals with the social decision about who owns what. Property law presides over the relationship between property rights among themselves (in the market) and before the state. It empowers and limits individuals or organizations that hold property rights in the reciprocal interest and in the interest of the other individuals in society.

The relationship between the institutions of the state, the market, and property, and appropriate location of property rights and property law within the market and the state, is the object of much theoretical debate which need not be discussed here.[14]

PROPERTY LAW: AN HISTORICALLY CONTINGENT AGGREGATE OF FORMAL AND INFORMAL CONSTRAINTS

Property rights can also be understood as a delegation of sovereign power. In modern societies, these powers belong to the state.[15] To be sure, in the course of the history of legal and political ideas many other conceptions have been advanced. Such conceptions are often variations of two great themes: (1) that property rights come from the state, the so-called positivistic conception, and (2) the "natural law" conception, that believes property rights supersede the state, are independent of the state, and must be respected to retain legitimacy of the state.[16] A book dealing with basic legal principles of property law need not devote much space to this debate, which belongs to the political–philosophic or jurisprudential tradition. It is enough to state that both alternative conceptions have some truth, and both are destructive in their extreme forms.[17]

First, property law does not need the existence of the state. Legal rules recognized by the community granting exclusive access and control by one individual (or group) over a given set of scarce resources not only preexist the state but even the development of language skills by humankind.[18] All social systems at various phases in their development have developed their property laws (in different forms) in order to prevent or solve conflicts over scarce resources.[19] For example, let us consider a simple social system, a legal system in the broad sense used here: the western nuclear family.[20] Two little sisters playing in a room usually disrupt the peace of their parents for one of the following reasons:

Hypo A: The first sister, Clara, does not want to share a toy with her sister Greta. Greta screams to obtain the toy.

Hypo B: Clara physically dispossesses Greta of the toy through violence or trickery. Greta will scream to receive restitution.

The parents wishing to restore peace and tranquillity must make a choice. In Hypo A, they may think the toy belongs to Clara, who has a right to resist Greta's attack. Or they may think that Clara is using a toy belonging to Greta and that she is justified in screaming. In the latter case, the parent is recognizing individual property rights over toys and, consequently, will force the nonentitled sister to return the toy to its owner. Some parents may not like to recognize individual property rights over toys. The rule in the family may be that all toys in the playroom belong to both Clara and Greta. They must either share the toy or take turns playing individually. The lengths of the turns will in this case determine the parents course of action. The parent may ban violence and screaming altogether by enforcing a first-come, first-served principle. In this principle, the sibling enters into possession and may keep the toy as long as she wishes. In this case, the parents will rule for Clara, who is under attack. Conversely, they may rule according to a principle that protects the supposedly weaker party, and in this case the parents may rule for Greta, because she is younger. In Hypo B, Clara's violent behavior may be repressed, and restitution of the toy will be granted independently from any abstract theory of who has the property right. In that case, a lawyer will say possession will be protected over property rights. Obviously, a parent wishing to be very tough on private property and to transmit a sense of the moral importance of defending it may allow the violence to protect the toy.

Whatever the content, the parent is making a proprietary choice. That is a choice aimed to solve (or prevent) a conflict over scarce resources. The aggregate of such choices, and the rationale that can be detected behind it (or not detected, if the father decides randomly and arbitrarily), is part of the law of property of that particular family, as much as the choice of a judge regarding who will keep the house in the case of divorce. Only a state-centric, severely provincial attitude makes modern lawyers consider law only the body of rules enforced (directly or indirectly) by state authority. No interesting comparative discussion can be based on such an arbitrary limitation of the subject matter of the law.[21]

What I have described shows property law does not need the existence of the state.[22] Therefore, rules of property law may be considered "natural" products of a spontaneous order whose idea is usually conveyed by the term "customary law."[23] As a matter of fact, the rules presiding over the allocation of scarce resources are extremely ancient rules, predating the idea of the state. Their content varies from place to place and from organization to organization, demonstrating the shortcomings of a natural law idea of individual property rights immutable through time and space.[24]

Rules of property can be found at play even in nonhuman organizations. Studies on ethology, the science devoted to the behavior of animals, are from this perspective an extremely rich reservoir of alternative property law. For instance, certain mammals (such as cats) delimit the territory of their hunting and love with their own scent or with other organic traces such as hairs. Similarly, pigeons, doves, and other birds establish a hierarchy when foraging for and consuming food by creating a precedence in favor of the senior members of the group over younger members. Examples abound. It is important to note that such rules of property law enjoy a high degree of effectiveness, perhaps more than certain property law statutes in some modern law systems. They may find enforcement in the group, usually by means of ostracism, or they may be effectively self-enforced by mysterious hormonal secretions that, in a fight, make the animal on the right side more effective than the wrongdoer.[25]

We must conclude by noting that property law, due to its particular nature, is usually a topic of extensive legal pluralism in a given geographic area.[26] Many customary rules are at play, both very old or very new.[27] Often these rules are in competition with official rules recognized by the modern state. Think of the rules of property that govern a gypsy community in a given town;[28] or rules internal to extended family networks such as those of many immigrant workers from different legal traditions; or even rules that govern a so-called "criminal organization."[29] I would go so far as to say that it is very rare that an individual is governed by only one system of property law. Imagine the organization of a law firm, that of a university, or that of a ministry. In such organizations, rules of seniority similar to those we have described for doves and pigeons will probably be at play in the allocation of spaces within the building or of other scarce resources, such as computers. This last example shows that in the informal background of all legal systems property rights develop over scarce resources in situations that legal professionals would find it difficult to conceptualize as property law. Of course, such rules are enforced in informal ways, but this does not mean that they are less effective than direct enforcement by the courts and/or by the police.[30]

Most people follow these kind of rules unconsciously, and many times they preempt formal legal intervention. The existence of informal, spontaneous property law is of crucial importance, because the courts cannot prudently bear the pressure of preventing and solving all possible conflicts over scarce resources. Informal rules of property work physiologically in social interaction. Simultaneously, rules of official property law, such as the ones that I will mostly describe in this book, tend to be detected at play in the pathology of it (such as when individuals go to court to litigate). Of course, these rules of official property law may and usually do determine the behavior of individuals outside of enforcement mechanisms: Most people do not trespass on another's garden because they instinctively know one should not enter another's property without permission.[31]

In conclusion, official property law works in the background of many different systems of rules presiding over the allocation of scarce resources. This should always be kept in mind, because, as we will see, an efficient system of property law should always try to follow closely what individuals would decide when bargaining among themselves over scarce resources.[32] Consequently, the absence of a rule of official property law, or the broad and vague wording of it, does not mean that there is no existence of property law for a given problem. It means that the state allows individuals to work out their own business in that particular area, perhaps developing a system of spontaneous property law because enforcing property law in courts is expensive. Occasionally, it is simply not worthwhile to allocate resources in that way.

However, "professional" property law has a story in itself that must be told before introducing the next chapter. The story illuminates the actors of a modern proprietary system. Of course, it would go well beyond the scope of an introductory book to follow in any detail the history of the law of property. However, what is important to consider is that property law has developed, as we see it today in advanced economies, by a slow and incremental process of accumulation of professional knowledge that has varied immensely around the world. Even if we narrow our focus on the modern system of official property law recognized as such by the professional lawyers in the Western legal tradition according to the local taxonomies, there are two different paths that we need briefly to discuss before seeking the description of common principles of property law.

In the following discussion my focus will be on the actors in the proprietary system that have played a comparatively larger role in their respective tradition. One should not be surprised if the history of the common law appears to be a story of competing political institutions, while that of the civil law mostly as the story of "some ideas." Both stories are needed if one wishes to capture common principles that cut across the two traditions.[33] Both aspects are at play in the civil law and the common law. Historically, one or the other have left more visible signs in the form (arguably much less in the substance) of modern professional property law.

COMMON LAW

The law of property, among all branches of common law, is the one that has remained most characteristically distinct from civil law systems. During the feudal period, the most significant features of the common law were developed in the area of the law of property.[34] Institutions arising in connection with land holdings represented the bulk of not only the law governing the relationship between private persons, but also the political organization of feudal England. The end of feudalism did not coincide with any commensurate revision of the legal structure that common lawyers had built around the relationship of feudal tenure. In contrast, in the development of English law, "equity," a parallel institutional system administered by the Chancellor, was grafted onto feudal tenure as reflected by the common law of property, so that today the legacy of England's feudal history is evidenced more in property law than in any other area.

The birth and development of equity jurisprudence is an historical accident. The writ system, around which the jurisdiction of the common law courts was organized during the reign of Henry II, became rigid around the end of the thirteenth century. It largely precluded the creation of new writs, and all common law remedies had to be fashioned within the structure of the existing writs. Covenants were not enforceable unless made under seal, and remedies like injunctions and specific performance were unavailable. With a few exceptions whose practical availability was impaired by the requirements of obsolete legal procedures (trial by battle), the only remedy available in a court of law were damages.[35] Typically, the writ system led to frequent acts of injustice. Eventually, the situation became intolerable and the Chancellor started to grant relief in the form of *in personam* orders to the wrongfully sanctioned defendant. By the fifteenth century, the Court of Chancery had formed and developed its own remedial devices. Thus, the dual common law–equity system, typical of Anglo-American law, was born.

The modern law of property characteristics were formed well before the reception in England of the modern doctrine of contracts.[36] Consequently, a large number of contractual relationships in civil law are grounded in the law of obligations (developed in the tradition of the classic Roman jurist Gaius), and belong to the law of property in the common law.

The private trust is the clearest example of a development in the area of the English law of property that is completely handled by contract in the civil law tradition.[37] Ordinary contractual instruments tend to be incapable of providing the practical results that common lawyers obtain using the trust. For example, the common law of contract did not offer protection to third-party beneficiaries until much later. Trusts, on the other hand, gave great protection to beneficiaries.[38] This proprietary nature of trust law that allows extensive protection of the beneficiary is due to an historical accident. It is nevertheless behind much of present-day success of the institution of trust.

The private trust is not the only phenomenon demonstrating that Anglo-American law of property extends well beyond the borders of the civilian notion of property law. The term "property," in the legal parlance of anglophone countries, covers a much broader concept, more similar to the economist's notion of a "property right." Consequently, it covers a variety of areas of the law which remain distinct under the Romanist tradition, and which no modern civilian lawyer would consider as constituting property rights. For example, insurance policies, stocks, and leases are all part of the common law notion of personal property.[39]

The law of property in common law countries is organized around the main technical dichotomy between real property and personal property. The division originates in the development of different remedies to assist in the protection of two different kinds of property. To understand this distinction, one must first recognize the confusion generated by the meaning of the dichotomy between real actions and personal actions. In the civil law tradition, it is known that the dichotomy is not the same as in the classical common law.[40] According to civilian taxonomy, the fundamental distinction between these two types of actions is that a real action protecting the thing (*res*) can be exercised against everybody, since a property right imposes duties of abstention to everybody in the world. In contrast, a personal action protecting the person can be exercised only against the particular person that is subject to the obligation. Contracts and torts which make up the bulk of the law of obligations impose duties only to the particular person who entered into the contractual agreement or who committed the tort. Therefore, real actions have an *erga omnes* (against everybody) characteristic when contrasted with personal actions. In comparison, the common law opposition is based on the structural characteristic of the remedy that one could obtain with the exercise of one or the other action. With a real action one could recover possession of the thing, whereas in a personal action it is only possible to obtain monetary compensation for the damage suffered by the loss. It would therefore be wrong to imply that an action which, according to common law, is classified as "real" would be likewise classified as such in the civilian tradition.

In the common law system, real property is protected by a real action while personal property is protected by a personal action. This distinction, originally quite clear, has been rendered obscure by two factors. First, the English Law of Property Act of 1925 partially unified the legal rules regarding real and personal property by eliminating the difference in available remedies upon which the partition was based. At the time, some English authors implied that the difference between the terms "real" and "personal" property corresponded to the civil law distinction between "movable" and "immovable" property. Such analogies are more misleading than useful. More sophisticated jurists recognize that the civil law tradition focuses on the connection with the physical thing that is the object of the property right. The common law, on the other hand, focuses not on the thing itself (e.g., land), but rather on some of the utilities that can be captured from it. Because the common law perceives property rights as an abstract entity (such as an estate or a term of years), the civil law approach is alien to the common law.[41] Although the value is mostly symbolic, one should remember that the theory in England is still that the absolute owner of all the land is the Queen. Second, the rise of equity, with its flexible and efficient remedies, introduced further confusion. One of equity's fundamental maxims is that "equity acts in personam." That is, the orders issued by the Chancellor are directed to the defendant in person and have no direct effect whatsoever on the structure of the legal relationship that is still governed by the common law. The defendant, however, is frequently ordered to comply with an injunction through some specific performance, which may well include an order of restitution. It follows that the locution *"in personam"* here has the opposite meaning than it has in the already explained classical common law terminology, where an order to give back the thing would make the action real and not personal.[42]

Despite such possible sources of confusion, real property and personal property are today perceived as such different and distinct aspects of the common law's law of property that they constitute two different areas of the law.[43] It is curious, however, that the effort at unification of property law pursued by the French post-revolutionary codification in its fight against feudal property rights, which quickly spread throughout the legal systems in the civil law tradition, stimulated the reformers of English property law as well, resulting ultimately in the more unified system of the Law of Property Act of 1925. In the United States this did not take place, with the paradoxical result that American law has preserved to a greater extent the traditional feudal features of common law. Throughout the whole common law tradition, on the other hand, the trust, a creature of real property, has penetrated the borders between real and personal property and has become applicable to the whole law of property.

Real property is organized around the concept of the estate.[44] The estate is only comprehensible within the historical evolution of the feudal relationship that bound tenants to their lords.[45] According to feudal theory, all land "belonged" to the king. The king tenured the land to the local lords, who became tenants-in-chief. In turn, the lords could seize other tenants. The chain could continue, but what is important to the structural relationship is that every person but the first and last subjects in the chain was lord and tenant simultaneously.[46]

The relationship between lord and tenant was known as "free tenure." In the classical feudal model, each free tenure could have different characteristics. On the one side, the lord would grant the tenant use of the land, while the tenant's obligations were variable in nature. For example, the tenant might be under a duty to provide horses and soldiers for the lord's army (known as military tenure), a tenant might be obliged by the terms of his tenure to perform certain religious services for the lord's soul (known as ecclesiastical tenure), or the tenant might be under a duty to pay a certain sum of money. Such different forms of the feudal relationship were known as "incidents of tenure." Some incidents were present in any type of tenure. The most important was the so-called "escheat," or the return of the land to the lord at the death of the tenant or (later) at the exhaustion of a certain line of succession, or in the case of felony.

While the content of the tenure was determined by its incidents, its duration was determined by the type of "estate" (from the Latin *status*) that the infeudation created in favor of the tenant. The main estates were the "life estate" (which came to an end with the death of the tenant), the "estate in fee simple" (the closest to the modern perennial idea of ownership), and the estate in fee tail, in which property was connected to a determined and specific line of succession. An example of the latter might be "fee tail male," in which the estate passed on only to male descendants.

Since escheat and other rights (i.e., wardenship, or marriage in the case of the death of a tenant leaving a minor child) were held by the king, the lord always maintains an interest in the estate, known as a "reversion," which is itself a property right. A reversion is an estate that does not give rise to a right to present possession of the land. For this reason, a reversion is classified as an estate in interest, as contrasted with the other estates briefly mentioned, which are said to be estates in possession. If the lord decided to dispose of a reversion by transferring it in favor of a third party, a relationship known as a "remainder" was created. A remainder is an estate in interest that will become an estate in possession only when the conditions are verified that would have brought about the escheat had the landlord not transferred his own reversion.

The feudal model's excessive complexity derives from the limitless degrees of subinfeudation allowed prior to the statute *Quia Emptores* (1290) promulgation. Each tenant could give rise to new tenures (within the limits of his title), different in both duration and content, all of which were property rights. For example, one who held a fee tail male in military tenure could create a life estate in socage in favor of a third party in exchange for a modest rent, and a remainder in favor of yet another person. This damaged the lord because it made his proprietary claims restricted and far away from actual control of the utility stemming from the property right. When the tenant died with a minor son, the wardenship (that otherwise would have allowed him the administration of the property until the coming of age of the minor) and the marriage (that would have allowed him to choose a wife for the minor who would best satisfy the interests of his family) were reduced to the claim of modest rent from a subinfeudated third party rather than to actual decision-making power.

The problem took on further complex developments that cannot be followed up in detail here. What is important to note is that by means of the remainders, conveyancers were able to bind future generations to the will of the deceased with inefficient results. Common law has developed a variety of techniques to take care of these kinds of problems (nowadays known as anticommons), the rule against perpetuities being the best known among them.[47]

Conveyancers were (and still are) those property lawyers who specialize in deeds, which are the fundamental instruments for the transfer of real property. From early on, the conveyancers were able to plan and control the transfer of a vast range of interests, and managed rather complex business requirements. The feudal origin system is not deprived of its impact on the modern law of property, a law that equity has rendered more flexible and functional. To this day, for example, the transfer of real property comes about by way of a unilateral formal act, the deed. The contract itself cannot transfer real property. The English Law of Property Act of 1925 limited possible estates at law to the term of years absolute and the fee simple absolute. However, consideration must be taken of two things: English law is only part of the entire common law model, and equity permits complex planning possibilities to survive within the law of property by means of the institution of trust.[48]

Conveyancers from the common law world tend to reason according to mental habits descended from the medieval law of property, as depicted by Littleton as early as the fifteenth century. This makes the common law path far different from the civil law. In civil law, the ideology of the French revolution has expelled most of the residues of the feudal structures from modern property law content as well as taxonomy. This surviving feudal subtradition in property law characterizes the greatest part of the differences between the civil law and its common law counterpart. Other subtraditions within common law have been identified which render the term "property" rich in meanings, making comprehension and comparison particularly difficult in this area.[49]

For example, the opposition between free and unfree tenure is still important and encompasses within the domain of the common law of property a large number of transactions that in civil law are purely contractual. The feudal lord could decide not to infeudate the land, but instead have a peasant take care of it to plow and grow crops. This other kind of property, the unfree tenure (villeinage or copyhold), developed outside of the feudal schemes of real property. Free tenure, with its feudal origin, always coexisted alongside other proprietary arrangements of different origin.

The estates theory is only conceivable in relation to real property (freehold). Today, freehold exists alongside nonfreehold, or leasehold (with which copyhold should not be confused). Leasehold is the modern relationship between a landlord to a tenant.[50] It constitutes a contractual relationship in the civilian law and is a branch of the law of property in the common law. Leasehold origins date back to commercial practice which aimed at evading anti-usury laws. Historically, it was not protected by a real action, and therefore was not classified as real property but instead as personal property. However, the action of ejectment subsequently gave the tenant a remedy to recover the property so that leaseholds were at odds within the category of personal property (also known as chattels).[51] Today, leaseholds are ambiguously contained in the ad hoc category of "chattels real," sharing some of the two main branches of property law.

Personal property covers several categories and is divided into several subcategories. The major dichotomy occurs between "choses in possession" (*chose* in law French, the language of the classic common law, means "thing") and "choses in action"; the former are movable goods capable of control and physical enjoyment, such as a book.[52] For a civil lawyer, on the other hand, the latter (a bank account, a bond, an insurance policy, etc.) have contractual nature.

The comparison of property law between civil law and common law is rendered more complex by the number of subtraditions developed in common law countries alongside the aforementioned technical ones. Such traditions are more common in the Western legal tradition and result from transnational circulation of legal and philosophical ideas. Alongside this technical, strictly professional meaning developed within the legal profession at Westminster Hall, the term "property" is used within the modern constitutional tradition (relevant mainly in the United States), where the natural law ideology, reflected in the French revolution and originally rooted in the civil law, becomes "enacted" in the common law.[53] Furthermore, analytical jurisprudence, a leading paradigm of Anglo-American property theory, speaks of property within a notion derived from German legal positivism.[54] Today, in the property-theory literature, both in the civil law and in the common law a much more uniform language than the one used by practical lawyers is spoken.[55]

CIVIL LAW

The technical evolution of property law on the European continent followed quite a different path. The development of the law was not in the hands of practitioners organized around a centralized system of justice. Instead, academic lawyers in universities were the leading force.[56] The law was not found in the register of writs but in the Justinian compilation, rediscovered more or less at the same time as the Battle of Hastings (1066). A dual legal system never arose in the civil law.[57] A general theory of contract as a source of obligations was developed early on by scholars, and the notion of obligation remained central to continental legal theory. Thus, in the Romanist legal tradition it was the law of obligations that played the most important role in the development of the technical legal tradition.[58]

Feudalism, politically defeated by the birth of the modern state, did not leave traces on the structure and taxonomy of the civilian law of property.[59] Perhaps because the law of property had never dealt with so many technical transactions, the French revolution was remarkably effective in giving technical content to its antifeudal crusade. In France, Italy, or Germany, the division of proprietary interests that is the essence of the theory of estate (and trust law) raises a number of problems, since it violates several taboos in civil law thinking.[60]

First, there is the so-called unitary theory of property rights. During the French Revolution, it became fashionable to consider the division of property rights as characteristic of feudalism. As a consequence, it was thought that the number of restricted property rights had to be strictly controlled and limited. The *numerus clausus* theory was developed, stating that divided interests in property must be strictly confined to a small number of well-defined types.[61] Although this idea was largely the product of the folklore and ideology of the French revolution and lacked a well-articulated rationale, it enjoyed tremendous success, even more than the Napoleonic Code (the document which many jurists say incorporates this idea).[62] For example, in the German BGB (which is not considered influenced by the Napoleonic Code, and which was enacted more than one hundred years after the French revolution) paragraph 90 carried the antifeudal attitude so far as to provide that only tangible commodities may be the object of property rights. As we have seen, many property rights in the feudal structure had a nontangible nature.

The idea that property is a fundamental of natural right (given wide distribution also in common law through William Blackstone's *Commentaries*) inspired much of the French revolutionary reform program.[63] The natural law idea of property was developed as a corollary to the notion of individual freedom.[64] A zone of individual sovereignty over property was considered the most effective barrier against unrestricted power of the state. Correlatively, the restriction of the absolute power of the state was thought of by the illuministic, rationalistic, and naturalistic schools as the institutional basis of a civilized society. Freedom of contract, proportionality of criminal punishment, and sanctity of property rights were in different areas the bulwarks and the tools of this program. The recognition and enforcement of the legal rights of each individual against all others was a necessary precondition for any organized society. Accordingly, it was believed that each individual should enjoy a right to control his body and his capacity to produce. The individual also had rights to commodities and services that he purchased in the marketplace.[65]

In this minimal institutional scenario, the state has the role of a watchdog and individuals may freely dispose of their rights. The naturalistic model is based on the idea of the free exchange of these rights. Rights acquire an exchange value which is determined by their market value. Yet the state has another goal. It must guarantee the execution of contracts that transfer rights once they are voluntarily entered. As mentioned before, this view dilutes the relevance of differences between property and contracts. The theory, as the famous comparative law scholar Professor Gorla pointed out, in fact "assimilates the transfer of property as [the] exercise of the power of a man over things to the act of entering into a contract as the exercise of the power of a man over his person, over his activity, over his own freedom."[66] Thus, the protection of property was the protection of freedom. Limits to property were limits to freedom.[67] This idea lives on in the political debate today and is familiar to the modern economist.[68]

While the idea may be extremely influential on the political and philosophical tradition of the law, the notion encounters severe limits in technical applicability. Consequently, the natural law notion of property was quickly challenged and abandoned by civil lawyers by the rise of the German Pandectist school in the nineteenth century. It was impossible for any legal system to guarantee the "airtight" rights required by the natural law model.[69] Every human action which might create an external effect should be banned in order to maintain an airtight right. Strictly speaking, damages cannot be considered as the protection of a right, but merely compensation for a taking.[70]

The same idea is asserted today by some law and economics literature by distinguishing the protection of a right from that of an interest. While damages protect the latter, they cannot adequately protect the former.[71] Consequently, to maintain the natural law model required a number of fictions. Nevertheless, before abandoning such a conception, lawyers developed a number of techniques to work around it. In continental Europe, the rhetoric of the French Revolution represented the apogee of the naturalistic model. It is common to introduce the French Napoleonic Code's conception of property as a direct creature of this naturalistic ideology.[72] Nonetheless, shortly after the enactment of Article 544 of the French Civil Code, such notions of property had to be abandoned. This provision, which contains the definition of private property most celebrated worldwide, states that ownership is the right to use and dispose of property in the most absolute way.[73] Despite the asserted completeness of the French Code, many practical necessities compelled the use of outside sources to fill up the many lacunae of the code.[74] This phenomenon—never acknowledged until the work of François Geny, the French founder of the so-called scientific school in the late nineteenth century—is clear in the domain of the law of property, where scholars and courts, in their work of limiting property rights, were influenced by the feudal tradition, Roman law, and contributions from other modern legal systems.[75]

Therefore, the naturalistic idea of property rights had influence on the jurisprudence theories of compact and individual property rights, but did not contribute to the framing of technical solutions. As one of the leading comparative legal scholars, Professor Antonio Gambaro, observed, natural law–inspired lawyers "after having declared that what belongs to an individual must be respected and guaranteed as the content of the proprietary power, have not cared to define such a content."[76] Lawyers resorted to the second part of Article 544, which allowed limits to property rights which were introduced "by law or by regulation." In so doing, they searched for the content of property rights in the bramble bush of administrative regulations and special statutes that were growing together with the authority and organization of the modern centralized state. These rules defining the actual content of property rights were treated as mere exceptions. This is a typical French approach to legal reasoning:[77] the giving of broad definitions and stating as many exceptions as necessary without worrying about the impact of the exceptions on the general rule.[78]

Consequently, the naturalistic theory of property was limited to celebrating the emphatic folklore soon created around the agrarian revolution and its code. Nevertheless, the actual law of property may be grasped by analyzing the detailed limitations on the general rule, which account for the many limitations that centralized regulations of public authority imposed on property rights. Further, they continued to develop at a highly technical level inaccessible to laymen. These lawyers' level of discourse always remained totally insensitive to the celebrated tautology of Article 544 of the Napoleonic Code. Recently, by applying the tools of comparative analysis, it is possible to understand the error of confusing a legal institution (such as property) with the rhetoric developed around that legal institution (such as the scholarly commentaries around the definition of a property right in Article 544 of the French Civil Code), or confusing the deceptively simple language of the Civil Code with the large body of private law which has developed around it. In other words, this was a confusion between the definitions of a property right stated within a given legal system and the law of property of that legal system.[79]

It is generally accepted that one of the breaks with the past introduced by the Napoleonic Code (in full harmony with the antifeudal character of the French Revolution) has been the separation between property rights and civil liability.[80] In the folklore of the revolution, it was unacceptable that property rights could be the source of obligations. The French Revolution aimed at dismantling the legal structure of feudal obligations linking persons to property in feudally prescribed ways. Property had to be considered a pure bundle of rights. For example, the owner's land use, as the exercise of a property right, should bar the liability rule contained in Article 1382 of the Napoleonic Code. In French tort law, the doctrine of "exercise of a legal right" has been used to limit the broad provision of the mentioned article according to which any act which causes a damage by fault obliges payment of compensation.[81] This proclaimed property right immunity was soon necessarily obliterated by the law in action. As pointed out by Professor Honoré, "French law initially gives a broad right by statute and then restricts its antisocial use by the Courts; to the contrary, in England when Courts announce the rights, they do so very restrictively. Consequently, there is little need for an equitable temperance of the exercise of such strictly specified rights."[82] According to this technique, for example, the old practice of prerevolutionary courts (Parliaments) of banning nuisances between neighbors as quasi-délits was never abandoned by French case law. Without caring for the critiques of contemporary scholars, courts have framed, in the complete absence of code language on the point, the theory of *troubles de voisinage* for the purpose of dealing with incompatible uses of neighboring property. Soon after the enactment of the Napoleonic Code, moreover, the French legislature enacted Décret 15, October 1810, which submitted to administrative authorization all polluting factories. This decree "transferred to the exclusive jurisdiction of the Administrative Agencies all collective interests threatened by industrial developments."[83]

One of the consequences of maintaining limits to property rights as exceptions to a natural law definition has been the complete divorce between private law and public law. Private law was viewed as distributing absolute property rights. Public law regulations were called upon to restrict individual selfishness in the cases of divergence between private costs and social costs. French private law courts (and many of the civil law systems which followed its tradition) did not claim until very recently any role in dealing with public policy problems. It was assumed that any matter of public welfare was in re ipsa within the domain of public law, as had always been the case since the impressive centralized administrative organization imposed by Louis XIV. Civilian legal thinking became increasingly concerned with technicalities, since the courts were precluded from policy discussions reserved to the government.

The German historical–pandectist school adopted a positivistic approach to law explicitly critical of the natural law approach, seen as universalistic and contrary to the notion of law as reflecting the spirit of the people in a given community.[84] The pandectists' concern was to build logically perfect legal taxonomies. They rejected exceptions and contradictions impairing the geometric precision of legal reasoning. They classified ownership within the broader category of "subjective rights," defined in various ways as a protected zone of sovereignty of one individual's will.[85] By enlarging the notion (already rooted in natural law) of a zone in which the individual will is sovereign, the right of ownership soon became the very paradigm of the so-called absolute subjective right. This conceptual framework made property rights paradigmatic prerequisites of two very different sets of private law remedies, both consequential to the notion that the legal system had to protect subjective rights. In the domain of the law of property, in a kind of injunctive and declaratory action, the so-called *Negatorischesklage* (*actio negatoria*) became available to the owner whose will was violated, aside from the action to recover the possession. In the domain of the law of torts, on the other hand, the violation of a property right (as paradigm to the absolute subjective right), was symptomatic of the unlawfulness of the wrongdoer's action. Such unlawfulness, together with damages and causation, was necessary to recover in torts.[86]

Friedrich Karl Von Savigny, the founder of the historical–pandectist school in the law, offered one of the most successful notions of ownership as "the unlimited and exclusive dominion of a person over property."[87] This conception was the technical translation of an idea already expressed by the German philosopher Hegel in his very influential work on jurisprudence. According to Hegel, collective interest is something ontologically different from the sum of individual interests. Private property therefore was not an institution recognized as promoting social progress, but merely a means of guaranteeing expression of individual free will.[88] This was the origin of the idea of inherent selfishness in the exercise of property rights.

This conception of ownership did not remain unchallenged. The leader of the efforts to introduce some limits within the notion of property in Germany was Rudolph Von Jehring, founder of the so-called "jurisprudence of interests," who is very well known in America, where his work has been imported by Roscoe Pound with the name of "sociological jurisprudence."[89] His impact, although important, only shifted the debate to the proper role of regulation to limit private property. An alternative private law notion of ownership, such as the one that in America is linked to the groundbreaking work of the Yale scholar Wesley Newcomb Hohfeld, was never articulated in the civil law tradition.[90] Duties and liabilities introduced by public law regulation were never conceived as "sticks internal to the proprietary bundle," but only external, exceptional restrictions.[91]

DISSIMILAR FORM AND SIMILAR SUBSTANCE?

At first impression, after reading this brief historical account, one could think that the development of the civil law and the common law in the domain of property have nothing in common and that it is therefore useless to try to describe common developments. The leading institutional actors are so different that the results are bound to be different. For example, the naturalistic conception of property rights was never shared, on technical grounds, by common lawyers. In England, the structure of property rights has been determined through the courts by incrementally solving individual conflicts. In England, no revolution ever marked a clean break with the past legal order. Much of the rhetoric and structure of the law of real property still has feudal features. As a consequence often repeated in literature of comparative law, the common law notion of property right is not absolute when compared with the civil law. Indeed, the very word "ownership" is of recent origin.

In the common law tradition, because of the practical needs of adjudication in courts of law, the notable divorce between property and liability which is a feature of the civil law "absolute notion" never occurred. The structure of the law of nuisance shows this difference, since it reflects the practical needs of creating boundaries between incompatible activities outside of a penetrating role of administrative regulation. In Anglo-American law, nuisance is a sort of synthesis between the law of property and the law of torts. The ownership of land in the common law is inherently limited by the need to use it in a reasonable way.

Every Anglo-American judge has been trained to detect whether a particular use of land may be considered reasonable in order to make the policy decision that in the civil law is made by administrative regulation. Consequently, doctrines such as the exercise of a right as a defense to liability stemming from the use of property, or its corollary doctrine of abuse of right, are useless and perhaps even senseless for the common lawyer, while perfectly logical for the civilian scholar worried to build a precise general taxonomy rather than to solve actual conflicts, dealt with by the public law.[92] Consequently, if one compares doctrines created by judges in common law with doctrines created by scholars in civil law (the leading actors of the two systems), the result will be a notable difference between the two approaches. If one then generalizes these observations to the whole law of property, oppositions such as the absolute versus relative idea of property will follow.

Nevertheless, if we compare homogeneous actors in the legal system we will find much more similar results than those we reach by comparing common law and civil law of property within monistic conceptions of the legal rule, as if property law was not a complex object of observation made by a plurality of competing legal formants. The very notion of the conception being more or less absolute loses much of its meaning. In Chapter 7 we will show, for example, that the law of nuisance, despite many formal differences, is fundamentally similar if one considers it in its function of delimiting property rights in similar social and economic contexts, such as advanced Western capitalistic systems. In other words, it is not that the owner in common law was "bound" while his civil law colleague was "free." Put simply, historically variable limits to proprietary freedom are introduced by courts of law in the first context, while by public law regulation in the second. The latter kind of limits are simply easier for private law scholars (leading actors of the system) to ignore in a tradition in which the public law versus private law dichotomy is deeply rooted. They consequently find it harder to be reflected in the traditional definitions of ownership.[93]

If we look at the story of legal ideas about property, we find more similarity and some more evidence of the substantial commonalities we are talking about. Modern property theory in the Anglo-American world describes an evolution from the "sole and despotic dominion" described by Blackstone to the "bundle of sticks" metaphor, sometimes described as the Hohfeld–Honoré notion and sometimes as the "relational idea" of ownership.[94]

Natural law, particularly through Blackstone, had tremendous influence on the way in which common lawyers, particularly Americans, began to describe their system. Descriptions and definitions, however, are the domain of scholars, and the mere fact of influencing scholarly writings does not necessarily imply meaningful penetration into the deep layers of the legal system which in fact determine the structure of property rights.[95] When between the two World Wars realist jurisprudence in the United States began a closer observation to the actual working of the judicial process, the Blackstonian definition of ownership, possibly accurate to describe proprietary freedom during the expansion westward in the United States, was quickly abandoned. The bundle of sticks metaphor indeed captures much better the reality of a system of property law in which judicial creativity (and the law of nuisance) plays an important role.

Similarly in the European Continent, beginning shortly before World War I as a consequence of the massive amount of special legislation and regulation impairing individual property rights because of the collective effort to prepare for the war, the individualistic definitions of ownership began to be abandoned in favor of more social ones. The bundle of sticks metaphor was not used, but ideas such as the social function of property rights or similar theories developed by leading scholars such as Duguit in France, Gierke in Germany, or Scialoja in Italy can be seen as equivalent "relational" ideas.[96] Consequently a common evolution in the domain of leading definitions of ownership can be detected as well.

Despite what can be seen as common, it remains true that the deep difference in the leading actors of the system plays a role in the way in which legal systems at similar stages of economic development react to new problems. In other words, I do not intend to deny that following the path of using judges rather than direct ex ante regulation to handle social problems affects the system. Such different paths clearly make lawyers dependent on them whenever they approach a new legal problem. An interesting example may be found in environmental law, with the rush of civilians to centralized administrative regulation and of common lawyers toward decentralized court-based systems.[97]

The aforementioned different historical developments in common law and civil law, beginning almost 900 years ago at the origins of the Western legal tradition, show to the modern observer two paths that make the area of property law one of the most challenging and difficult topics in comparative law. These early paths, grounded as they are in a radically different institutional structure, made the subsequent evolution of property law remarkably path dependent. Such institutional path dependency has conspired with the "difference seeking" professional ideology of much of the comparative law community, so that the already overwhelming formal differences between common law and civil law have been overemphasized and the substantial analogies have been overlooked.[98]

The important and substantial convergence has consequently been undermined by the mutual desire of lawyers belonging to one or the other tradition to surprise each other with radically different approaches. In this book, I will certainly acknowledge the main formal (and institutional) differences, but my focus will be on those common, shared principles that appear to be deeply rooted in the institutional system of those societies that have been able to develop an advanced economy. I believe that in the domain of property law significant analogies and differences are distributed rather randomly among different national legal systems. This calls into question the usefulness of the very distinction between common law and civil law if one's conception of property law is broad enough to capture the institutional background. Further, I believe that most of the differences cannot be located in substantive rules but instead are located in the legal process itself. In observing Western societies' substantive rules of property law from the perspective of market actors, they tend to introduce similar incentives despite their different form. Moreover, substantive rules tend to be negotiated around. The legal process, on the other hand, is the place to look for relevant differences between distinct systems of property rights. Substantive property law offers a large number of "common core" solutions.

NOTES

1. G. Hardin, *The Tragedy of the Commons*, 162 *Science* 1243 (1968).

2. This broad meaning is shared by the institutional economic literature. See, for an introduction, Y. Barzel, *Economic Analysis of Property Rights* (1989).

3. Such a broad meaning includes "informal" property law, as will become clear later. Informal reactions to commons problems are discussed in E. Ostrom, *Governing the Commons: The Evolution of Institutions for Collective Action* (1990), and in C. Rose, *The Comedy of the Commons: Custom, Commerce and Inherently Public Property*, 53 *U. Chi. L. Rev.* 711 (1986).

4. For a standard English-language black-letter treatment of such variations, see F. H. Lawson (ed.), *Structural Variations in Property Law*, in VI *International Encyclopedia of Comparative Law*, ch. 2 (1975), 3–284.

5. The tragedy of the commons is discussed in very similar terms by A. Gambaro, *La proprietà* 9 (1990).

6. See A. F. McEvoy, *The Fishermen's Problem: Ecology and Law in the California Fisheries 1850–1980* (1986); H. Scott Gordon, *The Economic Theory of a Common Property Resource: The Fishery*, 62 *J. Pol. Econ.* 124 (1954).

7. Ostrom, *supra* note 3. This book discusses a variety of alternatives for sustainable informal management of commons.

8. The classic cite is here to H. Demsetz, *Toward a Theory of Property Rights*, 57 *Am. Econ. Rev.* 347 (1967).

9. Of course, the literature on the definition and the concept of property and property law is monumental throughout the legal systems. No attempt will be made here to discuss it in any detail. For a first introduction to some famous thinking about property, see *Property: Mainstream and Critical Positions* (C. B. Macpherson ed., 1978).

10. See, most recently, M. A. Heller, *The Tragedy of the Anticommons*, 111 *Harv. L. Rev.* 625 (1998); id., *The Boundaries of Private Property*, 108 *Yale L.J.* 1163 (1999).

11. See, among many emphasizing private decision making as the essence of property rights, F. Michelman, *Ethics, Economics and the Law of Property*, 24 *Nomos* 3 (1982).

12. See, for example, D. C. North and R. P. Thomas, *The Rise of the Western World: A New Economic History* 23 (1973).

13. See A. Rapaczinski, *The Role of the State and the Market in Establishing Property Rights*, 10 *J. Econ. Persp.* 87 (1996).

14. The reader interested in further sophisticated discussion might want to read, in the English language, L. Becker, *Property Rights: Philosophical Foundations* (1977); J. Waldron, *The Right to Private Property* (1988).

15. See M. R. Cohen, *Property and Sovereignity*, 13 *Cornell L. Q.* 8 (1927).

16. See S. Buckle, *Natural Law and the Theory of Property: Grotius to Hume* (1991).

17. Further discussion can be found in many of the essays collected in J. R. Pennock & J. W. Chapman, *Property* 22 *Nomos* (1980).

18. See R. Sacco, *Mute Law*, 43 *Am. J. Comp. L.* 455 (1995); for the ethological foundations of territoriality and possession, see I. Eibl-Eibesfeldt, *Human Ethology*, §§ 4.11 and 4.12 (1989).

19. See P. Bohannan, *We, the Alien: An Introduction to Cultural Anthropology* 16 (1992).

20. The example involves two young animals belonging to the human species already framed by our Western culture. See R. Benedict, *Patterns of Culture* 12 (1934).

21. See *Law in Culture and Society* (L. Nader ed., 2d ed., 1998); U. Mattei, *Three Patterns of Law: Taxonomy and Change in the World's Legal Systems*, 45 *Am. J. Comp. L.* 5 (1997).

22. See R. C. Ellickson, *Order Without Law* 123 (1991).
23. See F. Von Hayek, *Law, Legislation, and Liberty* (1973).
24. I tackle this problem in U. Mattei, *Comparative Law and Economics* (1997).
25. See Sacco, *supra* note 18.
26. See M. Guadagni, *Legal Pluralism*, in *The New Palgrave: A Dictionary of Economics and the Law* vol. 2 p. 542 (P. Newman ed., 1998).
27. Of course, customs need not be ancient. What makes customs, as all other rules discussed thus far as "legal" is their ability to convey signals that affect the behavior of market actors fearing the enforcement. In this book, I have no special worry to distinguish legal from nonlegal sanctions as has been relentlessly done by much American realist and law and society literature. See, for a recent survey, E. A. Posner, *The Regulation of Groups: The Influence of Legal and Non Legal Sanctions on Collective Action*, 63 *U. Chi. L. Rev.* 133 (1996).
28. See *Gypsy Law Symposium*, 45 *Am. J. Comp. L.* 225–442 (W. O. Weirauch ed., 1997).
29. See Heller, *supra* note 10, at p. 635, recognizing the Mafia as a relevant formant of transitional property law in Russia.
30. See, for many examples, H. De Soto, *The Other Path: The Invisible Revolution in the Third World* (1989); for a case study, see J. Ensminger, *Making a Market: The Institutional Transformation of an African Society* (1992).
31. See R. Cooter et al., *Bargaining in the Shadow of the Law: A Testable Model of Strategic Behaviour*, 11 *J. Legal Stud.* 225 (1982).
32. See the discussion in Chapter 3.
33. The classic book developing comparative legal history as the story of different professional groups in civil law (professors) and common law (judges) is J. P. Dawson, *The Oracles of the Law* (1968). For some general background, one should also consult H. J. Berman, *Law and Revolution* (1983).
34. Cf. J. H. Baker, *An Introduction to English Legal History* 255–357 (2d. ed., 1990).
35. The literature on the English legal history is very abundant. It is not in the nature of an introductory work to take care of many details. The classic works are F. W. Maitland, *Equity and the Forms of Action* (1909) and F. Pollock & F. W. Maitland, *The History of English Law: Before the Time of Edward I* (2d ed., 1898).
36. See J. Gordley, *The Philosophical Origins of Modern Contract Doctrine* (1991).
37. See H. Kotz, *National Report for Germany*, in *Principles of European Trust Law* 85 (D. J. Haiton et al. eds., 1999); M. Graziadei, *Trust*, in *Introduction to Italian Law* (U. Mattei & J. Lena eds., forthcoming).
38. Cf. H. Hansmann & U. Mattei, *The Functions of Trust Law: A Comparative Legal and Economic Analysis*, 73 *N.Y.U. L. Rev.* 434 (1998); for a reconstruction of trust law focusing on its contractual rather than proprietary nature, see J. Langbein, *The Contractarian Basis of Trust Law*, 105 *Yale L.J.* 625 (1995).
39. Cf. F. H. Lawson & B. Rudden, *The Law of Property* (2d ed., 1982).
40. For a classical discussion, see W. W. Buckland & A. D. McNair, *Roman Law and Common Law: A Comparison in Outline* (2d ed., 1952).
41. See B. Rudden, *Things as Things and Things as Wealth*, 14 *Oxford J. Legal Stud.* 81 (1994).
42. See F. H. Lawson, *Remedies of English Law* 15–16 (2d ed., 1980).
43. M. Bridge, *Personal Property Law* (2d ed., 1996).

44. J. Stevens & R. A. Pearce, *Land Law* (1998).

45. See, generally, A.W.B. Simpson, *A History of the Land Law* (2d ed., 1986).

46. See Baker, *supra* note 34, at 283.

47. See R. Ellickson, *Property in Land*, 102 *Yale L.J.* 1315, 1374 (1993). "To deter destructive decomposition of property interests the Anglo American Legal System has developed a complex set of paternalistic rules." See also Heller, *supra* note 10, at 664.

48. In 1996, the Trusts of Land and Appointment of Trustees Act made important changes in the English law relating to trusts of land; see J. G. Riddall, *Land Law*, 142 (6th ed., 1997).

49. Cf. A. Gambaro, *Property*, in A. Candian et al., *Proprieté Property Eigentum* (1991); the more theoretical literature on property law develops notions at a level of generality that makes them useful for describing both traditions. See A. M. Honoré, *Ownership*, in *Oxford Essays in Jurisprudence* 107 (A. G. Guest ed., 1961). It remains true, however, that within each system the notion of property as used in constitutional law is very different from that used in the technical legal discourse. For a discussion in English of the development of a constitutional notion of property different from the one defined in the civil code, see G. F. Schuppert, *The Right to Property*, in *The Constitution of the Federal Republic of Germany* 112 (1992).

50. S. Bright & G. Gilbert, *Landlord and Tenant Law* (1995).

51. Actually, the term of years was originally neither more nor less than a contractual relationship between lessor and lessee: The lessee had probably no remedy at all against third persons. From Edward II's reign onward, the lessee was protected against ejectors by a variety of the writ of trespass known as the *writ de ejectione firmae*, but he could only recover damages for the ejectment and not the land itself; only toward the end of the fifteenth century was it beginning to be thought that a lessee could recover the land itself by this action. Since *ejectio firmae* was a form of trespass, the simplest and most satisfactory action in the Register of Writs, soon freeholders came to compare their misfortune in having to use the older real actions with the happy position of the termor. In the course of the next two centuries, a series of fictions enabled them to use the termor's remedy, which came to be called the action of ejectment. See W. S. Holdsworth, *An Historical Introduction to the Land Law* 71, 230 (1927); A.W.B. Simpson, *A History of the Land Law* 68, 135 (1961).

52. See for a classic treatment R. H. Kersley, *Goodeve's Modern Law of Personal Property* (London, 1949).

53. See B. Ackerman, *Private Property and the Constitution* (1977); F. Michelman, *Tutelary Jurisprudence and Constitutional Property*, in *Liberty, Property and the Future of Constitutional Development* 127 (E. F. Paul & H. Dickman eds., 1990).

54. In America today it is fashionable to talk about the Hohfeld–Honoré notion of property claiming a local origin of such approaches. See, for example, L. C. Becker, *Property Rights: Philosophic Foundations* 7–23 (1977); see also J. Waldron, *The Right of Private Property* 49 (1988); A. Reeve, *Property* 14–21 (1988).

55. The bundle metaphor can easily be adapted to describe any technical notion of property. It will be enough to clarify that different sticks might be missing in different legal systems. See J. E. Penner, *The Bundle of Right Picture of Property*, 43 *UCLA L. Rev.* 711 (1996).

56. The classic is Dawson, *supra* note 33.

57. See R. B. Schlesinger et al., *Comparative Law* 197 (6th ed., 1998).

58. See R. Zimmermann, *The Law of Obligations: Roman Foundations of the Civilian Tradition* (1996).

59. See A. M. Patault, *Introduction Historique au Droit des Biens* (1989).

60. See J. H. Merryman, *Ownership and Estate: Variations on a Theme by Lawson*, 48 *Tul. L. Rev.* 916 (1974).

61. A *numerus clausus* theory never developed in common law, although some functional analogies can be found as means to reduce anticommons problems. See, in general, B. Rudden, *Economic Theory versus Property Law: The Numerus Clausus Problem*, in *Oxford Essays in Jurisprudence* (J. Eekelaar & J. Bell eds., 1987); Heller, *supra* note 10, at 664–665.

62. For a different position, see J. Gordley, *Myths of the French Civil Code*, 42 *Am. J. Comp. L.* 439 (1994).

63. The blackstonian definition of property, clearly inspired by continental writings, is contained at the very beginning of Volume 2 (Rights of Things) of his treatise of 1766: "that sole and despotic dominion which one man claims and exercises over the external things of the world, in total exclusion of the right of any other individual in the universe"; 2 W. Blackstone, *Commentaries on the Law of England* (1766).

64. For a longer discussion and bibliographical details, see Mattei, *supra* note 24, at 33–40.

65. See M. H. Kramer, *John Locke and the Origins of Private Property* (1997).

66. See G. Gorla, *Diritto comparato e diritto comune europeo* 182 (1981).

67. In the French Civil Code this idea went so far as to erase an ancient and important institution like emphiteusis.

68. I discuss its relevance in modern law and economics in Mattei, *supra* note 24, at 27.

69. See F. Parisi, *Liability for Negligence and Judicial Discretion* 90 (1991).

70. See J. Coleman & J. Kraus, *Rethinking the Theory of Legal Rights*, 95 *Yale L.J.* 1335 (1986).

71. See R. Cooter & T. Ulen, *Law and Economics* 93–94 (2d ed., 1997).

72. See C. Atias & A. Lavasseur, *The French Civil Code: An Insider's View* (1987).

73. Article 544 defines ownership as "the right to use and dispose of a thing in the most absolute way, provided that one does not so against a law or a regulation." This definition obviously is tautological, since the rule and a full exception are contained into it.

74. See A. Gambaro, *The Abuse of Right in the Civil Law*, in *Aequitas and Equity* 375 (A. Rabello ed., 1994).

75. See J. Bonnecase, *Le pensée juridique française de 1804 a l' heure presente* 561 (1933).

76. See A. Gambaro, *Ius Aedificandi e nozione civilistica della proprietà* 99 (1976).

77. For a recent comparative description, see M. Lasser, *"Lit Theory" Put to the Test: A Comparative Literary Analysis of American Judicial Test and French Judicial Discourse*, 111 *Harv. L. Rev.* 621 (1998).

78. This phenomenon has been described as a synecdoche. See R. Sacco, *Legal Formants: A Dynamic Approach to Comparative Law*, 39 *Am. J. Comp. L.* 1 (1991); P. G. Monateri, *Régles et techniques de la definition dans le droit des obliga-*

tions et des contrats en France et en Allemagne: La synecdoque française, Rev Int Droit Comp 7–57 (1984).

79. See Gambaro, *supra* note 74, at 81.

80. See F. Lawson & B. Markesinis, *Liability for Unintentional Harm in the Civil Law and Common Law* (1982).

81. See, in English, the discussion in Parisi, *supra* note 69.

82. See A. M. Honoré in 7 *Irish Jurist* 138 (1972).

83. See Gambaro *supra* note 74, at 150. References to case law in Mattei, *supra* note 24, at 36 n. 27–28.

84. See F. Wieacker, *A History of Private Law in Europe* (T. Weir tr., 1995).

85. See J. Q. Witman, *The Legacy of Roman Law in the German Romantic Era* (1990); M. H. Hoeflich, *Law and Geometry: Legal Science from Leibniz to Langdell*, 30 *Am. J. Legal History* 95 (1986).

86. See Schlesinger et al., *supra* note 57, at 617.

87. F. K. Von Savigny, *Sistema del diritto romano attuale* 337–367 (V. Scialoja tr., 1886).

88. G.W.F. Hegel, *Lineamenti di filosofia del diritto* 362–363 (F. Messineo tr., 1974).

89. Roscoe Pound was the prophet of Sociological Jurisprudence in America. His work, as he freely admitted, rested heavily on continental, especially German scholarship, and the extent of his own originality is still an open question. See W. P. La Piana, *A Task of No Common Magnitude: The Funding of the American Law Institute*, 11 *Nova L. Rev.* 1085, 1111 (1987).

90. See W. N. Hohfeld, *Fundamental Legal Conceptions as Applied in Legal Reasoning and Other Legal Essays* (1919).

91. See Gambaro, *supra* note 74.

92. See Gambaro, *supra* note 74.

93. Another example of convergence between common law and civil law systems (in a field in which there are profound historical and theoretical differences) can be seen in the evolution of the rules concerning residential leases in the last decades; see M. J. Radin, *The Revolution in Residential Landlord–Tenant Law: Causes and Consequences*, 68 *Cornell L.Q.* 508 (1982); A. De Vita, *Lease*, in X *Digesto Discipline Privatistiche. Sez. Civile* 443 (1993).

94. See literature cited *supra* note 54.

95. Evidence that the natural law conception of property is not rooted in the technical discourse of the common law (despite Blackstone's contribution, and despite that of Madison to the American Constitution) may be grasped from other areas of the law as well. For example, most European codes provide a detailed set of rules determining the distance between buildings, trees, plants, and so on. The formal respect of such rules is strictly enforced by courts which do not enjoy discretion. Even a slight violation of such distances, albeit reasonable and innocuous for the neighbor, compels destruction of the building or eradication of the offending plants. In the common law courts, a standard of reasonableness would guide decision-making in this area. This short analysis suggests how the common law conception of property handles externalities. The law of nuisance is a structural characteristic of the common law notion of property rights. The American developments are very interesting and are a classic topic of law and economics literature. In *Boomer v. Atlantic*

Cement Co., 26 N.Y. 2d 219, 257 N.E.2d 870 (1970), a factory creating externalities was not enjoined from operation, provided it could internalize its costs. In *Spur Industries v. Del Webb Development Co.*, and in the very notion of "coming to the nuisance," the flexible boundaries of common law property rights are clearer still. *Spur Industries v. Del Webb Development Co.*, 108 Ariz. 178, 494 P.2d 700 (1972). See *infra* 149 sq.

96. See C. Salvi, *Il contenuto del diritto di proprietà* 33 (1994).

97. See S. R. Ackerman, *Controlling Environmental Policy: The Limits of Public Law in Germany and the United States* (1995).

98. See R. Schlesinger, *The Past and the Future of Comparative Law*, 43 *Am. J. Comp. L.* 477 (1995).

CHAPTER 2

Sources

CONSTITUTIONAL LAW

If compared with simple systems of property law, modern legal systems show both increases in the number of individuals or organizations that compete for scarce resources and in the number of institutional actors that are enabled to make proprietary choices. In other words, the increase of social complexity also increases the complexity of the legal process that frames property law. From the two girls of the example discussed in Chapter 1, or from a few landlords in feudal England, we shift to several million people who theoretically have access to the resource. From parents entrusted to decide family property matters, or from a small and homogeneous Bench in Westminster Hall, we shift to a complex organization of individuals placed in different official capacities, who are called upon to make property choices, usually by interpreting legal texts or sets of precedent. Moreover, in these cases, the content of different property choices, and ultimately of property law, may vary with the ideology of different decision makers. Consequently, legal systems struggle to obtain consistency, neutrality, predictability, and, ultimately, legitimacy by a series of institutional mechanisms.[1]

To begin, there is a tendency detectable at early stages of social development to formalize a constitution of property and to solidify it by deeming it immutable. The reason for this fiction is obvious. Property law deals with fundamental distribution issues, and since there is no general agreement regarding the legitimacy or rationale of the distribution of resources within the society (why the rich should be rich and the poor should be poor), distribution issues related to property cannot be rediscussed beyond certain limits.[2] If they were, excessive social instability would follow. Often, the political process reshuffles property rights and wealth among different social groups. This can be done by increasing certain tax liabilities and decreasing others, or by regulating or prohibiting certain uses of property in the interest of a community.

However, this redistribution activity always faces limits, one being the domain of political revolution. Indeed, all political revolutions can be regarded as redistributions of property rights beyond the constitutional limits of the previous social organizations. The French Revolution, for example, seized property interests from the nobles in favor of the bourgeoisie, beyond the proprietary constitution of the ancien régime.[3] Similarly, the October Revolution nullified the former proprietary constitution through massive nationalization.[4] Again, the post-socialist legal systems have overcome the socialist proprietary constitution by privatization and redistribution of property and wealth.[5] Thus, each revolutionary movement immediately tries to formalize these shifts of economic power, limiting the discretion of the "officials" charged with making choices related to property.

Immediately after a revolution, new fundamental redistribution of wealth is forbidden. Once again, as before the revolution, nonowners (according to the new order) are required (and forced by the law) to respect the property rights of the new owners, no matter how the latter have acquired them. Peace and order are at stake in this social dynamic.

Of course, I use the phrase "proprietary constitution" in a broad sense, independent from the existence of a written constitution. For example, the proprietary constitution in most African customary law is based on a rule of collective land tenure, accompanied by the inalienability of individual parcels of land outside of the extended family group.[6] This rule, made sacred by the respect for the deceased members of the group who are buried in the land, can be seen as a fundamental constitutional guarantee for the unborn future members of the family. Both the traditional chief and the modern political authorities are limited, de jure or de facto, by this fundamental constitutional structure of African customary law.[7]

In modern law, the desire of immutability is usually pursued by the introduction in constitutional texts of provisions devoted to property, which are considered hierarchically superior to other sources of law. Such constitutional provisions contain the fundamental distributional choices of the society. For example, the few socialist constitutions left maintain a ban on the privatization of the means of production, and usually of land. The first Western constitutional experiences tended to emphasize the opposite choice, by introducing private property into fundamental values of the society. For example, the French Constitution presently in force reiterates the famous provision of the revolutionary Declaration of Human Rights, in which private property is sacrosanct, at the same level as freedom, security, and resistance to political oppression.[8] In the United States, the Fifth Amendment and the Fourteenth Amendment to the Federal Constitution do the same thing, by putting private property within the three fundamental values, together with life and liberty.

An intermediate option is reflected in other constitutional experiences, including the German and the Italian, which display the so-called "social functionalization" of private property.[9] They recognize and protect individual property rights as a matter of principle, but they limit their exercise and acquisition in order to avoid excessive social inequalities. It is important to note that this intermediate attitude is wisely followed today by the constitutions of most former socialist countries, including Russia, the Czech Republic, Hungary, and Poland. In these countries, private property, despite its intrinsic contradictions and its unsolvable political tensions, is leading the transition from the planned to the market economy.[10]

The importance of the text, however, should not be exaggerated. Property law is always tracing a balance between the political needs of redistribution and stability. The political decision making relates to redistribution, while the technical legal decision making attempts to maintain stability. The point of equilibrium in modern political organizations is found somewhere between the extremes of pure market and planned economies. Such a point of equilibrium may be well expressed, as it is done in the mentioned constitutions following Duguit's terminology, as the social function of private property.[11] This notion can be considered a basic principle of property law: Property rights should have their share of social responsibility.[12]

In abstract, the language of a constitution tells us very little about what practical choices regarding property rights institutional actors will carry out. The different machineries of justice and administration grant decision-making power to a variety of officials, whose authority is not effectively limited by the broad language of the constitution. This decision-making activity frames the concrete law of property of different legal systems.

A comparative example may clarify the picture. For historical reasons, France and the United States use similar constitutional languages about property rights. The two systems, however, are unrelated in terms of the practical mechanisms of constitutional protection of property rights. In the United States, any judge can strike down a statute, administrative regulation, or judicial precedent as unconstitutional. Constitutional issues therefore arise at any moment, and may involve all aspects of public decision making that affect property rights (i.e., the activity of any one official exercising the power of proprietary decision making can be constitutionally challenged). Consequently, property rights have strong constitutional protection against any regulations affecting them, and limits to property rights can be considered unconstitutional by an American judge. Accordingly, an official making a decision affecting property rights must prepare to justify and rationalize this choice (police power).[13]

In France, there is no Constitutional Court where an individual property owner can bring a constitutional challenge. Moreover, ordinary judges have no power of judicial review. Rather, the Conseil Constitutionnel checks ex ante the constitutionality of a statute following legislative enactment. After this initial judicial review, the statutes cannot be challenged on constitutional grounds. However, the French owner of property may attempt to challenge an administrative regulation in administrative courts as unconstitutional. This surrogate protection is weak and is widely considered inadequate.[14] The protection that private property receives by these mechanisms is weak for a number of reasons.

First, it is very difficult to predict in abstract, ex ante, the ways a statute may affect individual rights. Only the practical interaction of the statute within the legal system defines its impact. The more a system of constitutional adjudication is open to individuals, the more likely it is that a concrete violation of rights will be known by the decision maker.[15] Second, a statute is subject to an ex ante check enveloped in its full and fresh political force. When a statute has just been approved by the political power it is less likely that a technical body can overrule it. In contrast, old statutes lack political force and are easier to strike down as unconstitutional.[16] Finally, the members of the Conseil do not have the guarantee of independence from the political power that tenure of office provides the U.S. judiciary. The decisions of the Conseil Constitutionnel declaring constitutionally admissible the massive nationalizations carried out by the Socialist government in the early 1980s, demonstrate the impact of this type of constitutional adjudication of property rights, despite the constitutional rhetoric around them.[17] The structure of the legal process gives property rights more protection in the Austrian, German, and Italian systems, and most post-socialist countries. In these countries, the language of the constitution is less favorable to private property than in France, but constitutional adjudication plays a more significant role.[18]

From the discussion so far it is clear that there are different choices related to property rights competing with one another for determining the legal status of a given resource. For instance, African traditional chiefs compete with modern political officials who aim to free property rights from the traditional rule of inalienability.[19] The intentions of the framers of a constitution compete with different political majorities that may use statutes or regulations. The political intentions of these majorities compete with the techno-legal culture of a court of law such as a Constitutional Court or an administrative tribunal, which by invoking the constitutional choice may defeat the political decision. The techno-legal choice of judges may compete with the bureaucratic choice of the public administration or of an administrative agency, which may modify, through regulations, the intent of the legislature.[20]

Similarly, practical institutional mechanisms can be much more important in describing the property law of a given legal system than the text of a statute or code. In certain countries (e.g., France and Italy), a separate administrative justice system may demand the last word over the content of individual property rights. In administrative courts, judges are not as independent in front of the political power as they should be. Consequently, property rights may change their nature depending on whether the conflict over scarce resources is between private individuals or between an individual and the government.[21] For example, in Italy or France, an owner's powers over resources are often frustrated when public law starts to play a role.[22]

Finally, it must be emphasized that legal writers make many choices delineating property law. These decision makers without an official role are extremely important in framing the law of property. Their role varies from legal system to legal system, but it cannot be neglected in accurately understanding the principles of property law. Many of these principles and entire chapters of property law in the Western legal tradition were found in the opinions of legal scholars and adopted in actual official choices related to property.[23] A most important example that we will discuss later in the domain of remedies is the French Astreinte or the doctrine of *Troubles de Voisinage*. In both these cases, scholarly writings led to innovation eventually received by the legislator and case law, respectively.[24]

Of course, each of the actors in the property system tends to perform its role and make choices that are coherent within its institutional structure. Therefore, it is crucial to find common principles that can be used to describe this structure. Between the textual extremes of the sanctity of property rights that we find in the French and U.S. models, and that of the ban on private property of socialist law, lies the notion of property law as a "social function." This idea, introduced in legal thinking by the French scholar Duguit in the early twentieth century, seems to capture the reality of modern property law systems. The same idea seems to be reflected in the Anglo-American tradition, by including general liability toward third parties within the typical sticks of the proprietary bundle.[25]

Between the structural extremes of constitutional adjudication open to all judges (as in the U.S. model) and of no constitutional adjudication (as in Great Britain and France), lies the choice of most modern systems to develop special constitutional courts. This compromising option deserves attention since it captures most of the structural characteristics of constitutional adjudication as a synthesis between political and technical decision making. Such an intermediate option is a sound equilibrium between two extremes. The phrase, "political decision making in matters of property" is used to describe the political decisions that redistribute property rights and scarce resources between individuals (i.e., a project of nationalization or a land-use regulation). Further "technical decision making" describes the check on the compatibility of such redistribution with the need for stability of property rights (as presently distributed in society), whose protection is the province of the judiciary.

In constitutional adjudication, the fundamental principle (established in the celebrated 1803 U.S. case *Marbury v. Madison*) is that constitutional provisions prevail in case of a conflict with any law of inferior ranking. A number of modern systems, however, do not follow the American way of granting to any judge the power of directly applying the former over the latter. In such systems (Germany, Austria, Italy, and Spain being paradigmatic), the ordinary judge faces only the duty to stay the procedure and refer the case to the Constitutional Court for a decision on the hypothetical conflict.[26] As a practical matter, systems vary on what type of preliminary ruling the ordinary judge can enter. In other words, an amount of discretion is always open to the judge deciding on whether to stay the procedure. However, the systems do agree that such discretion cannot be extended. Otherwise the ordinary judge would have de facto power to consider a statute's constitutionality. Generally, judges can decide against referral of a case to the constitutional court if either the constitutional issue is irrelevant to the practical merits of the case or the constitutional issue seems implausible on its face. For example, the Italian legal system removes most of the ordinary judge's discretion, compelling the judge to refer the case whenever a constitutional issue is not meritless on its face. Other systems, in Germany, Spain, and Austria, grant a higher degree of discretion to the ordinary judge in deciding whether to defer to the Constitutional Court.

However, in all cases, such a solution does not in practice preclude ordinary judges from interpreting the law in compatibility with the constitution if it is possible to avoid a constitutional conflict. Nonetheless, the effort to avoid constitutional conflict through interpretation compatible with the constitution must be exercised with sound discretion, whether it is done by the ordinary judge asked to stay a proceeding or by the Constitutional Court in deciding the issue. The Constitutional Court's decision to allow the statute to survive, provided that a certain meaning is given to it, may invade the prerogative to interpret the law that is given to the top of the ordinary judiciary. In Italy, for example, the *Corte di Cassazione* and the *Corte Costituzionale* often conflicted with each other.[27] However, some conflicts are acceptable, as is usual when a number of institutional actors play similar roles within the machinery of justice.

To be sure, certain systems, following the German model, allow the Constitutional Court to decide outside the mechanism just discussed, by granting direct access to individual complaints. These systems, however, do not completely give up the primary check of the ordinary judge, since the door of the Constitutional Court is open to direct complaints only when all ordinary means to reach the court have been exhausted.[28]

Constitutional Courts enjoy a high degree of prestige among the institutional actors asked to carry on proprietary choices. They are usually staffed with highly qualified lawyers, although the technical qualifications of their personnel are somewhat tempered by a political element. Judges of the Constitutional Court are usually appointed from jurists with important political connections or with high political visibility. This political influence is not only ex ante in the process of appointment, but continues ex post. Constitutional judges typically serve for a term of years and do not enjoy the same privilege of tenure during good behavior as their American colleagues, or even as their colleagues in most ordinary judiciaries. Consequently, their decision making, particularly in politically charged cases such as nationalization or privatization of broadcasting frequencies, may not be as nonpolitical as one would wish.

Decisions of a Constitutional Court enjoy a higher standing than that of ordinary legislation. As a consequence, the structure of their holding is usually general, abstract, and forward looking.[29] Therefore, the decision making of Constitutional Courts contains not only a decision on the present conflict over scarce resources, but a directive aimed at leading the future decision maker (a court, legislator, or administrative agency). In other words, the main function of the decision of a Constitutional Court is to create a prospective program for the distribution of resources that reflects formalization within the constitution. The results of a decision are not simply a concrete redistribution of resources in the case at bar; political considerations still play a significant role, even if they do not go so far as to modify the described structure of constitutional adjudication.

First, the court is in a position to consider constitutional issues that would not otherwise be foreseeable ex ante, thereby guaranteeing the informational advantages of a system of decentralized decision making. Second, the ordinary judge maintains the power to filter, through his or her traditionally technical (sometimes bureaucratic) legal culture, the demand for redistribution of property rights arising from societal demands. Similarly, this system prevents a completely political decision-making power from sacrificing rights that should otherwise be respected.

The formalistic mentality, still common among judges in the civil law tradition, creates doctrines that, in certain legal systems, allow the Constitutional Court to rule only on what is recognized as a statute in the formal sense.[30] Such a narrow reading, based on the theory that administrative regulations other than statutes may be challenged as unconstitutional in front of administrative judges, has a high cost for the system. For instance, there are no guarantees whatsoever that the structure of administrative adjudication will bring results similar to the constitutional adjudication structure. As a paradoxical consequence, an administrative regulation (a hierarchically inferior source) may become much more resistant to constitutional scrutiny than a formal statute.[31]

In any system with a constitutional guarantee of private property, the crucial issue that constitutional adjudication must face is the selection from a variety of regulatory decisions that have redistributional character of those that directly or indirectly affect property rights. Some such redistributions are considered "takings" requiring compensation, while others are not and consequently do not allow for such. For instance, a zoning ordinance that decides that no buildings can be constructed in a certain area has the same intrusive impact on private property as an expropriation that grants a nominal compensation for the taking of edified land. While the latter would be considered plainly unconstitutional in most legal systems, the former may have more chances of surviving on theories similar to what Americans call "police power." Indeed, legal systems have to recognize that in our crowded society private property sometimes must be sacrificed in the interest of the collectivity. Police power theory and its analogues strive to find some principle distinguishing between cases in which compensation is granted and those in which it is not.[32]

From the perspective of the individual owner, what matters most is the economic impact of a given activity on the value of the property. For example, a decision authorizing the construction of a freeway will similarly affect both those individuals on whose land the freeway will actually run and those whose property is so close to the freeway as to become practically unusable (e.g., a quiet summer house). While it is true that not all limits which public decision making imposes on property rights will need to be indemnified, it is also true that dilemmas such as redistribution require indemnification and cannot be solved using formalistic reasoning. The special mixture of political legitimacy and technical skills found in the Constitutional Courts should be exploited outside any formalism, for the purpose of sound proprietary decision making.

CODES AND COMMON LAW PRINCIPLES

In modern legal systems, property law is heavily codified or, one might better say, property rights are intensively regulated by statute. It is sufficient to consider a building code, a zoning ordinance, a regulation for the protection of the environment, a statute that imposes on the owner of a car the duty of periodical safety tests, a regulation that imposes on farmers a certain slaughtering process, and so on. This is true both in the civil law and in the common law tradition, so that nowadays it would be impossible to distinguish, from the volume of regulation and statutes, a civil law from a common law system. Indeed, property law can be considered codified in a relatively general sense even in England (Law of Property Act 1925), the crib of the common law tradition.[33] In the civil law tradition, however, the law of property has been generally organized around the code system. Such a system contains not only rules, but also the conceptual framework that the lawyer needs in order to make reasonable property law choices. The code in the system of a civilian property law can be considered as the background of the techno-legal decision making related to the distribution of property. It plays much of the same role that broad common law principles play in Anglo-American law.[34]

While detailed rules of property law within the codes may change substantially from legal system to legal system and are often modified by subsequent special legislation, the function of the code that must be emphasized is to organize legal discourse and to trace the fundamental principles of property law. Indeed, the code can be seen, much as the fundamental framework of the common law, as the ultimate attempt to introduce impartial and neutral decision making in property issues, taking for granted the actual distribution of resources. In principle, a property law decision based on the code does not redistribute property rights. Its principal purpose is to protect property rights as the judge finds them in front of him. True, each concrete judicial decision about property may be considered yet a new allocation of property rights, particularly because usually a conflict arises from the less than clear boundaries between various rights.[35] However, it remains true that the fundamental characteristic common among the systems of codified property law is their attempt to organize a system of decision making related to scarce resources, as insulated as possible from the political pressures of redistribution.[36]

While most of the following chapters will be devoted to discussing in some detail the principles that ground technical decision making regarding property, we need here to introduce two fundamental general aspects found at play in every property system. One has an economic flavor and sheds some light on the intimate relationship between market principles and private law. The other, more grounded in the legal tradition, is at the root of the Western taxonomy of private law and deals with the structural distinctions between property, contracts, and torts. They will both be explored in greater detail later, but deserve special attention now.

Civil codes may contain rules and principles related to property in different parts of their organization. For example, the French Code (1804) entitles two of its three books to property (Book 2 on property, Book 3 on the different ways of acquiring property). Book 3 covers tort law, contract law, and the law of successions. In Spain, the body of law that the French paradigm treats in Book 3 is more coherently divided up in two books of the Civil Code (1889), one devoted to obligations, and one to successions. Most of the codified property law is consequently left in Book 2. In the German BGB (1900) we can find rules of property in Book 1 (the famous General Part) and in Book 3, entirely devoted to property. Likewise, the Italian Civil Code devotes its Book 3 to property law, although many important rules related to property matters can be found in Book 4 (obligations) as far as the transfer of property is concerned, and in Book 6 (evidence) for many of the remedial devices. Again, the new Dutch Civil Code (1992) devotes one of its books (Book 5) to property, but scatters many rules of property in Book 3 (as a sort of general part), as well as elsewhere.

Considering that many rules of property law can be found either in commercial codes (in those systems that adopt separate commercial codes) or in the parts of the codes devoted to commercial law, it is easy to see that property remains crucial to the general system of civilian private law. The two fundamental principles we are talking about are, however, common everywhere, and are considered part of the metapositive structure of modern systems of private property.[37] Such principles are at the root of the common law of property as well.

The fundamental economic principle that governs property law is the fight against externalities created by private activities. Codes are aimed at protecting individual choices consistent with property rights already allocated by decision makers. In other words, proprietary freedom is encouraged by systems of ownership aiming to develop a market economy.[38] Yet this freedom must be reconciled with liabilities that any choice affecting the interests of third parties carries. By so doing, the premises for the proper functioning of the market are enshrined at the core of the private law organization, with benefits for the public interest consistent with private-property guarantees. Of course, to obtain this result, property law cooperates within the whole system of private law, mostly with the law of contracts and the law of torts.

The structure of property rights is different, both from contractual rights and from interests whose protection is the province of tort law. Only a property right is the guarantee of a completely idiosyncratic sphere of the owner. No one is entitled to challenge his or her choices as absurd or unreasonable. To explain in simple terms, although it may be considered absurd or unreasonable to buy a book and not to read it, nobody is entitled to challenge the choice of an owner who buys books only to cut their pages and make funny pen drawings in them. No public authority could take his or her books away on this rationale. Tort law, on the other hand, does not work to protect an interest when such an interest has no social value in the market. In the case of the faulty destruction of vandalized books, the idiosyncratic owner can obtain no substantial damages from the wrongdoer.[39]

Moreover, the structure of property rights may cause the owner to claim that they should be respected throughout society. They pose a legal duty of respect of a given property right to all individuals in the present and in the future. Property rights survive the life of their owner, and are not related, as contractual rights, to a given personal relationship among individuals. Civilian systems talk about real rights (i.e., rights that run with the thing), as opposed to personal rights (i.e., rights that can be exercised only against one given individual). Although common law countries give the notion of real versus personal rights a different meaning, much of the same idea exists within them when they talk about remedies in rem versus remedies in personam.[40]

We do not need to enter into the subtleties of comparative discussion to say that property rights do affect the allocation of scarce resources in a much deeper way than contractual rights.[41] This is one of the reasons behind the civilian theory of the *numerus clausus* of real rights that precludes the parties from creating limited property rights (such as servitude, etc.) outside of the typical scheme provided by the code. Whenever a property right is created over a scarce resource, there is a need for public notice that could not be provided as effectively if complete creativity were allowed.[42] When a property right rather than a contractual right is created over a resource, everybody is bound by it, not just the individuals who actually entered into the contract. Much of the same need to limit the permanent impact of property rights over scarce resources is behind the "rule against perpetuities" and other rules against "extreme decompositions" of property rights that in common law countries try to limit the impact on future generations created by the absence of the *numerus clausus* principle.[43] Such "permanent impact factor" limiting the free decision making of future generations is the other structural characteristic that makes property law different from other major branches of patrimonial private law.

SPECIAL STATUTES

Politically organized pressures (lobbying) may and usually do find their way into the system of property law. However, they usually take the form of special statutes that are the product of pressure groups, and therefore are not aimed at neutral decision making regarding scarce resources.[44] A statute that limits the rent tenants must pay landlords, or a statute that introduces minimal terms in rural leases or that exempts from pollution liability certain industrial activities forces the judge into a pattern of decision making that favors certain interests over certain others. This philosophy opposes that which is transmitted to judges through general codes or common law principles. Indeed, such a philosophy, being grounded in the political decision making of a parliament rather than in the techno-legal decision making of a code (which is more the product of scholarship rather than of the political battlefield), is stronger as a matter of legitimacy than technical decision making aimed at neutrality.[45] This explains why, in all modern systems of law, in case of conflicts, special statutes prevail over codes (principle of specialty) and why, exactly for the same reason, statutes prevail over the common law.

On the other hand, special statutes, although politically stronger, are much more difficult to use when decisions related to property rights are beyond their scope. If one abolished all special statutes, a system of technical property law would still exist if the code (or the common law) were left. Conversely, if one abolished the code (or the common law) while maintaining all special statutes, the system would not be able to guide technical decision making. This may explain, among other things, why reasoning through analogy is usually banned in the interpretation of special statutes.[46] Indeed, analogy extends principles contained in legal provisions beyond their original scope by applying them to factual situations that can be approached within the same rationale. Since the rationale of special statutes is usually to advantage certain political groups over others, it makes perfect sense that they are confined to the factual situations that the political process was actually contemplating.

While the fundamental characteristics of technical property law, as recognized by the codes (and by the common law) despite all the formal differences, connect the technical decision making of the judge with the proper functioning of the market, this is not the only option available for the legislator. Even in Western systems historically committed to the market economy, special statutes may be inspired by a coherent redistributive philosophy. When such a philosophy is present, one can detect subsystems of private law (alternative to the code) in which much of the same interpretive options are open to the judge (including reasoning through analogy and principled decision making). In this case, the code loses some of the power that it gets from being the main source of default rules. Examples may be statutes introducing rent control, protecting farmers against landowners or the consumer against the producer, and so on. Such systems may be inspired by a philosophy of protection of the weaker party that, although at odds with market principles, may well be a political option capable of grounding a pattern of technical decision making by the judge.[47] Thus, it is imperative to grasp the fundamental principles that are involved in the codes, as well as the fundamental taxonomy that allows discussions of property law.

LOWER REGULATION

Codes have the force of law. Formally, they are statutes, yet as a practical matter they can be weaker than special statutes because they yield to political decision making. On the other hand, they enjoy a higher status within the legal system, since codes can guide judges in their approach to special statutes. Many times, however, rules of property law are contained neither in the codes nor in special statutes. Rather, many rules of property law are contained in lower administrative regulations, such as an ordinance issued by a mayor, the decision of a city council limiting store hours within a commercial district, or a city-planning ordinance. These lower-level regulations abound in modern legal systems, and may be as intrusive and disruptive of individual property rights as any decision made on a higher hierarchical level.

The practical mechanisms legal systems use to grant some protection of property rights against this sort of decision making vary greatly from system to system. Some systems may allow the ordinary judge to review administrative regulation (in the United States, for example), while others use special administrative courts. Systems with two sets of courts, like France or Germany, may differ on the criteria they use to grant jurisdiction to the public law or to the private law courts. It is extremely hard to find common principles from this perspective.[48] A few generalizations can, however, be attempted. In many situations, civil codes expressly delegate lower regulations the authority to intervene, the most famous example being the very definition of property within Article 544 of the French Code, which expressly mentions regulations as sources of limits to proprietary powers.[49] Such delegation of power to lower-level decision making is a consequence of the very semantic structure of the code. Codes may not be too detailed; their semantic level is located midway between the casuistic approach of Anglo-American common law and statutory discourse and the very abstract level of discourse that is typical of the civilian scholarly tradition. All codes, as a consequence, must yield in some cases to lower-level decision making.

All modern legal systems have worked out some systems of review, usually checking the coherence of administrative regulation within the legal framework, much in the same way constitutional decision making checks the coherence of the legal framework within a constitution.[50] Indeed, "judicial review" means, in England, the control of administrative regulation, while in the United States it means the control of the constitutionality of a statute.

Civil law systems (as well as common law ones) have not codified public law and the domain of lower-level regulation.[51] Many reasons account for this exception to the typically (modern) civilian attitude of major efforts of codification. An "official" explanation is that noncodification allows for flexibility. Such an explanation is, however, contradicted by the historical observation that the decision making of ordinary judges based on a code can be as flexible (or as rigid) as that of administrative judges based on precedent. Another explanation could be the fear of governments (which are usually favored by the private law vs. public law dichotomy) to put their obligations toward individuals in writing, similar to the traditional reluctance of the English legal system to put a Bill of Rights in writing.[52] Whatever the explanation may be, it is a fact that the public law of property remains largely the province of case law and of bureaucratic decision making.

The sources of this public law of property are special statutes, lower-level regulations and decision making, and administrative case law. This structure reflects the separation of jurisdiction of the different levels of government (central, local, etc.), resulting in a high level of complexity and unpredictability. In order to master such complexity, one should not consider public and private law of property as completely separate fields, as civilians tend to do. There are areas of the law that are at the core of the private law of property (e.g., incompatible uses among neighbors) and of the public law of property (e.g., takings) that share many common features.[53] Yet in more than one legal system (possibly not only in the civil law traditions) the analyses of one field excludes the other. Scholars must try to create methods of interpreting policy capable of coordinating different property subsystems. Thus, scholars could reach a more thorough understanding of the legal status of a given resource, possibly distinguishing principled decision making from random byproducts of some bureaucratic fiat.

To offer an example, the so-called "power of eminent domain" (i.e., to take property from individuals in the name of the public interest) has always been counterbalanced, in the Western legal tradition, by a number of due process guarantees.[54] This system of formal protection is of great importance, since it guarantees the substantial value of individual property. Of course, due process rights must also be guaranteed against lower-level decision making that can disturb them. It would be absurd to remove low-level decision making from judicial and constitutional scrutiny, simply because constitutional adjudication is admitted only against formal statutes. In the case of such due process violations, administrative judges (as in Italy), or even ordinary ones (such as in France), should be able to protect individual rights by broad policy reasoning, rather than hiding behind formalistic reasoning based on a hierarchy of the sources of law.

Bureaucratic officials often make public choices directly affecting property in administrative hierarchies. Such bureaucrats usually pursue the circumscribed interest that is behind each lower regulatory instrument, without any global perspective. They tend to forget that (even in the French administrative model) each administrative decision should always respect the rights of the individuals. This sort of decision making, difficult to justify even within the active bureaucracy (which competes with individual owners over scarce resources), becomes completely unbearable and subversive of the rule of law when accepted by judges charged with reviewing the administrative process. No good policy decision can be obtained by a compartmentalized bureaucratic interpretation in which each of the circuits of decision making already discussed (constitutional, judicial, administrative, national, local, etc.) is sealed from all the others, ignoring the impact of their decisions on the legal status of a scarce resource. It must be remembered that property rights, being of central importance to market systems, are particularly sensitive to unjustified inequalities of treatment. For example, if housing property is subject to regulations more restrictive than similarly located office property, the whole housing market of a given area may be disrupted, since investments will privilege offices over housing. This result should not be the contingent consequence of different bureaucrats acting in reciprocal ignorance.

The decisions of such low-level bureaucrats are the most common type of contact between the individual owner and the legal system.[55] Owners have to deal with this whenever, for example, they wish to modify their buildings. In such cases, the administration is interested in obtaining some benefit from the project of the owner just as the owner seeks to benefit from it too.

Occasionally, administrative choices affect the property rights of an individual while carrying out administrative objectives; administrations pursue their particular interests over the general interests of sound proprietary decision making.[56] For example, an administration can send an order to a property owner to create a give structure that facilitates the use of water for the fire brigade. Such a structure will benefit a number of properties which should all pay pro quota for the job. However, it is cheaper for the administration to require one owner to do it rather than dividing up the cost. When a bureaucrat makes these proprietary choices, the damage it causes is limited since it can be considered only lightly redistributive. It simply imposes on the owner the cost–benefit analysis of challenging it in court. However, the court must vigorously reestablish that each owner should pay for its own benefit and not the benefit of other owners, or the result is that important choices like the social distribution of scarce resources will be left to bureaucrats. Unless the principle is reestablished, these bureaucrats receive incentives not to worry about the public interest but only about the interest of their office (e.g., saving the costs of getting contributions by all the owners that benefit from that given pump).

MACHINERY OF JUSTICE

Property law, far from being confined to an abstract set of principles and rules, is rooted in institutions that may or may not be able to enforce those rules. These institutions vary greatly from one system to another. For example, a perfect civil code, containing the best possible abstract regulation of property law, would have no impact on the market in Eastern Europe outside of a global reform of the institutional system which presides over property law.[57] In other words, the law in the books does not affect the markets and what matters is which law is applied. For instance, if a legal system does not have a decently organized system of courts, equipped with qualified lawyers, or if it does not have a reasonably efficient system of law enforcement, its system of property law will be severely affected. In the case of Central and Eastern European countries, for example, the reform of private law (and more specifically of property law) declares the aim of building up the legal infrastructure needed for an efficient local market.[58] Consequently, the importance of the legal process cannot be disregarded. In general, whichever solution we propose in terms of substantive law, we must consider the problems posed by its implementation. This requires a serious effort to provide plaintiffs with a set of legal remedies easy to enforce (i.e., both cheap and effective).[59]

Property law, in all modern legal systems, is not limited to private law, but rather also involves public law. Economists tend to disregard this point, which is crucial for lawyers. Lawyers see private and public law as cooperating in defining property rights. Economists have a tendency to see private law as creating property rights and public law as affecting them by lowering their value.[60] Indeed, in the standard neoclassical economic approach, private law is the province of the market, while public law is the province of the state.[61] From this assumption usually follows a strong antipublic law bias.[62] In more sophisticated economic terms, property law is justified as a cure for externalities (i.e., those behaviors which by affecting third parties without their consent determine the failure of the market).[63] Property rights are given to individuals in order to avoid consumption of resources outside market mechanisms. Each market actor should pay for his or her consumption of scarce resources without passing the cost along to his or her neighbor.

It is necessary to stress that a system cannot deal with externalities defining property rights in a pure private law approach, nor in a pure public law way.[64] This is only the translation on institutional grounds of the impossibility of a "pure market" and of the related impossibility of the "absence of a market." Each legal system will therefore establish, in addition to a private law one, a more or less extended public law cure for externalities, which is reflected in a larger or smaller role of administrative regulation and enforcement.[65]

A good system of property law should take into account this assumption as well as the role that public law actually plays in the system in which it is to be applied. Comparativists distinguish two different approaches to public law within the Western legal tradition: While civil law jurisdictions, based mainly on the French or German model, tend to rely very extensively on public law regulations, common law jurisdictions tend to be much more private law oriented. Such a traditional view is slowly disappearing, since public law is taking on an increasing role and scope everywhere.[66]

However, the impact of this distinction on the legal process still has important applications: While civil law systems organize and select a different body of administrative judges, common law systems tend to keep a unitary judiciary. There are a few policy advantages for the latter model. First, there may be a tendency to staff administrative courts with public servants less sympathetic toward individual rights, and therefore less inclined to make the needs of the market prevail over those of bureaucratic control. Second, because the existence of a unitary judiciary tends to make judicial decisions more grounded in terms of public policy, judges are conscious that the primary responsibility toward public policies resides with them and not with entities such as administrative courts or agencies. As a result, we find a better kind of judicial creativity and responsibility, and bureaucratic judicial reasoning is strongly discouraged.

The choice between public law and private law in framing property rights should not therefore be conceived in abstract terms, but grounded in solving concrete problems. Public law regulation in the form of command and control is cheaper in terms of administrative costs, but more expensive in terms of enforcement costs. Drafting a clear-cut rule is rather cheap for a technical bureaucracy. However, we must also take into account the fact that the state must provide monitoring, control, and sanctions for any violation. Private law regulation is more expensive in terms of administrative costs (coming out with a rule or standard as a result of litigation is much more expensive than drafting the rule ex ante). However, it is much cheaper in terms of enforcement costs since, as a matter of fact, it passes most of them along to private parties.[67]

Keeping this trade-off in mind, property law must strike the right balance between public and private law for each problem. Where transaction costs are very high, for example, in pollution cases, it is difficult in general to rely on private law and it is very unlikely, in particular, that property-based remedies such as injunctions would work at all.[68] Private property cannot be understood as a fundamental legal institution without considering its nature as a cure of externalities. When property rights do not pay for the social costs that they impose, the legal system has not developed a property law. Power brings with it liability. As a result, in order to understand property law, liability rules should be a part of the very idea of property rights together with powers and immunities that are traditionally considered the essence of property rights. This analytical device (considering liability rules as part of the structure of property rights) can be translated on the normative ground. For example, the law (e.g., against a taking or requisition) should not protect property rights over an industry unless social security, insurance, and a decent wage are offered to workers. This is a concrete economic formulation (no property rights without internalization of social costs) of the widely known, but sporadically applied, theory of the social function of property rights.[69]

NOTES

1. In general, on institutional change one can consult D. North, *Institutions, Institutional Change and Economic Performance* (1991).

2. See, generally, M. Kelman, *A Guide to Critical Legal Studies* 259–260 (1987); C. M. Rose, *Canons of Property Talk, or, Blackstone's Anxiety*, 108 *Yale L.J.* 601 (1998).

3. See *infra* Chapter 1.

4. See W. E. Butler, *Soviet Law* 169 (1983); G. M. Armstrong, *The Soviet Law of Property* (1983); for an insider's view, see V. Knapp, *Structural Variations in Property Law: Socialist Countries*, 6 *Int. Enc. Comp. Law* 35–66 (F. H. Lawson ed., 1975).

5. See W. G. Frenkel, *Private Land Ownership in Russia: An Overview of Legal Development to Date*, 3 *Parker Sch. J. Eur. L.* 257 (1996); M. A. Heller, *The Tragedy of the Anticommons*, 111 *Harv. L. Rev.* 625 (1998); G. Ajani, *Il Diritto Postsocialista*, in *Trattato di Diritto Comparato* (R. Sacco ed., 1998).

6. See, still a classic in detecting basic principles going beyond the peculiarities of the many systems of customary law in Africa, T. O. Elias, *The Nature of African Customary Law* 162 (1956); see also N. Rouland, *Antropologie Juridique* 252 (1988).

7. See U. Mattei, *Socialist and Non Socialist Approaches to Land Law: Continuity and Change in Somalia and Other African States*, 16 *Rev. Soc. L.* 17, 22 (1990); R. Sacco, *Il diritto africano*, in *Trattato di diritto comparato* 81, 199 (R. Sacco ed., 1995).

8. The present French Constitution of 1958 expressly refers to the Revolutionary Déclaration de Droits de l'Homme et du Citoyen. See, generally, J. Bell, *French Constitutional Law* (1992).

9. For the German experience, see G. F. Schuppert, *The Right of Property*, in *The Constitution of the Federal Republic of Germany* 112 (1992); for the Italian, see A. Candian et al., *Property Law in Italy*, in *Italian Studies in Law* (A. Pizzorusso ed., 1990).

10. See R. Frydman & A. Rapaczinsky, *Privatization in Eastern Europe: Is the State Whithering Away?* (1994).

11. The French scholar Duguit, writing early in our century, was the first to develop a theory of "functionalized" private property. See L. Duguit, *Les Transformations génerales du droit privé depuis le Code Napoleon* 147 (1912).

12. To carry on the parallel driven at the closing of the previous chapter, liability toward third parties is one of the sticks in Honoré's bundle. See A. M. Honoré, *Ownership*, in *Oxford Essays on Jurisprudence* 112–128 (A. G. Guest ed., 1961).

13. The classic work on this is B. Ackerman, *Private Property and the Constitution* (1977).

14. See A. Stone, *The Birth of Judicial Politics in France: The Constitutional Council in Comparative Perspective* (1992).

15. See F. Von Hayek, *Law, Legislation, and Liberty* (1973).

16. See G. Calabresi, *A Common Law for the Age of Statutes* (1982).

17. See Cons. Cost 16-1-1982, *D.* 1983, 169 and JCP 1982 II 1978 and Gaz. Pal. 1982, 1, 67.

18. See R. Schlesinger et al., *Comparative Law* 408 (4th ed., 1998).

19. See E. Le Roy, *Enjeux Foncières en Afrique Noire* 135 (1983).

20. See P. G. Monateri & R. Sacco, *Legal Formants*, in *The New Palgrave: A Dictionary of Economics and the Law*, vol. 2, 531 (P. Newman ed., 1998).

21. See Schlesinger, *supra* note 18, at 539.

22. See A. Gambaro, *Il Diritto di Proprietà* 235 (1995).

23. See P. G. Monateri, *Legal Doctrine as a Source of Law: A Transnational Factor and an Historical Paradox*, in *Italian National Reports, International Academy of Comparative Law Conference* (1986).

24. See *infra* Chapter 7.

25. See *infra* Chapter 1.

26. See M. Cappelletti, *The Judicial Process in Comparative Perspective* (1989).

27. See J. H. Merryman & V. Vigoriti, *When Courts Collide: Constitution and Cassation in Italy*, 15 *Am. J. Comp. L.* 665 (1967).

28. See Schlesinger et al., *supra* note 18, at 410.

29. See A. Barak, *Judicial Discretion* (1989).

30. See Cappelletti, *supra* note 26.

31. This is the case, for example, in Italy. See Gambaro, *supra* note 22.

32. See F. Michelman, *Property Utility and Fairness: Comments on the Ethical Foundation of Just Compensation Law*, 80 *Harv. L. Rev.* 1165 (1967); Ackerman, *supra* note 13.

33. Codification has gained in the comparative law literature a specific meaning, mainly used to refer to the civilian nineteenth-century general codifications. This is not, of course, the one that I am using here. It remains true,

however, that certain statutes such as the English Law of Property Act can be considered as examples of piecemeal codification, since they meet the usual test: They are general enough and they aim to substitute the previous order. Examples of this kind of codification are the Israeli experience and the Dutch (in Holland, piecemeal codification was eventually incorporated in a new general civil code). See, generally, H. Kotz, *Taking Civil Codes Less Seriously*, 50 *Mod. L. Rev.* 1 (1987). See also F. H. Lawson, *A Common Lawyer Looks at Codification*, in 1 *Selected Essays* 48 (1977) and F. H. Lawson, *Further Reflections on Codification*, in 1 *id.* 96 (1977); A. Gambaro, *Codice civile*, in 2 *Digesto Discipline Privatistiche. Sez. Civile* 442 (1988). The International Academy of Comparative Law devoted one of the panels of the 1982 Conference in Caracas to codification.

34. See Schlesinger et al., *supra* note 18, at 583.

35. See *infra* p. 44; 163.

36. See U. Mattei, *Comparative Law and Economics* 73 (1997).

37. See the discussion in Gambaro, *supra* note 27, at 225.

38. Note that nine of the eleven fundamental incidents of ownership described by Honoré, *supra* note 12, encourage proprietary freedom.

39. Put in other terms, property rights are fully satisfactory of the value of affection. Such value cannot be compensated in torts. After the accident, a property right lowers to a mere interest. See R. Cooter & T. Ulen, *Law and Economics* 261–270 (2d ed., 1997).

40. In common law terminology, real property could be protected by real actions (i.e., could be recovered), while personal property could be protected only by personal actions (i.e., you could get only damages and not the restitution) on remedies *in persomram* as opposed to remedies *in rem*. See F. H. Lawson, *Remedies of English Law* 15–16 (2d ed., 1980).

41. The point was recently developed by Heller, *supra* note 5, at 664, discussing what he calls "restrictions on extreme decomposition."

42. See B. Rudden, *Economic Theory versus Property Law: The Numerus Clausus Problem*, in *Oxford Essays on Jurisprudence* 234 (J. Eekelaar & J. Bell eds. 1987).

43. See Heller, *supra* note 5, at 664.

44. The literature known as "public choices" is very extended. No attempt will be made here to reach any level of sophistication in handling problems that have been so deeply discussed. In general, one can refer to J. M. Buchanan & G. Tullock, *The Calculus of Consent: Logical Foundations of Constitutional Democracy* (1965); *The Political Economy of Rent Seeking* (C. K. Rowley, R. D. Tollison, & G. Tullock eds., 1988); A. Ogus, *Regulation: Legal Form and Economic Theory* (1994).

45. The issue of legitimacy of different kinds of decision making is approached within the legal process school. For a recent scholarly update on this movement, active in the 1950s mostly at Harvard, see N. K. Komesar, *Imperfect Alternatives* (1994).

46. On this kind of reasoning in civil law, see Schlesinger et al., *supra* note 18, at 637; in general, see W. Twinings & D. Miers, *How to Do Things with Rules: A Primer of Interpretation* (1976).

47. Much of this different "philosophy" can be seen at play, for example, in European consumer regulation. See U. Mattei, *Efficiency and Equal Protection*

in the New European Contract Law: Mandatory, Default and Enforcement Rules, 39 *Va. J. Int. Law* 537 (1999).

48. See, for introductory material, H. J. Abraham, *The Judicial Process* (2d ed., 1968).

49. See the discussion in Chapter 1.

50. See P. S. Atiyah, *Law & Modern Society* 47 (1995).

51. See Schlesinger et al., *supra* note 18, at 539.

52. See Atiyah, *supra* note 50, at 157.

53. See *infra* Chapter 7.

54. See discussion *infra* Chapter 9.

55. See K. Llewellyn, *The Brumble Bush* (1930).

56. See the classic study by W. Niskanen, *Bureaucracy and Representative Government* (1971).

57. See G. Ajani & U. Mattei, *Codifying Property Law in the Process of Transition: Some Suggestions from Comparative Law and Economics*, 19 *Hast. Int'l. & Comp. L. Rev.* 117 (1995).

58. See P. Brietzke, *Designing the Legal Framework for Markets in Eastern Europe*, 7 *Transnat'l Law.* 35 (1994).

59. From this standpoint, as we will see, a system of property law inspired by remedial creativity administered by courts of law is preferred. Remedial devices, such as injunctions (both mandatory and negative), astreintes, and interlocutory orders could be introduced for the purpose of creating an efficient system of justice. See Chapter 7.

60. I develop this point in Mattei, *supra* note 36, at 53.

61. See M. Blaug, *Economic Theory in Retrospect* (3d ed., 1978).

62. See Brietzke, *supra* note 58.

63. See *infra* Chapter 3.

64. See G. Calabresi, *Tort: The Law of the Mixed Society*, 56 *Tex. L. Rev.* 519 (1978).

65. The point is clearly made in *id.*; see also B. A. Akerman et al., *The Uncertain Search for Environmental Quality* (1973).

66. See J. Vining, *Legal Identity: The Coming Age of Public Law* (1978).

67. See M. Polinsky, *Introduction to Law and Economics* (1994).

68. See R. Cooter & T. Ulen, *Law and Economics* 138–146 (2d ed., 1997).

69. See Duguit, *supra* note 11.

CHAPTER 3

Economic Analysis

In this chapter we shall discuss some economic assumptions on the subject of property. No extraordinary familiarity with economics is necessary to understand the following material, as it has been presented at a simple level. The following pages serve two purposes. On the one hand, I would like to emphasize once more the inseparable nature of the connection between economics and property.[1] On the other hand, I will offer some basic economic tools for the interpretation and explanation of property law. The economic analysis of property law has become an essential tool of legal discourse in the last twenty years.[2] Since property is a fundamental institution of market capitalism, it is now shared wisdom that an understanding of how the market works and reacts in the shadow of the law is crucial for policy analysis, legal drafting, and legal interpretation.

EFFICIENCY AS A LEGAL PRINCIPLE

It would be naïve to claim that the legal system already contains all of the possible property decisions. Many of these are still open to the judge, who completes them by interpreting the law. It is a fundamental understanding of legal systems aspiring to democracy and the rule of law that the judge is not authorized to introduce his or her own political views into the ambit of his or her decision making. Political choices are the province of government and of the legislature, not of the judiciary. This is true also when the judge is dealing with property rights.[3]

The judge—at least as a matter of theory and in principle—should guarantee a neutral decision-making process.[4] He or she should not substitute his or her own policy preferences to those expressed within the politically legitimized agencies. He or she should look for the technical form to implement substantial policymaking. The judge's job is to detect which one of the parties involved in the controversy should prevail according to law and public policy. This policy is contained in the rules and standards, which the judge is called to apply to specific cases.[5] On such activities the judge must concentrate. I do not mean, of course, that the judge should not care about the general impact of his or her decision. The decision of a judge, as any other institutional decision making, should avoid bad social consequences.

Economic analysis suggests that, within the field of property, efficiency is the tool that the judge should use for the purpose of fulfilling the difficult task of offering solutions that are respectful to the political options which are taken elsewhere (in politically legitimated agencies).[6] At the same time, the judge should be cognizant of the need to develop a good, market-friendly legal structure of property rights. A large number of scholarly contributions demonstrate how efficiency might constitute an important guiding light for a judge who is aware of this role.[7] Redistribution by means of court decision is expensive and random. A system aiming to minimize wastes should prefer taxation for the purpose of redistribution.

Although efficiency is open to a number of different, more or less technical definitions, it would be well beyond the nature of this book to discuss its meaning.[8] For our purpose it is enough to observe that the minimization of wastes is one of the least arbitrary criteria of decision making that a judge can use in the implementation and control of the public policies found in the rules upon which he or she bases his or her decisions.[9] Moreover, even without endorsing a particular idea of efficiency, important insights might be gathered by looking at the law of property as a system of incentives. This simple fact suggests some familiarity with economic tools.

In accepting the criteria of efficiency, the judge need not feel he or she has abandoned fundamental principles of justice which have historically acted as his or her guide. Even the efficiency-aware judge may choose not to apply a regulation which he or she finds obviously unjust because it violates, for instance, equal protection. An administrative judge, in legal systems that grant this power, could even annul such an unfair regulation. Sometimes the judge has the power to raise the question of constitutionality before the Constitutional Court, and a constitutional judge may even annul the unjust statute, as is the power in some jurisdictions, most important, U.S. law.[10] But these are only rare cases, not the daily functions of the judiciary.[11] Outside these hypotheses, on a daily basis, a judge may properly assume that the public policy elaborated in the law conforms at least to a minimal, generally shared standard of justice. He or she may assume, in principle, that the law (or the regulation) in which public policy is formalized is "fair." In the application of law according to criteria of efficiency, he or she will only contribute to the selection of the best fair rule proper for the solution of the property conflict which he or she must resolve.[12] Moreover, if efficiency is interpreted in a sufficiently advanced way, it takes into account fundamental notions of justice and fairness that are imbedded in society and that actually determine the behavior of self-interested individuals.[13]

To use the idea of justice beyond the institutional limits indicated would result in the improper substitution of the judge's politics for policy decisions made in politically legitimized institutions.[14] A substitution of this nature, whatever the authority that in practice the judiciary could claim, could be perceived as arbitrary and subversive of the rule of law.

EFFICIENCY AS WASTE PREVENTION

The economic analysis of the law reclaims a vast ambit of application.[15] Many of the criticisms offered against the economic approach to the law focus on the excessive "commodification" of the legal discourse which, according to these critics, should be guided by other, superior ethical, moral, or constitutional values.[16] Without taking sides regarding this criticism, we will only observe that they cannot target someone proposing the use of economic tools in approaching the domain of property law. Indeed, the legal discipline of goods constitutes the very base of the patrimonial relationship between individuals in any kind of organized society, so that the economic interpretation of the law only adds some technical tools to a discourse that is already economic in its nature.[17]

To be sure, there are cultures and societies in which some goods are not considered property being subtracted from the market. African traditional conceptions of land might be an obvious example, and even in Western societies certain goods assume a symbolic value that might put them de facto out of the market.[18] Not many Italians would pledge the family grave in mortgage, even if the scarcity of burial spaces confers on it high market value. Nevertheless, the fact that some goods are, for cultural reasons, out of the market does not justify the neglect of the market as an institution for all other goods. Approaching property law from an economic perspective is no different from using any other methodology. It is worth using as long as it improves our understanding. Of course, should we have the possibility to rewrite history by preserving the very sophisticated culture of pre-Colombian Indians or of the fifteenth-century Timbuktu reign, mostly based on sharing and ignoring individual property rights, the economic analysis would be completely misplaced.[19] The economic analysis of property law is no more corruptive (if at all) than the institution of private property itself. Once we have politically accepted individual property rights protected by the institution of private property, we might well want to use the best available tools to understand those rights and to make the best social use of them.

Judicial rules and standards, drafted by judges in the process of interpretation of property law, should tend to eliminate economic waste. This basic notion of efficiency will guide our analysis of basic principles of property law. It is particularly harmless to the fundamental values of the legal system. None of these fundamental values (equality, social welfare, etc.) claim that wasting is a good policy. According to this standard of efficiency, a rule will dictate the best possible solution for a controversy regarding a scarce resource, inasmuch as it reduces the amount of resources rendered useless instead of profitable for everybody. This particularly simple principle becomes more meaningful in light of a series of corollaries that have been extensively studied in the literature.[20]

PROPERTY LAW: DEFAULT AND MANDATORY RULES

On the subject of property, the fundamental principle is that most legal rules have a default nature. They constitute a program of social allocation of resources from which the parties are in principle able to negotiate alternative, more efficient solutions.[21] The so-called "Coase Theorem" demonstrates that, whenever the parties are left free to negotiate and have the possibility to do so without being restricted by excessive costs, they will reach efficient solutions independently of the legal rules which underlie their relationship to each other.[22]

Efficiency is favored by an agreement, which assures that a scarce resource is allocated to whomever values it the most judged by willingness and ability to pay. To know who values a resource more, the simplest way is to let the parties bargain between themselves to see who offers more for the resource. The law should not decide for the individuals unless there is a strong reason to do so such as the protection of third parties. Also, the law should always consider that self-interested individuals will obey its precepts only if they have enough incentives to do so. Whenever the structure of incentives (including sanctions) allows bargains, self-interested parties will negotiate solutions between themselves that make both of them better off. This is the reason why banning the use of a resource able to produce utility for individuals (e.g., cocaine, vodka, etc.) has as a necessary consequence the birth of a black market which is extremely costly to prevent and monitor.

Lawyers usually distinguish between coercive rules (*ius cogens*) and yielding rules (*ius dispositivum*). Individuals cannot change the former (provided that the legal system is effective and that its sanctions introduce strong enough incentives), but are left free to modify the latter.[23] For example, a rule that protects a minor by limiting his or her possibility to contract for labor is *ius cogens*. An employer cannot contract with a minor for a labor contract which imposes longer hours than the maximum limit prescribed by law. Such a contract would be void or voidable in favor of the minor according to the different legal systems. To the contrary, a rule establishing certain typical standards of care for a contract performance is *ius dispositivum*, since the parties are free to agree on higher or lower standards. In Western legal systems, most rules of private law are *ius dispositivum*, including a large percentage of those related to property rights.[24] In the domain of public law, most provisions are traditionally considered *ius cogens* by protecting so-called "general interests." A great deal of public law is involved in modern property law, so the question of distinguishing between the two kinds of legal provisions (coercive or yielding) might arise. The different nature can in principle be detected by focusing on third parties. Rules must be considered *ius cogens* if they are aimed at avoiding the transfer of costs from the bargaining parties on third parties or on the collectivity in general. This includes inducing third parties to rely on misleading appearances. For example, the *numerus clausus* doctrine of property rights that will be discussed in Chapter 5, aimed as it is to protect third party reliance, can certainly be considered coercive in nature.

By considering the efficiency implications of the Coase Theorem and challenging the notion of a general interest as different from the algebraic sum of all individual interests of society, economic analysis suggests that unless a rule is clearly *ius cogens* it should be considered *ius dispositivum*. Accordingly, the parties should be left free to change if they reach an agreement to do so. In other words, the political choice to make a provision coercive should be clearly taken by the legislature, which should face the political responsibility for its potentially inefficient choice.

JUDICIAL INTERPRETATION AND PRIVATE BARGAINING

We have stressed the importance of allowing individuals to bargain with each other in order to reach efficient results. Often, however, individuals encounter grave problems of communication with one another. Sometimes such problems arise from the distance the parties must travel to communicate in person and the high costs of such travel. Sometimes communication problems may derive from one party's hostility toward the other. Sometimes it is costly to get enough information, either about the trustworthiness of the other party to the bargain or the object about which they are bargaining. Due to lack of information or excessive cost of obtaining information, one or both parties might lack confidence to enter into a bargain.

In general, the law should be a part of the solution to these problems, so that these costs, known in economic jargon as "transaction costs," are reduced or allocated to the party which is in the best position to face them.[25] In this way, the parties can be encouraged to negotiate an efficient property arrangement.[26] To the contrary, the legal system itself sometimes creates problems of communication and discourages individuals from entering otherwise efficiency-enhancing bargains. This happens, for example, when unreasonably formalistic requirements are introduced for transfers of property or for other transactions.

From this perspective, one can first see that the comparison of transaction costs can lead to important suggestions from the point of view of the legal process. Considering courts as one of the institutional alternatives available to lower transaction costs, one can first of all see that sometimes it can cost a lot more to resolve the dispute in court than by means of an administrative agency. For example, in the case of urban land use, transaction costs suggest the superiority of zoning ordinances supervised and enforced by administrative agencies over private law alternatives administered by courts. Litigation is expensive, time consuming, and piecemeal; and it is not wise to leave decisions about urban planning, which they are not equipped to take, to judges. Naturally, this general proposition does not mean that in urban land use disputes it is necessary to introduce a rigid, unchangeable zoning system.[27]

Of course, even when efficiency suggests using public law (zoning ordinances) rather than private law, this does not completely marginalize the judge. The rules of property that the judge uses to settle conflicts can also move in the direction of an efficient solution by lowering transaction costs. Transaction costs are wastes that efficiency suggests reducing, not so much for the conflict actually in front of the judge. The mere fact that the parties have appeared in court demonstrates their present inability to arrive at an agreement. The decision of the judge is, however, particularly important for the future, since it creates the structure of property rights on which future transactions might rely.[28]

MINIMIZING THE COSTS OF FAILURES IN NEGOTIATION

As suggested, the rules of property law contained in codes and judicial precedents are to be considered dispositive until proved otherwise. This does not mean that the parties will, in every possible case, reach an efficient agreement that is better than the default rules contained in the code. If this were the case, a system of statutory or judicial rules of property law would be useless, which makes such a conclusion counterintuitive and indeed absurd.

To begin with, private negotiations can result in inefficient results for a variety of reasons well documented in microeconomic theory: Imbalances of power, monopolies, strategic behavior, externalities, and lack of information are the economic counterparts of some of the traditional problems that justify the existence of a system of private law. In more familiar terms for the lawyer, it may be the case that an agreement is obtained with fraud or malice, by extortion, or by an obvious economic imbalance between the parties and so on. Evidently, to resolve these problems a number of different areas of law—not only property but also contract and tort—must work together.

Moreover, most of the time it would be very costly and time consuming for individuals to frame their own property law system. It is usually convenient to assume a system of law that regulates property relationships with other individuals, rather than working it out from scratch each time. Parties only have incentives to change the system of default rules marginally to make it fit their special needs. For the bulk of their relationship, they can save huge transaction costs by being able to rely on a system of property law.

As noted, negotiations might fail for any number of reasons. Thus, rules of default, which come into play unless there is some other agreement, should be shaped in a way that best avoids waste. Suppose John constructs a building in good faith, which slips just slightly over the border between his property and the property of Jane. Should this building be maintained or should it be destroyed? In such a case, if transaction costs were low and parties could negotiate whatever the legal rule on the point, the building would stay if John values it more than Jane values her property free from it. If the opposite were true, the building would be demolished.[29] Indeed, in the first case, John would pay Jane enough to persuade her to keep the building even if she had the power to destroy it. In the opposite case, Jane would pay John enough to persuade him to demolish the building (or to relocate it) despite his or her right to keep it. While legal systems depart from the point of view of the solution adopted, such differences would not concretely determine the result in terms of efficiency (whether the building will stay or go).[30] At most, it would determine whom between John and Jane will be better off after the transaction. The legal regime would affect the distribution of wealth but not the efficiency of the transaction.

The scarcity of judicial decisions on this point everywhere in Western legal systems seems to confirm that cases similar to this one are resolved out of court by negotiation in a manner similar to that described. Jane could, however, hate John (suppose he had once broken his engagement to her) and thus refuse any of his reasonable offers to buy the right to violate her property line. If French law was to be applied, Jane could in such a case force John to destroy his or her building. French law is indeed very strict in protecting an owner's boundary lines.[31] In German or Italian law, Jane could not insist on destruction if John had acted in good faith. She could only get an indemnity.[32] The German–Italian rule, which grants to John the right to keep his or her building, is to be preferred from the efficiency perspective over the French rule, especially when one considers that destruction of John's building would result in an enormous waste of resources. As illustrated in this case, the rule of efficiency dictates a formula completely compatible with the demand for justice that a number of French commentators, severely critical of Cassation's jurisprudence on this point, have invoked in order not to overpenalize one, who like John, constructs a building in good faith.[33]

PROPERTY RIGHTS AND INTERNALIZATION OF SOCIAL COSTS

In Germany, a fundamental economic principle of the subject of property is well summarized with the constitutional phrase, "ownership obligates."[34] In Italy, the same idea is expressed by the notion of the "social function of ownership" contained in the second paragraph of Article 42 of the Constitution. From the standpoint of constitutional definitions, this language represents a notable shift from the rhetoric of the French–American model, which flourished following the French Revolution.[35] From an operative viewpoint, such a constitutional evolution cannot remain without effects. In order to explain its significance, it is necessary to reflect on the economic foundations of private property. Thus we are able to approach at once the functions and limits of property law seen from the perspective of an economist.

As to the function of property, private property justifies itself as a remedy to the so-called "tragedy of the commons." Each individual will attempt to acquire as much of a resource as possible, because he or she will always keep the benefits of such an attempt, whereas the costs of such unlimited acquisitions will be shared with a number of other individuals.[36] The opposite extreme, excessive use of the individual right to exclude, can also have "tragic" results in terms of wastes and justifies a disparate array of property law doctrines.[37]

Another economic justification of property is that it introduces incentives for investment. No farmer would seed a field knowing that the harvest will be taken by his neighbor: Here lies the strongest argument for protection of property rights.[38] Historical examples of catastrophes serve well to highlight the importance of this principle. The *kolhoz* cooperative organization was never able to get enough products to the Soviet marketplace because the farmers abandoned their large fields in favor of small, personal ones. They did this precisely because the fruits of the large fields went to the cooperative, while anything grown in a personal garden could be consumed as personal property or sold on the black market.[39]

As to the limits of property, the example used by economists to show that sometimes property law is not enough to introduce proper economic incentives is that of the lighthouse. There is indeed a structural difference between those goods that, from an efficient perspective, must be objects of private property and other goods which cannot be anything but public property. So, as no one would cultivate in order to give away the harvest to the first person that passes by, no one builds a lighthouse, thus assuming the costs of construction and maintenance, without the promise of future profits. Since it is impossible to exclude any sailor from enjoying the lighthouse and it is also impossible to charge ships passing by in the high ocean for the use of it, no lighthouse would be built unless the state grants power to levy taxation like charges on boats in nearby ports.[40] The lighthouse, as well as the protection against an enemy's airforce attacks, are "public goods" by their nature, and private property in the case of public goods is not an efficient institution.[41]

These short examples teach various important lessons. Ownership of goods is allocated to private individuals because of the benefits that they are able to gain from the appropriation of what those goods produce. Work and investment are thus stimulated, with numerous benefits to society. It is not always the case that personal interests serve the interests of the community. The tragedy of the commons (and that of anticommons) demonstrates that no one individual should impose upon the community the costs of his or her choices. Likewise, not all goods are managed best by individuals. In a few particular cases, public intervention is necessary (as in the case of military protection); in other cases it is merely recommended (e.g., roads, ports, etc.).

This approach shows that, in modern complex market economies, as long as there is no official statement to the contrary, goods are presumably owned privately. Such private ownership carries with it a strong social responsibility. Any private owner of goods should be seen as an agent who, while satisfying his or her own private interests, at the same time satisfies the interests of society as a whole. Good institutions are those able to channel individual greed to the benefit of the community.[42] Good institutions should never assume the existence of giving, sharing, good-hearted, altruistic people in society. Maximum attention must consequently be paid to assure that each property bears its own costs to avoid tragic consequences. For an economist, property law should be framed to avoid all externalities (i.e., costs imposed by the self-interested individual on the society). This is not only true when goods are allocated in private property, but also when they are kept in public ownership for any reason. The fundamental economic principle of property law is that each market actor should bear his or her costs and not be allowed to transfer them onto other parties outside market transactions.

COLLECTIVE AND DECENTRALIZED SYSTEMS TO AVOID EXTERNALITIES

In economic terminology, "negative externalities" or "external diseconomies" are terms used to describe when a property right imposes its own costs on other property rights. The clearest example is the problem of industrial pollution: One party (the polluting factory) consumes a scarce resource (peace and quiet, clean air, fresh water) without bearing the costs of this consumption.[43] On the other hand, an externality may be positive. For example, whenever a private party beautifies a landfill (e.g., transforming it into a garden), it renders a benefit not only to the private party, but also to all the owners of property nearby, who will enjoy a new environment without having borne the costs of making it so. Or further, consider when a condominium owner renovates, at his or her own expense, the shared parts of the building: All the other owners will benefit from the newly added value without having borne the costs. Both in the case of positive and negative externalities, a transfer of wealth between two or more individuals has taken place, outside the world of the marketplace.[44] The marketplace fails in its primary function of efficiently allocating resources, inasmuch as the system of prices transmits incorrect information. The ultimate result of this failure is that there will not be enough or that there will be too much of a given commodity than the amount it would be efficient to supply. In our example, without a system of property law able to avoid externalities, there will be too much pollution and not enough beautiful gardens. Consequently, economists are concerned with both types of externalities. The reason for the existence of externalities resides in the difficulty in completely separating property rights; thus, in our crowded world, rarely does the behavior of one owner of property fail to affect others.

Lawyers more commonly focus on negative externalities, the ones that are likely to produce social conflicts. Consequently, positive externalities go relatively unnoticed. Often the negative externalities appear as damages or risks. Sometimes public law directly tackles some externalities (e.g., the many regulations regarding nuclear plants and related activities). Sometimes private law is called upon to react against them. These private law rules can be found in civilian codes or in the general common law of property and tort. Usually the literature talks about collective control of externalities by the direct regulation of the first kind, of decentralizing control by the private law model.[45] In Western legal systems, collective controls are carried on by a process of decision making which is brought to life collectively (politically) by groups of people, through political institutions and the democratic process. These choices tend to reflect the power struggles present internally in political organizations, and they often end up redistributing resources considerably beyond the mere internalization of externalities.[46]

The private law rules, on the other hand, are administered by the courts, and constitute a system considered "decentralized." This means that a property right confers upon every citizen some power in his or her dealings with others. This power becomes effective in court whenever the property-right holder claims to be a victim of negative externalities. For example, if I own an apartment, I may complain in court against my neighbor's noisy use of his apartment at night. The rules of property law that derive from resolutions of these conflicts (e.g., absolute quiet use after midnight) are not choices made directly by a collective political body (such as allowing or forbidding nuclear plants to operate). They are the result of a series of independent decisions made by the courts in the resolution of a number of different conflicts between individuals. In this sense, the power of the owner is decentralized, carried on outside collective political institutions, and used by every owner which is sovereign in relation to some decision making related to the scarce resource he or she owns. Theoretically, the judge is not exercising independent political power, so the struggle against externalities, and not redistribution, should guide the courts in this work.

The opposition between collective choices and decentralized choices, developed in the scholarly tradition of law and economics especially within the American common law, discounts the simplification that exists due to the absence of administrative courts. In the process of transplanting the terminology and the method of investigation in an institutional system such as the civil law, rendered much more complex from the reduced role of ordinary courts, it is necessary to keep in mind that administrative justice constitutes a system of decentralized choices. Therefore, the rules of property law that the civil law creates maintain the nature of incidental results reached while solving controversies involving individual property rights. Administrative justice administered by courts, in other words, does not share a redistributive nature with direct administrative regulation.[47]

PROPERTY RULES AND LIABILITY RULES

Concretely, an owner will go to court in order to obtain one of the following results: (1) the restitution of his or her property taken by others, (2) an injunction to cease the activity which is creating prejudice to his or her property, or (3) the restoration of the situation relating to his or her property that was altered in some way by the behavior of others.[48] All these activities affect the utility that the owner can get from his or her property. An economist would say that they "push the owner on a lower indifference curve."[49] In less esoteric terms, this simply means that property is less valuable to its owner whenever it is unjustly taken, polluted, or subjected to a risk, or whenever it is altered in any other way contrary to the desires of its owner. If the owner does not receive protection against activities that are prejudicial to his or her property, the marketplace takes account of his or her failure to protect his or her property right. This failure is consequently reflected in the market's valuation of the property in question. An owner can make less money in selling an occupied apartment than he or she would make in selling the same one vacant, precisely because the market reflects the fact that the property law of modern societies includes restrictions on the power of the owner to evict tenants. Whatever is given to the tenant in terms of legal protection against sudden and arbitrary eviction is taken away from the value of the property to the owner. A house near the freeway is less valuable than one in a quiet part of the city, because the market takes into account that a property owner has no control over the noise made by cars: He or she usually cannot sue in court and stop it.

The owner, at least in theory, has a remedy against each activity that may threaten the value of his or her property. We will see a variety of remedies that different legal systems frame for the purpose of offering complete protection of property rights against prejudicial activities. Specifically, of course, there are limits to the power of the owner to seek a judicial remedy against an activity that he or she considers prejudicial.[50] The time necessary to obtain one of these remedies also affects the value of a property right. A defendant, knowing that the owner will need years to obtain a remedy, may act in disregard of the property right. Precisely to face this problem, modern legal systems have framed a variety of interlocutory remedies that the owner can obtain as a precaution without waiting for the end of a full-fledged trial.

Whenever an owner succeeds in obtaining one of these remedies (or any of their functionally similar counterparts), the law will have returned the owner to his or her status quo ante.[51] He or she will again be able to obtain the same utility from his or her property, so that economists would express this notion by saying that the owner has been restored to the previous indifference curve. To the contrary, if the law refuses or cannot supply a remedy, this means that one's property right has been limited in favor of another.[52] An example can be found between landlords and tenants in eviction actions subject to a stay so that the landlord cannot effectively evict the tenant for a term of years. Clearly the legal system guarantees a property right to the tenant by limiting that of the landlord. Until the landlord is able to evict the tenant, his or her ownership is guaranteed only as a "future interest," as an Anglo-American lawyer would say, or as a "naked property right," as a civilian jurist would qualify this situation. Indeed, the common law, more pragmatic, has always considered leases to fall under the law of property, while civilians, more interested in grand theory, have been reluctant to recognize the proprietary nature of leases.[53]

Another example, equally clear, is that whenever an owner loses in an action to recover his or her property, this means that as far as that property is concerned, he or she is no longer recognized as the owner. The law has granted the property rights to the defendant. Take, for example, an action brought by Article 1153 of the Italian Civil Code or by Article 2279 of the French Napoleonic Code, which we will discuss thoroughly in Chapter 5. In this case, the true owner cannot recover his or her movable property against a third-party, bona fide purchaser from the nonowner. The fact that he or she is no longer considered the owner does not at all preclude his or her possibility to recover damages against the nonowner who transferred the property to the bona fide purchaser. In this case, it is clear that the remedy of damages by itself is no protection of ownership as a property right. The owner can be redressed economically by mean of damages, but he or she has still lost ownership against the good-faith purchaser recognized by the law as the new owner of the property.

More generally, as this last example demonstrates, the full proprietary protection (property rule) is made of a number of components: the action to recover possession plus injunctive relief against prejudices plus action to reestablish the status quo ante plus damages. If this complex protection is substituted by the damages (liability rule), the legal system does not protect the original owner's property right. In the law of property, as a consequence, protection by means of a mere liability rule does not have a different nature than an indemnity for taking. It compensates the owner for the loss of his or her full property right, but it is not a full protection of it. When an injunction is denied in a nuisance case, damages are merely the internalization of costs that the defendant is imposing over the plaintiff. Consequently, a judge faced with a claim of an owner–plaintiff will find himself confronted with the choice between (1) protecting the owner by means of a proprietary protection (property rule), or (2) granting to the plaintiff a mere liability rule which compensates the owner for an externality but does not defend his or her right. How should a judge choose between these options?[54]

Of course, this choice of the judge cannot be arbitrary. In order to guide the judge's discretion, efficiency considerations offer some guidelines. The focus of the judge should be on transaction costs that might preclude the possibility of the parties from finding an efficient agreement between them. When transaction costs are low, the property-rule protection should be favored. When transaction costs are high, the liability rule is the best remedy.[55]

Consider the case of low transaction costs. If the property-rule protection is followed, the judge will end up granting the property right to the person that values it most with both private and social benefit. The damage remedy internalizes externalities that might have happened in the past and the parties will negotiate among themselves the most efficient solution for the future. For example, in a case of nuisances created by a factory, let us consider that the defendant values at 100 his or her possibility to carry on polluting activity after having internalized all its costs, and the plaintiff values at 80 the enjoyment of his or her land free from pollution. There will be space for an agreement by which the factory buys for, say, 90, the right to pollute. If the parties will agree on this solution this is efficient because both parties are moved to a higher utility curve without anybody being moved down. In other words, the cooperation between the two negotiating parties will produce a benefit of 20 if compared to the status quo previous to the negotiation. If, on the other hand, the polluted plaintiff values the right to be free from pollution at 110, the nuisance will stop because the full internalization of costs still leaves a social cost of 10. There will be no space for an efficient agreement.

The more difficult cases, as well as the more usual, however, tend to happen when transaction costs are high. In this case, the liability rule proves to be the best remedy because there is no possibility of the parties renegotiating the decision of the judge to grant the injunction. Consequently, if the judge grants a property rule and the defendant values his or her polluting activity more than the plaintiff values the freedom from it, the high transaction costs will preclude the efficient agreement from happening and the judicial solution will be inefficient. Moreover, when the nuisance affects a large number of possible plaintiffs, the property-rule protection will favor strategic behaviors, themselves inefficient and to be disfavored. The factory might well be able to buy its right to pollute from nine owners out of ten. The tenth owner will obviously find himself or herself in a very strong bargaining position because he or she might be able alone to force the polluting activity to shut down. As a consequence, he or she can insist on an unreasonably high amount of money for selling the right to be free from pollution. As a consequence, each one of the plaintiffs receives an incentive to be the last one to settle, so it is extremely unlikely that the agreement will ever take place. The harsh and inefficient consequences of property-rule protection will consequently remain.

When transaction costs are high, therefore, the liability rule is the proper remedy. The liability rule is sufficient to internalize the costs imposed by the polluting defendant over the plaintiffs. It avoids, however, the inefficient consequences of the overprotection by means of the property rule. The liability rule, indeed, judicially establishes the price by which the plaintiff can sell the right to pollute to the defendant, avoiding the "blackmail power" of the last plaintiff to settle.[56]

Naturally, liability rules also present some problems. As already discussed, denying property-rule protection corresponds to an expropriation of the property right of the plaintiff. The liability rule, short of being a protection of the polluted property, becomes a shelter for the polluting activity against too strict a protection of opposing property rights. This, of course, does not mean that in the long run this kind of expropriation is not favorable to the institution of property. The market positively reflects the possibility of using property rights in productive (although nuisance-creating) activities without the constant threat that a plaintiff (with whom negotiation is impossible) can enjoin them. In the long run, this is the same economic logic that allows us to see that the institution of property is (paradoxically) favored by the rule that protects the good-faith purchaser for value as a new owner against the "true" owner of a movable property.[57]

EFFICIENCY AND SECURITY OF PROPERTY RIGHTS

The efficiency of property law is a function of the costs of the enforcement of property rights. Since litigation is costly and destroys resources, a system of property rights should be structured in a way to avoid litigation as much as possible. In other words, the more a system of property law is self-enforcing, the more it is efficient.[58] In order to make property law as self-enforcing as possible, economic analysis offers a clear suggestion: Property rights should be clearly separated and the rules of property law should be as clear as possible. Confusion and doubt in the rules of property create incentives to litigate, because each conflicting individual hopes that he or she will end up being favored by the judicial decision.[59] Clear-cut property rights, to the contrary, reduce litigation because the parties will already know who will lose and who will win so that they will avoid spending money on a litigation the outcome of which is already clear ex ante. Clear-cut property rights, in other words, do create incentives to negotiate (and find an efficient agreement) rather than litigate (and waste resources).

As a consequence, in the domain of property law the stability of legal rules is more efficient than their mutability. Whenever courts, regulations, and other proprietary decision makers redistribute property rights, they sacrifice efficiency for the purpose of redistribution. This is obviously a legitimate task when required politically. It is, however, costly. This observation is confirmed by the incremental evolution of the common law. In Anglo-American property law, the rule of *stare decisis* that requires courts to follow precedents whether they like it or not is interpreted in a particularly strict way. American commentators who usually criticize *stare decisis* do agree that in property matters it has a value.[60] Continental courts should follow this lesson of the value of stability as well.

Sometimes, as a consequence of the necessity of stability, some rules of property subtracted from the negotiation of the parties might also be advisable from the perspective of economic efficiency. As a consequence, some environmental regulations completely ban developments in areas of particular natural beauty. A ban on all building activity on the shore of a sea or a lake or in mountains beyond a certain height would introduce a clear signal of what is possible and what is not possible to do, avoiding litigation. The same rationale of discouraging costly litigation is behind other aspects of property law. For example, the terms of adverse possession are not negotiable. The same is true in some legal systems that protect lessees as far as the lengths of certain lease agreements that cannot be shorter than a minimum period of time. In all these cases, the purpose is to send clear signals that make the law self-enforcing.

CLEAR SOCIAL SIGNALING IN MOVABLE AND IMMOVABLE PROPERTY

In the real world, it usually happens that whoever has physical control over a piece of movable property is also its owner. The rules of property law reduce transaction costs by following a fact situation that is valid in most cases.[61] It is more efficient for rules of property law to introduce presumptions valid in most cases rather than complicated formal requirements to prove the title. We will see in the domain of movable property a variety of choices in the conflict between formal property and possession. The most efficient solutions to this conflict include those that favor possession. Suing the possessor is discouraged. The possessor and his or her opponent receive an incentive to negotiate, because the latter knows that he or she will face a particularly onerous burden of proof.[62] If the law recognizes physical possession as establishing a good title, the value of property rights will increase because the market reflects the security of legal transactions that are introduced. More generally, economic analysis helps to see that the more a system favors possession, the more the owner will receive incentives not to lose physical control of his or her possession. The more the legal system protects the title, the less the owner will receive this incentive and the more the prospective buyer will have to invest in investigating the quality of the title that he or she is considering acquiring.[63] Consequently, many efficient transactions might be discouraged by the transaction costs introduced by this need to check the formal quality of the title.

While the first alternative is efficient for movable property, there are reasons to believe that the particular nature of the scarcity of land calls for different choices. In the case of immovables, only in a very limited set of cases does the person who physically finds himself or herself on a given piece of property turn out to be its owner. If Brian locates a piece of land he likes, he cannot approach Miriam who is farming it and by a simple handshake buy the land, being reasonably certain that he has dealt with the owner. Much more often on each piece of the surface of the earth one finds individuals dwelling whose title is different from that of owner. As a consequence, the law, in order to obtain the certainty of property rights, must use a legal tool that is different from mere physical control.[64] Differently than in the case of movables, physical control does not offer an economically efficient prima facie presumption of ownership. If the law used possession of immovables as evidence of title, owners would have to invest an unreasonable amount of resources in policing their land in order to avoid the possibility that some Miriam could enter into it and transfer it to the first Brian passing by. In other words, in the case of immovables (differently than in the case of movables) the cost of uncertainty following the use of possession as a prima facie signal of ownership is higher than the cost of creating a formal institutional system to recognize ownership from mere possession. An economist would say that delimiting and making certain property rights in the case of immovables is a public good that can best be created by the state. Clearly, while a private individual can reasonably face the cost of excluding everybody else from his or her movable property, the same is not possible for immovables.

This is the reason why all legal systems use different rules for movables and immovables when it comes to the rights of third parties acquiring title. It should be immediately observed that, as already mentioned, the subversion of property rights has itself a social cost, so that in the domain of movable property there is also space for some difference between ownership and possession. As we will see, all legal systems introduce some limits to the presumption that the possessor is also owner to discourage theft and other opportunistic behaviors. Similarly, in the domain of immovables, physical control does not remain devoid of all legal implications. The rules on adverse possession are the most obvious example.

Moreover, there are areas of the law in which the regime of property law reflects a different economic rationale. Some movables are treated in a way similar to immovables as far as the impact of possession on the transfer of ownership. Cars, boats, and airplanes, for example, cannot be transferred with a simple handshake. While the reason is often indicated in the particular value of these commodities, this is obviously not the best economic explanation: An old car may be much less valuable than an antique piece of furniture.[65] The rationale of the regime is consequently to be found in the particular liability rules that are attached to these pieces of property. This kind of property creates externalities in the form of danger. Should the danger become outright harm, it becomes necessary to allocate it to a particular individual: the formalized, registered owner.

EFFICIENCY AND THE NATURE OF PROPERTY

While most of the rules of efficient interpretation of property law touched on in the previous paragraphs do apply to all kinds of property, regardless of its nature, we have started to see that sometimes the different nature (movable–immovable, fugitive–static, material–immaterial, etc.) of property might requires different rules. To begin with, between movables and immovables there are important economic differences as far as the separability of consumption is concerned. Such separability is tendentiously complete in the case of movable property: It is very difficult to imagine that my use of a book may create externalities. To the contrary, separability is usually a problem in our crowded society when it comes to immovables. It is very unlikely that my next door neighbor is indifferent to the way in which I use my apartment. If my neighbor organizes wild parties or simply has a different schedule from mine as far as sleeping and being awake, the peaceful use of my apartment might be impaired.

Generally speaking, one can say that while externalities are the rule as far as immovables are concerned, they are the exception in the case of movables. While abandoning a Coca Cola can in a bush is an example of an externality created by means of movable property, one nevertheless can easily see that, in the case of immovables, externalities happen because the nature of the property makes separability difficult, while in the case of movables (such as the Coke in the bush) you need an abusive behavior to create the external effect. This different structural nature of the externality problem is reflected in many areas of property law which differentiate (or should differentiate) between movables and immovables.[66]

When it comes to immaterial property (such as a copyright, a patent, or a software program which is not tangible like a book or a piece of gold), its nature must be reflected by an efficient legal regime.[67] The nature of property rights in this case is not particular: It is still the power to exclude everybody else that gives economic value to them. The problem is that the exclusion can be (and usually is) very difficult. As a consequence, many of the rules that centuries of legal evolution have framed having in mind material property are difficult to adapt to these different entities.

Property law nevertheless remains the key legal institution to encourage economic development and the efficient allocation of resources. Clearly, much less investment and energy would be invested in inventing new software programs (or, generally speaking, in research aimed at innovation) if such programs could not enjoy a particularly strong legal protection. Anyone is able to reproduce such programs just by touching a few keys of a personal computer, which explains why many resources are devoted to sophisticated self-protection programs in the absence of sufficient legal protection. For a lawyer, these are very old problems that appear in a new form. Sometimes the landowner puts broken glass or dangerous devices on the top of a fence in order to discourage unauthorized trespasses. Similarly, the owner of a computer program might introduce disruptive viruses that attack computer programs reproduced without authorization. The law in such cases can be called upon to avoid excesses in this self-protection.

Economists face problems due to the particular nature of information as property. In order to develop a market, it is necessary to give to the inventor a sort of monopoly on his or her idea. This necessity stems from the fact that whoever first purchases an innovation (such as a computer program) which is very easy to reproduce is then able to take away from the inventor all of the expected gains from the invention by competing with him or her in selling it out. Moreover, the price of the invention cannot reflect this possibility, because the buyer only knows its value once he or she has bought it so that he or she will not purchase it at a very high price and risk that it is worthless to him or her. Due to this huge problem of information asymmetry, the parties will not find a price that satisfies both of them and the market will not develop unless the law protects the inventor with a special monopoly. Such a monopoly allows the inventor to sell the idea to different individuals without fearing the competition of each customer. In other words, since innovation is much more costly to produce (it needs research) than to reproduce, a monopoly (usually limited in time) is necessary to have a market develop.

Obviously, this different nature of information as property might itself limit the applicability in this area of some traditional tools of property law. For example, the rules developed for recovering possession are not easy to apply to a property whose intangible nature makes possession an odd concept. Nevertheless, one should not conclude that property law works only when its object is tangible. Most of the general principles of efficient property law can be applied by analogy if the interpreter is creative enough to understand in which areas differences in economic nature are crucial and in which areas they are not.[68]

Some other kinds of property have a "fugitive" nature that also requires partially different efficient rules. Water, oil, gas, energies, and so on, in order to be allocated efficiently, need rules of property law that reflect their fugitive nature. In theory they can be allocated to the individual who is able to exert physical control on them. Alternatively, they can be connected in some way to the ownership of land.[69] Both of these alternatives have advantages and disadvantages from the point of view of efficiency. The first rule risks encouraging excessive investments in physical control at too early a stage. There is no ownership until someone does the kind of activity that the law requires in order to prove physical control. On top of the risk of tragedy of the commons, individuals are consequently encouraged to invest only in activities required in order to have physical control. This happened in America in the nineteenth century during the development West, when the law granted ownership to the first people that fenced land. A lot of fencing rather than a lot of development followed from those provisions! On the other hand, a rule based on physical control or first possession is efficient as far as it is extremely clear and easy to enforce, consequently discouraging litigation. A classic example is the conflict between two hunters, one who saw the fox first while the other shot, killed, and took possession of it. It is obviously more efficient to give legal title to the latter.

The rule that links ownership of fugitive goods to that of the land introduces other kinds of disadvantages. In the case of oil or gas in the subsoil it is extremely difficult to know under which land it dwells. Consequently, property rights cannot be clearly delimited. On the other hand, an advantage of this rule is that it links ownership to already allocated property rights so that it avoids the tragedy of the commons and does not encourage excessive investments. As in many other cases, economic analysis can be useful to clearly see advantages and disadvantages, but does not offer a clear-cut answer to the abstract question of which regime is efficient.

Finally, the easy or difficult replaceability of a commodity on the market (fungible or nonfungible nature, in the civil law tradition) also calls for some different rules.[70] For example, specific performance in this case is not a proper remedy, since it introduces wastes due to the need to monitor it. It would be absurd to use the law in order to give the plaintiff the very dollar bill subtracted from him or her or exactly that new television set. If a commodity can be easily replaced on the market, money damages are always the efficient remedy.[71]

NOTES

1. See *infra* Chapter 1.
2. See, in general, Y. Barzel, *Economic Analysis of Property Rights* (1989); B. Ackerman, *Economic Foundation of Property Law* (1975); R. C. Ellickson et al., *Perspectives on Property Law* (2d ed., 1995).
3. The issue of legitimacy is central to jurisprudence and political theory. A general, rather classic overview can be found in J. Plamenatz, *Consent, Freedom and Political Obligation* (1968).
4. Judicial neutrality and even its theoretical possibility is challenged in many circles. See, recently, D. Kennedy, *A Critique of Adjudication* (1997).
5. See, for an introduction, A. Barak, *Judicial Discretion* (1989).
6. See R. Cooter, *The Best Right Laws: Value Foundations of the Economic Analysis of the Law*, 64 *Notre Dame L. Rev.* 817 (1989).
7. See N. K. Komesar, *Imperfect Alternatives* (1995).
8. The literature on efficiency as a legal tool is very abundant. Some authors question the very idea that efficiency has or should have a role in judicial thinking. One interested in deepening his or her understanding might consult some or all of the sources cited in R. Posner, *Economic Analysis of Law* 31 (5th ed., 1998).
9. See U. Mattei, *Comparative Law and Economics* (1997).
10. See M. Cappelletti, *The Judicial Process in Comparative Perspective* (1989).
11. On the need for restraint of the judiciary, see A. M. Bickel, *The Least Dangerous Branch: The Supreme Court at the Bar of Politics* (1959); for a broader transnational perspective, see Barak, *supra* note 5.
12. See Cooter, *supra* note 6.
13. See E. E. Zajac, *Political Economy of Fairness* (1995).
14. See Barak, *supra* note 5, for a judge aware of these limits. A classic on the (broad) limits of judicial decision making remains B. Cardozo, *The Nature of the Judicial Process* (1927).
15. See R. Cooter & T. Ulen, *Law and Economics* (2d ed., 1997).
16. See, in the domain of property, F. I. Michelman, *Ethics, Economics and the Law of Property*, 24 *Nomos* 3 (1982). For a discussion of the American literature on commodification, see R. Rao, *Property Privacy and the Human Body* (unpublished manuscript). In the civil law literature similar concerns are expressed in many quarters. See, for example, many of the writings that appear in Symposium, *Le muove frontiere del diritto di proprietá*, 15 *Rivista critica del diritto privato* 5–156 (1997).

17. See *infra* the discussion of "the tragedy of the commons."

18. On the issue of inalienability, see S. Rose Ackerman, *Inalienability and the Theory of Property Rights*, 85 *Colum. L. Rev.* 931 (1985).

19. See H. Zinn, *A People's History of the United States* 7 (1980). Nonetheless, economists also made important contributions in the understanding of commons. See E. Ostrom, *Governing the Commons: The Evolution of Institutions for Collective Action* (1990).

20. Such literature has developed an insight produced in the so-called "Coase Theorem." See R. Coase, *The Problem of Social Costs*, 3 *J.L. & Econ.* 1 (1960).

21. See G. D. Libecap, *Contracting for Property Rights* (1989).

22. The literature on the Coase Theorem is very extensive. The interpretation that I am using here is that developed by R. Cooter, *The Cost of Coase*, 11 *J. Legal Stud.* 1 (1982); an interesting reflection of what the author meant and what has been retained is in R. Coase, *The Firm, The Market and The Law* 178 (1988).

23. See R. B. Schlesinger et al., *Comparative Law* 659–660 (4th ed., 1998).

24. See U. Mattei, *Efficiency and Equal Protection in the New European Contract Law: Mandatory, Default and Enforcement Rules*, 39 *Va. J. Int'l L.* 537 (1999).

25. Transaction costs are a central concern of modern neoinstitutional economic theory: see, in general, D. North, *Institutions, Institutional Change and Economic Performance* (1991); O. Williamson, *The Economic Institutions of Capitalism* (1987).

26. See Libecap, *supra* note 21.

27. See W. Fishel, *The Economics of Zoning Laws: A Property Rights Approach to American Land Use Controls* (1985).

28. See, generally, R. C. Ellickson, *Order Without Law* (1991).

29. I also discuss this example in Mattei, *supra* note 9, at 133.

30. See, for a detailed discussion, *infra*, Chapter 6, 137 sq.

31. See C. Atias, 2 *Droit civil, les biens* 333–334 (1982).

32. See Para. 912 BGB; Aer 938 C.C.

33. See A.Weill et al., *Droit civil, les biens* 219 (3d ed., 1985).

34. See Art. 14, Basic Law.

35. See *infra* Chapter 2.

36. See also *infra* Chapter 1.

37. See M. A. Heller, *The Tragedy of the Anticommons*, 111 *Harv. L. Rev.* 625 (1998).

38. See D. North, *Structure and Change in Economic History* 90 (1981).

39. See V. P. Mozolin, *Property Law in Contemporary Russia* (1993).

40. The puzzle of the existence of private lighthouses is approached by R. Coase, *The Lighthouse in Economics*, 17 *J.L. & Econ.* 357 (1974).

41. See P. Samuelson, *The Pure Theory of Public Expenditure*, 36 *Rev. Econ. Stat.* 387 (1954).

42. See C. L. Schultze, *The Public Use of Private Interest* (1977).

43. See Cooter & Ulen, *supra* note 15, at 38–40.

44. See, generally, D.J.H. Hullet, *An Analysis of Market Failures: Externalities, Public Goods and Mixed Goods* (1977).

45. This terminology is developed by Guido Calabresi, *The Cost of Accidents: A Legal and Economic Analysis* (1970).

46. See Chapter 2.
47. See, for a description, Schlesinger et al., *supra* note 23, at 539.
48. See G. Calabresi & D. Melamed, *Property Rules, Liability Rules, Inalienability: One View of the Cathedral*, 85 *Harv. L. Rev.* 1089 (1972).
49. A basic introduction to microeconomic tools for the benefit of the lawyer is offered by Cooter & Ulen, *supra* note 15, at 9–42.
50. See *infra* Chapter 7.
51. See, for similar rhetoric in different traditions, A. Di Majo, *La Tutela Civile dei Diritti* (2d ed., 1993), and F. H. Lawson, *Remedies of English Law* (1980).
52. See J. Coleman & J. Kraus, *Rethinking the Theory of Legal Rights*, 95 *Yale L.J.* 1335 (1986).
53. S. Bright & G. Gilbert, *Landlord and Tenant Law* (1995); N. Horn et al., *German Private and Commercial Law* 98 (1982).
54. See *Symposium. Property Rules, Liability Rules, and Inalienability: A Twenty-Five Years Retrospective*, 106 *Yale L.R.* 2081 (1997).
55. Full demonstration in Calabresi & Melamed, *supra* note 48.
56. See, however, for more nuances, E. Krier & S. J. Swab, *Property Rules and Liability Rules. The Cathedral in Another Light*, 70 *N. Y. U. L. Rev.* 440 (1995).
57. See the discussion *infra* Chapter 4. See also A. Gambaro, *Perspectives on the Codification of the Law of Property: An Overview*, 5 *Eur. Rev. Private L.* 497 (1997).
58. See Ellickson, *supra* note 28.
59. See R. A. Epstein, *A Clear View of the Cathedral: The Dominance of Property Rules*, 106 *Yale L.J.* 2091 (1997); however, for a more nuanced position, C. Rose, *Christals and Muds in Property Law*, 40 *Stan. L. Rev.* 577 (1988).
60. See *Stare Decisis*, 34 *Harv. L. Rev.* 75 (1920). For a discussion, see U. Mattei, *Stare Decisis* 216 (1988).
61. At least in most of the controversial cases in which the possessor not only has physical control but also intention to keep it in front of his or her opponent. On the ambiguity of delivery without intention, see K. Reid, *Obligations and Property: Exploring the Border*, 225 *Acta Iuridica* 237 (1997).
62. Thorough comparative discussion appears in R. Sacco, *Il possesso* (1988).
63. See Cooter & Ulen, *supra* note 15, at 128–133.
64. This explains the origin of land registers. See Horn et al., *supra* note 53, at 180.
65. See J. Carbonnier, *Droit civil, les biens* 88 (14th ed., 1991).
66. See *infra* Chapter 7.
67. See Posner, *supra* note 8, at 43.
68. See M. A. Heller & R. S. Eisenberg, *Can Patents Deter Innovation? The Anticommons in Biomedical Research*, 280 *Science* 698 (1998).
69. See Cooter & Ulen, *supra* note 15.
70. See Carbonnier, *supra* note 65, at 96.
71. See A. Kronman, *Specific Performance*, 45 *U. Chi. L. Rev.* 351 (1978).

CHAPTER 4

The Object of Property Rights

TAXONOMY

The physical object of a property right may have a very different nature. A piece of land, a book, a water basin, an animal, a computer program, a human embryo, a television frequency, a portfolio account, a negotiable instrument, a cubic meter of clean air, and so forth are all scarce resources. From a social science perspective they may be considered as objects of property rights. Of course, all such different objects of property do not and should not share the same legal regime. Traditionally, lawyers have been called upon to group together such different scarce resources in more or less broad legal categories to make it possible to handle in a simple way the legal discourse related to property. Possibly in no area of the law does one find more diversity among legal systems than in the domain that we may call "the object of property."[1] In this context, what differs is the taxonomy; that is, the classification that is needed to deal intellectually with a complex reality (such as property law).

Not only is the diversity high in terminology, but the conceptual framework varies significantly between legal systems. For example, in Germany, technically speaking, the object of property may only be a tangible thing (Section 80 of the BGB). France and Italy share a different view from the German one. In these two countries, a property right may also have as its object an intangible thing such as an original idea or energy.[2] Common lawyers, on the other hand, are not as fond of taxonomy as civilian jurists are. Consequently, they have not developed a conceptual framework to distinguish a property right from its object.

If one goes beyond taxonomy and tries to capture principles of the law in practice, it will be easy to perceive that all legal systems converge in handling within proprietary notions a variety of things other than tangible objects. The linkage between a property right and a physical object may be absent (e.g., a copyrighted idea) or only abstract (e.g., a nondivided coownership). More specifically, property rights may have as their object limited economic attributes of one thing both in time (e.g., a usufruct or a time-sharing condominium) and/or in extension (e.g., a servitude or the common areas of a condominium). Many intangible objects, such as intellectual property, are handled within a proprietary paradigm in all legal systems, whatever the official taxonomy may be.[3] On the other hand, all legal systems resist the idea of considering as the object of property rights certain kinds of material things that may have a very high economic value. Among these things are nonreplaceable parts of the human body (e.g., kidneys) or, in many cases, embryos, adoptable children, and so on.[4] There is an underlying fear of commodifying things that we ethically resist to address within the rhetoric of property law. Also recently, with the development of the public law regulatory state, yet another entire area of legal relationships has been approached within the proprietary paradigm: the so-called "new properties," entitlements on job security or on administrative licenses which certainly share certain structural aspects of property rights.[5]

In this book I do not discuss the more controversial areas in which, arguably, the notion and the language of property may offer some insights but which legal systems resist in approaching within proprietary frameworks. I also do not address those areas that, although clearly linked to property law, have developed a somewhat specialized flavor, such as copyright law or negotiable instruments law. I would rather dwell on the core problems of property law, on rules of property that pertain to objects that most legal systems would regard incontrovertibly as part of the area of private law usually referred to as property.

Given the high degree of formal divergence among legal systems in matters of property law, I will try to develop a terminology and a taxonomy that can be employed to understand and transfer knowledge from one system to another.[6] This taxonomy may not be at work as such in any one legal system, but I claim it can be used to approach and understand all legal systems. The taxonomies of the legal systems, in other words, may be considered as variations on the general notions that will be presented here. The terminology and the taxonomy that I use are consequently rather simple to grasp and understand.

Ownership and Property Rights

"Ownership" in this context refers to the legal right that a legal system grants to an individual in order to allow him or her to exercise the maximum degree of formalized control over a scarce resource.[7] This notion stems directly from the Roman law definition of *dominium*. A definition of this notion can be found in the rather emphatic language of the famous Article 544 of the Napoleonic Code, according to which ownership is the right to use and dispose of a thing in the most absolute way. A similar emphatic definition can also be found in the most influential common law treatise, that written by Sir William Blackstone at the end of the eighteenth century. According to Blackstone's definition, ownership had to be considered the sole and despotic *dominium* of an individual over a thing.[8] Despite this definition, common law countries have been traditionally cautious to emphasize the extent of the owner's powers, always employing the idea of reasonableness to limit him or her in the interest of his or her neighbors. It is no surprise therefore that the most important contribution of Anglo-American legal scholarship to property law is the metaphor of the bundle of rights. This clever metaphor defines ownership (and property) as a bundle of rights (and duties) enjoyed by an individual over a thing.[9]

To maintain some terminological precision while accepting the lessons of a more realistic approach to the law of property,[10] in this study I will use the notion of ownership to denote the highest possible legal right granted by the legal system to an individual over a certain scarce resource.[11] For example, the owner of a house is the person who exercises over it the most extended right recognized by a given legal system willing to admit individual property rights. Ownership is then recognizable from other lower property rights such as usufruct, coownership, servitudes, terms of years, or the like.

Ownership must be protected by the most effective set of legal remedies that are available in the legal system given the circumstances. Typically, the owner will be protected against (1) dispossession (by a remedy that allows him to recover the commodity), (2) behaviors that interfere with the exercise of the property right both temporarily (nuisances) or permanently (destruction) (in this case the legal system will use the most effective protection that is available given the circumstances—typically injunctions and other specific remedies—rather than mere damages), and (3) claims both explicit or implicit of incompatible rights over the object of ownership. This last protection is the key to the conceptual difference between ownership and limited property rights, whose enjoyment the owner always monitors. Consequently, the holder of a limited property right must always confront the possibility of the owner's incompatible claims based on his or her residual rights.

Indeed, one notion that allows one to capture the essence of ownership as opposed to other property rights is the notion of the elasticity of ownership. Whenever a limited property right is extinguished (e.g., by death of the usufructuary or change of physical circumstances of the land brought by a servitude), ownership recaptures the value that used to be the object of the opposing property right.[12] An easy metaphor can be that of a course of water limited by a dam. As soon as the dam (limited property right) is removed, the water (ownership) retakes its full course.

Property Rights and Personal Rights

As the previous examples illustrate, the notion of property rights refers to a broader category that includes but is not limited to ownership. In other words, the relationship between property rights and ownership is that of genus to species. All ownership includes property rights, but not all property rights include ownership. While ownership can be considered the queen of property rights, the two notions should not be confused (as they usually are). A servitude, for example, is a property right, not an ownership right. The notion of property rights can be better understood under the traditional civilian idea of absolute rights as opposed to obligations, or of property rights against personal rights.[13] A property right, in this sense, commands respect and abstention from all the members of a community and can be brought against all of them. To the contrary, an obligation merely reflects duties and rights that the legal system recognizes and protects between two parties.[14]

Accordingly, if I have a mere personal right in relation to a particular thing, I can only claim this thing against the person who is obliged to me.[15] If John promises to let me use his home in the countryside until his death, it is important to know whether he is granting me a real right (a usufruct) or only a personal (contractual) right. In the former case, I can claim my property right against everybody including Tom, a third party who bought the house from John and who moves into the property. The legal system will protect my property right (usufruct) by evicting Tom. If my right is only personal, I cannot evict Tom. I can enforce my contract only against John and claim the property from him (he is obliged toward me), but I have no remedy against Tom because he has no obligation toward me. In other words, my personal right is not against Tom. Consequently, I will only be able to sue John and, if John is not in a condition to persuade or to force Tom to leave, I will not be able to recover the property.

Another example of a property right that differs from ownership is the servitude.[16] The nature of a servitude can also be better understood by comparing this situation with that of a personal right (a contract) with the same content. Suppose that I have a right to cut my neighbor John's trees whenever they obstruct the beautiful view of the Danube that I enjoy from my balcony in Pest. Again, in a case like this it is crucial to know whether I have a property right (a servitude) or a mere obligatory (or personal) right. Only in the case of a servitude will my right survive when John sells his property to Sam, allowing me to keep cutting Sam's trees. If my right to cut the trees is personal and only obliges John, the transfer of ownership from John to Sam will terminate my right.[17]

In the two examples that I have discussed, legal systems may diverge in different details and may introduce different exceptions to these principles. What is important here, however, is the principle behind the difference between property rights and personal rights. That is, the principle that a property right can be claimed against the whole world whereas a personal right can only be claimed against the obligee is crucial to understanding the conceptual framework of Western property law.[18]

Property and Possession

Another quite simplified notion that I will use in this book is that of possession.[19] Legal systems diverge extensively in the use and the definition of possession.[20] However, a factual comparative study I have made with Professor Gordley from the University of California at Berkeley demonstrates that, in both common and civil law, "possession" contains the power of control over a scarce resource that tends to yield before ownership because it receives a legal protection whose justification is different from the one that legitimizes ownership.[21] The usual description of possession as a situation of fact corresponding to the exercise of ownership should therefore be rejected as a misleading legacy of useless conceptualizations. It is obvious that the possessor has rights which are sometimes very extended. Hence, in my terminology, possession is also a property right whose protection by the legal system is simply less intense than that of ownership.

Possession connotes physical control over a given object.[22] This physical control receives a more or less intense protection from the legal system, depending on the way in which it is acquired, the way in which it is exercised, and the nature of the legal interest of whoever is challenging it. Possession is a difficult legal category to capture, partly due to the schizophrenic nature of its coexistence with ownership. Possession is sometimes an institutional arrangement that facilitates the control of the owner over his or her property because it is a simple way of social signaling.[23] Possession in this sense cooperates with ownership (the owner is usually also the possessor, and his or her possession signals his or her ownership). Indeed, the owner may find it convenient to enforce his or her possession as a way to enforce ownership. But sometimes possession plays a rather antagonistic role against ownership. In some cases the possessor may even prevail against the owner. In this case, the possessor who prevails against the owner becomes the owner. This is why possession is an important way to acquire ownership.[24]

It is also important to consider that one cannot only possess ownership, but also possess a property right in general. For example, if someone rents my home which is subject to a servitude to the view on the Duna, the renter will possess my home as well as the servitude during the term of the rental agreement.

Property Rights and Interests

A final notion that needs to be introduced here, although it will be explained in more detail later, is the difference between a right and an interest.[25] As explained in Chapter 1, when the legal system protects a right it does so because it seeks to allow a zone of individual decision making over a scarce resource. Consequently, the legal system protects the subjective value and the subjective decision making on how to use the right. The legal system that recognizes the right to own a book will not take the book away from its owner because the owner is using the book as a decoration on a coffee table instead of reading it. When dealing with rights, the legal system protects idiosyncratic preferences. But when dealing with interests, the legal system protects only a given share of welfare.[26] The typical protection of an interest is compensation at market value. The right of ownership of the book would be protected as a mere interest to read the book should the legal system take away the book from its owner at market value on the rationale that he or she is not using it properly.

Typically, an interest and not a right is protected when the system denies full protection while granting only a limited one. For example, my right to use John's property for life, discussed in a previous example, ends up being protected as a mere interest (e.g., to obtain damages from John) in the case in which the legal system recognized the right of Tom to stay in John's home. Another example might be when the legal system refuses to grant me an injunction to prevent my neighbor's factory from polluting my river on the assumption that the factory creates jobs. In such a case, the legal system that uses a liability rule (e.g., granting me compensation for damages) is not protecting my ownership as a right, but as a mere interest.[27] In other words, two conflicting, incompatible rights cannot be recognized over the same scarce resources by the legal system. In case of conflict, one of the two rights usually declines into a mere interest to a share of welfare.[28]

It is not at all unusual that within the dynamic of a living legal system some property rights (or some aspects of them) are reduced and protected as mere interests. However, the remedy of damages as opposed to more specific remedies does not necessarily mean that the legal system is reducing a right to a mere interest. In certain cases, there is no possibility for the legal system to protect a right other than by granting damages. If, for example, a unique piece of antique furniture is burned and cannot be physically restored to its previous condition, the remedy of damages is the only possible protection of the right of ownership. In this case, ownership is not reduced to a mere interest but is still protected as a right. This is why the protection granted by ownership is described as the highest available within a legal system, given the circumstances.

Immovable Property versus Movable Property

A crucial taxonomic distinction that is at play in the modern law of most legal systems is that between immovable and movable property.[29] The first category includes the legal regime of land and fixtures, while the second can be defined only negatively by saying that property which is not immovable is movable. Indeed, legal systems disagree on many details, particularly on what can be considered a fixture. We should not overstress the difficulties stemming from these details. In describing Western property law, one finds at play much more crucial divergences, such as the lack of agreement between common law and civil law even on what can be classified as property in general, let alone the different taxonomies of detail within the law of property. The problem can be solved with a careful choice of the materials that one wishes to cover.

In this book, I am discussing principles that are common to a variety of legal systems in order to facilitate the communication among them. Consequently, my focus will be mainly on the subject matter that a plurality of legal systems regard as property, and I will exclude those areas in which systems disagree, even on this very fundamental choice. For example, I will not discuss here the law of leases, which are considered property in common law countries but are considered part of the law of obligations in civil law countries.[30] This choice may be challenged as unsound when seen against the evolution of many modern civil law systems (including France and Italy) to protect the rights of the tenant against the landlord by securing his or her position in an increasingly more effective way.[31]

Similar political choices are also present in some post-socialist legal systems. In the new Armenian Civil Code, for example, a provision has been included that compels the buyer of a privatized residential property to conclude a lease with the tenant who was in possession of the privatized immovable. Of course, when a lease resists a transfer of ownership it may well be considered a property right in the sense that we have just discussed, because its value extends beyond the relationship between the two contracting parties. However, most legal systems do not carry the choice to protect the tenant so far, and probably the modern landlord–tenant relationship is still better captured by the traditional contractual structure.[32] On the other hand, most legal systems agree that land can be the object of ownership. Practically all of them, including many of the residual socialist countries in Asia and Africa, do agree that a usufruct or other long-term grant can be considered the object of a property right.[33]

Consequently, I will mainly discuss the area of immovable property, although I will describe those fundamental principles that, particularly in the domain of transfer of property, make the law of immovables and movables significantly different and rather difficult to capture within the traditionally civilian unitary framework. This choice is not only dictated by the need to capture common principles at play in a plurality of legal systems. What constitutes immovable property is more clear and its boundaries are easier to describe.[34] The category of movable property is so variable among legal systems that in focusing only on what is common between them one could exclude all of the more interesting and revealing problems.[35] Indeed, systems do not agree on important issues, such as whether a stock can be considered property, a part of the body can be owned, or the like. The result would be that the few objects which legal systems agree to consider movable property would be so simple (a book, a pen, a simple toy) that nothing particularly interesting and revealing could be observed by their study.

On the other hand, the structure of immovable property, even if one were to focus only on land, seems more complex and interesting. Indeed, a large portion of public law may be involved in its structure.[36] As already mentioned in the first chapter, another important basic feature of different legal systems lies in the distinction between private law and public law. Although most of the rules and principles of property that I discuss in this book are traditionally part of private law and should apply both between individuals and in transactions between an individual and a public authority, there is one crucial area of property law that is part of public law in all developed legal systems. These are the rules devoted to the loss of property rights (usually immovables) that follow expropriation for public utility. I will discuss this area, the only one in which there are structural reasons to differently treat individuals and the public authority, in the final chapter of this book.

IMMOVABLE PROPERTY

Land

Legal systems do agree that land is an object of property of particular importance. Although it is clearly false in modern societies that land constitutes the most important form of wealth—important wealth is nowadays made of stocks and other forms of movable property—it is nevertheless true that the rules related to land can well be used as the paradigm of modern property law.[37] Indeed, a large part of modern private law has developed its present features around the land tenure revolution that characterized the demise of the feudal organization of society. A system of free land tenure is one of the fundamental institutions of a market economy made of individuals that compete with one another, as opposed to a feudal economy in which the hierarchy rather than the market rules the society.

On less sociological and more technical legal grounds, there is no doubt that land law is possibly the most complex area of traditional property law for a number of economic reasons that we have summarized as being externalities to the rule rather than the exception in transactions related to immovables.[38] Of course, many things other than land (in the sense of soil) are contained by the notion of immovable property of different legal systems (e.g., buildings and other fixtures in almost every system). Indeed, in common law terminology, land includes buildings. It is therefore important to see whether there are some reasons, other than the accidents of historically developed taxonomies (that change from legal system to legal system), why certain objects should share the legal regime of land although they are distinguishable from it. Before entering into that discussion, let me first dwell briefly on land.

All through the Western legal tradition, land is part of what can be owned as immovable property. Of course, as we have already mentioned, the common law notion of "real property" does not perfectly coincide with the notion of immovable property.[39] However, in the historical common law, most land could be defended with a real action (and was therefore real property) and also those limited areas of England in which land was not in free tenure (and technically a copyhold not defendable with a real action) were very soon accommodated in legal regime with the real property. A real action could be used specifically to recover land, while a personal action only opened the door to a claim for damages.

Many legal rules have been historically thought of and developed keeping land in mind. Indeed, land is a psychological entity that enshrines the ideals of immobility, perpetuity, and absence of risk.[40] Land absorbs the economic utilities of the evolution of humankind and, except for occasional revolutionary circumstances, this process of wealth stratification in the long run cannot take a negative step. Even taking into account the bitter and realistic observation of the great Lord Keynes, "In the long run we will all be dead," the risk-averse investor will nonetheless be keen in acquiring ownership of land, because even after death he or she will still be able to increase the wealth of his or her progeny (note the ancestral analogy with the African constitutional structure of property).

As it is very well known and demonstrated in economic theory, risk aversion is the rule in the majority of individual market actors, so that the importance of land as an object of legal organization appears obvious. Indeed, the minimal conditions that are needed in order for land to maintain its characteristic of safe investment is the existence of stable, albeit rudimentary, legal institutions. No human society can be considered organized if it cannot guarantee the exclusivity of an individual or of a group of individuals on certain economic utilities that stem from land. Someone who has invested his or her money in buying an apartment in Mogadiscio, Sarajevo, or Beirut just before the beginning of political turmoil can tragically be witness to this point.

Land is the object of continuous incremental transformations in the long run. This is very easy to observe focusing on urban land, but it is no less true in the countryside. The English country landscape, for example, although it may seem very natural, is nonetheless the product of continuous physical transformations carried on by one generation after the other.

Fixtures

The last observation in the previous section explains why the legal regime of land is strictly linked with the legal regime of what is connected in a stable way with it. Indeed, the communist (as well as the colonialist) regimes, which excluded land from ownership while allowing property rights on buildings, were introducing a counterintuitive legal solution only dictated by symbology.[41] As we will see in our chapter on the loss of property, a residual power of the state over land is a structural necessity of modern organized societies and stems from the very need of a relatively stable political organization to put in place a system of property rights. Modern legal systems, however, have evolved to make sure that the exercise of such power is not carried on in a way that can impair the crucially important institutional characteristic of the security of property rights. Security, of course, does not mean sanctity. However, in order to attract investment and the development of a market, security of property rights is as important to land as it is to fixtures which can be regarded as investments permanently modifying land. There is no rational point in distinguishing the two regimes.

The more land is transformed, the more it will become a complex object, and this increased complexity will be reflected by the law which has to discipline the allocation of the returns that may be obtained therefrom. Indeed, while for rural land the only legal problem may be the delimitation of borders of the fields, if land is transformed into a skyscraper with hotel, shopping malls, and office space, the complexity of its legal regime has to grow enormously. It may become necessary to regulate parking, to decide on opening and closing times for public-access facilities, and to allocate the costs of security, heating, and the like among the different owners. This is the reason why, in the first decades of the twentieth century, most Western legal systems were forced to enact laws, either in the form of special statutes or in the outright form of code amendments, to take care of the added complexities introduced by the widespread use of condominium apartment buildings.[42]

If we wish to express this idea in economic terms, not only do externality problems increase with the complexity of use of a given resource, but lump investments and the economies of scale also modify the picture. Externalities can also be created when an activity is connected with land in a purely occasional way. Consider the legal and economic activities involved in the establishment of a circus in town. There is still a difference between a circus and a stadium. If one focuses on the lump investments, the circus cannot be correctly considered a structure that permanently modifies land. It will not be difficult therefore to see that a stadium is an immovable because it is a stratification in land use that changes the land's economic value.

While it is true that modern technology could allow us to transfer the Kremlin to Japan, it is nonetheless true that the economic effort needed to do so would be utterly exceptional exactly because of the nature of the Kremlin as a permanent transformation of land in the center of Moscow. The same nature of exceptional effort is not true for other structures of amazing dimension and weight, such as a drill to build the Channel Tunnel or the military buildup preceding Desert Storm. The important point to retain from this discussion is that it would not make sense for a legal system to diversify the legal regime of the Kremlin and Red Square on which it is grounded.

The German Civil Code well reflects these structural observations in its taxonomy. Paragraphs 93, 94, and 95 of the BGB are devoted to the definition of immovable property. Under paragraph 93, the parts of a thing that cannot be separated without the destruction of the whole thing (essential constitutive parts) cannot be the object of different rights. Under paragraph 94, essential constitutive parts of land are things permanently and firmly attached to it, particularly buildings or the products of land until they are attached to the land (in our example, the Kremlin or a stadium). Finally, under paragraph 95, those things that are attached to the land only for a transitory purpose (in our example, the circus tent) are not to be considered constitutive parts of the land.

Italian law offers an example of a taxonomy that, far from improving the German one, creates serious problems for the interpreter, since it does not reflect the economic reality of the transactions it is called upon to discipline.[43] The Italian Code made an attempt to eliminate the abstract notion of "essential constitutive parts" by introducing a mere list of examples of immovable property. According to Article 812 of the Civil Code of 1942, the list includes land, sources of water, rivers, trees, buildings, and "everything that is attached to land either in a natural or in an artificial way even if for a mere transitory purpose." Hence, Italian law breaks with tradition and incorporates in the same category the Kremlin and the circus tent! The list continues in the second part of the article of the Italian Civil Code, and includes mills, baths, and all the floating objects that are permanently connected to the shore. According to Italian law, this last category of objects, although not immovable by its nature, is immovable by their "goal" and therefore should share the legal regime of immovables.

This article is interesting because it shows how the abstract mentality of civil lawyers ends up building abstractions even in those areas in which there has been a clear attempt to get rid of some of them.[44] In fact, lawyers have introduced a distinction (which is often the object of a question in first-year law school examinations) between immovables by nature (such as land or buildings) and immovable by "goal" (such as floating secured objects, or the circus tent). Of course, considering floating objects and tents as immovables when the costs of their separation from land are so low does not make any economic sense and one wonders what the purpose of such taxonomic subdistinctions could be. Indeed, it only serves the purpose of failing a first-year law student at the cost of losing the centrality of such a commonsensical and economically sound distinction as that between movables and immovables.

MOVABLE PROPERTY

In General

As mentioned before, movable property is a broader, less-defined residual category that contains whatever things different legal systems do not consider as immovable. Legal systems therefore have developed a variety of different subtaxonomies in order to capture and to handle the great structural variety of movable property.[45] In legal discourses throughout different legal traditions, one can find many of these notions, which include (1) "intangible goods" to refer to things such as copyrights and ideas, as opposed to tangible goods such as a book or a bottle; (2) "fungible goods" to refer to things whose economic nature makes them perfectly interchangeable with other things of the same kind (e.g., one pound of screws of a given kind), as opposed to nonfungible things which do not share this characteristic (e.g., a piece of antique furniture or a house); and (3) "consumable goods," such as those things whose value is captured by a one-shot perfectly rival use (e.g., a loaf of bread) as opposed to nonconsumable goods (such as a car).[46]

Of course, all of these taxonomies are neither precise nor strict and their variety is staggering if one describes a multiplicity of legal systems. It is important to consider at our level of abstraction that different things may fit in a variety of taxonomies. The use of such taxonomies is justified by the need to handle with precision, to accommodate, and to submit to common rules objects whose nature may be different but whose legal regime for certain purposes should be the same. For example, a brand new car is a fungible, nonconsumable, tangible good. A pound of bread is a fungible, consumable, tangible good. What would a three-year-old horse, a brand-new piece of furniture, or a used bicycle be?

In dealing with problems of transfer of property and the obligations for the parties involved in them, it may be useful to be able to use certain categories in order to distinguish legal situations from a technical viewpoint. Although on a nontechnical level they may seem governed by the same legal principle, in the technical life of the law they may involve completely different problems and questions.[47] For example, a proposition (or a legal principle) such as "when you borrow something from your neighbor you have to return it" has an entirely different meaning in the case of a consumable or a nonconsumable thing. If one borrows a pound of bread or six eggs from his or her next-door neighbor, the understanding is that he or she will have to return another pound of bread or another six eggs. On the other hand, if I borrow my neighbor's used car I will not be on the right side of the law by returning (unless he or she specifically approves this solution) my old used car or even another used car similar to the one borrowed. Putting it in economic terms, the default rules for consumable and nonconsumable goods are and must be different, given the different nature of such things.

Only a couple of general things may be said about movable property across legal systems. To begin with, the different, more complex taxonomy that must be used to handle them is the result of higher variety and complexity in the nature of movable property. While immovable property can be physically described as land plus fixtures, movable property is a category that may contain the entire world of things having some economic value, and therefore its content as a legal category is contingent on the taxonomic options of different legal systems.[48]

Second, and very important, it seems that in dealing with movable property the distinction between ownership and possession tends to blur. Most modern legal systems have followed, although along different formal paths, the principle clearly stated by the French Civil Code, according to which in the domain of movable property possession equals ownership.[49] Indeed, there are strong efficiency reasons to do so and the protection of possession against ownership in the domain of movable property is one of the most important institutional evolutions that have guaranteed the development of efficient markets in Western societies.[50] The reason for such evolution is easy to grasp if one compares immovable with movable property. While the most important (and legally complex) transaction over immovable property lies in its use and in its transformation, the same is not true for movables. The most important transactions relating to movables lie in their market transfer. Efficient legal institutions therefore are those which facilitate the transfer of movables. Such transfer is motivated by the protection of possession over title and ownership.[51] Indeed, if title and ownership are protected over possession, the transaction costs for the buyer involved in monitoring the chain of previous transfers to be sure that he or she is acquiring ownership (i.e., that the seller is the true owner) would be prohibitive. It is efficient to assume that the social signal coming from possession is enough to guarantee that the buyer will prevail over possible previous owners who have lost control of the property for different reasons. It is no wonder that the legal merchant has pushed the evolution in favor of actual possession and not ownership in the domain of movables. Because the most important aspects of movable property are related to its transfer, we will deal with some details in the next chapter.

Vehicles

What I have just mentioned about the sufficiency of possession as a legal regime for movable property is subject, in most legal systems, to an important qualification. Sometimes certain kinds of movables are subject to a legal regime structurally more similar to immovable property. This happens practically everywhere in the case of motor vehicles such as cars, motorcycles, airplanes, boats, and so on.

To keep track of these movables, legal systems usually organize some public system of ownership registration. The name of the owner of this kind of movable property must be entered in the registry. Consequently, the transfer of these movables is subject to more or less stringent formalities, ranging from the need of notarial form, as in Italy, to the simple mailing of a signed form to the Motor Vehicle Department, as in California and other American states. Movables are also objects, most of the time, of special regimes of liability. In these particular cases, the notion of ownership as opposed to possession reacquires its importance, even in those systems, such as the German one, which create a special kind of legal entity to deal with the particular liability problems created by movables. Indeed, the so-called "Halter" responsible for damages created by vehicles in Germany is usually, although not always, the owner in the technical sense.[52]

Generally, registered movables share a legal regime similar to that of immovables for a number of purposes. As already mentioned, the rationale of this choice is the special regime of liability due to the dangerous nature of the use of vehicles. The particular value of some of these objects, such as airplanes, may be another reason to be careful in allowing completely unsupervised transacting over them, as in the case of other movable property.

Movables Equated to Immovables

The case of vehicles is not the only one in which for some purposes legal systems choose to equate the legal regime of movables to that of immovables. Indeed, although the difference between movables and immovables is to be considered structural and the legal regime of property should reflect its structure in order to be efficient, sometimes legal systems decide that certain movables should be considered as immovables for given purposes. French law offers us the clearest terminology for this purpose when it distinguishes immovable property "by its nature" from immovable property "by goal."[53] This terminology suggests that while certain property is immovable, certain other can be made immovable by institutional choice. An object which is per se a piece of movable property may be expressly finalized (*affecté*) to serve in the use of an immovable. In these cases, the legal regime of both the objects will be the same. The movable will follow the fate of the immovable.

What is the rationale of such a decision? Once again, it is possible to find it within the institutional function of lowering transaction costs.[54] The rationale is obviously the pursuit of clear property rights in the case of transfer of a complex piece of property. If I sell "a milk factory," the understanding will be that I will sell not only the land and the buildings but also whatever it is that makes it a factory. I cannot sell the milk factory and, before passing the keys to the buyer, take away all of the machinery. Unless we agree otherwise, the legal regime of the immovable part of the factory (land and fixtures) will be extended also to the movable parts, which are aimed to its use. An even clearer example would be that of a car. The legal regime of the registered property will be extended also to the parts of the car that are independent movable property by themselves. A buyer will expect to find the spare tire in the car unless he or she agrees to buy the car without it. The car will be the principal property and the spare tire will be the accessory property following the principal's regime. A classic example would be a tractor on a farm. Unless expressly separated (or sold by itself), the tractor will follow the regime of the farm. Such default rules lower negotiation costs because they do not force the contracting parties to go through specific negotiations on each of the component parts of a complex object (such as a factory), unless they are willing to do so.[55]

Of course, since the function and the justification for equating these two legal regimes is the simplification and ultimately the clarity of property rights, it is essential to have available criteria that clearly tell us in what circumstances an object can be considered an accessory to another. What makes an object accessory to another? Is a tractor always accessory to a farm? Is an oven an accessory to a bakery? Legal systems wrestle to define such criteria. The French and Italian Civil Codes appear to use a subjective standard, according to which what determines the nature of accessory property is the will of the owner of the principal thing. Italian law, adopting the classic French view, describes the accessory property as "functionalized in a stable way to the service or the ornament of another property." The civil code makes clear that "accessory property may be the object of separate legal transactions," clearly recognizing the nature of default of such regime.[56]

Many commentators who see the "objective approach" of the German BGB as a much more advanced attempt to pursue clarity have criticized such a standard based on the decision making of the owner of the principal thing.[57] Indeed, according to the letter of paragraph 97 of BGB, "Accessories are movable things that without being essential parts of the principal are aimed at serving the economic purpose of the principal thing and are in a spatial relationship with it that corresponds to such an aim. A thing is not an accessory if, in the usual transactions, it is not regarded as such." According to the so-called objective approach, what matters is the social (objective) perception of the relationship between the things rather than the individual (subjective) decision making of the owner. This makes substantial sense given the nature of the default regime of such rules. Indeed, if the principal owner's decision making was clear enough to determine the accessory status, the very nature of default rules would yield to it.

The German BGB proceeds to the task of objective clarity by offering an exemplifying list of accessory movables. According to paragraph 98,

Aimed to serve the economic goal of the principal thing are:

1. In a building permanently devoted to industrial activity, such as a mill, a foundry, a beer brewery, or hardware house, the machinery and the tools that are used for the purpose.
2. In a farm, the tools, the animals that are used in the agricultural process, the agrarian products that are necessary to keep on the production until the time in which similar products will be presumably produced, as well as the existing fertilizers made within the farm.

In general, we may observe that a legal regime that assimilates movables to immovables is justified only if the clarity it introduces lowers transaction costs more than how it raises them by introducing a divergency between the economic nature and the legal regime of property.[58] Consequently, the objective reading is to be preferred only if it is clear that the owner is free to expressly alter it. Generally, on the legal ground, it is interesting to observe that all of the civilian codifications have felt the need to introduce a special regime for accessorial property. Possibly such a special regime can lower transaction costs only in a limited number of socially perceivable circumstances, such as the ones described in the German Code. In all other cases, short of introducing clarity it only introduces confusion.

Technically, we may conclude by observing that ownership of accessories is transferred together with the ownership of the principal property without the need to expressly mention them. A third party who claims a possessory right over the accessories must prove his or her right with strong evidence (usually a written instrument) which antedates the moment of transfer of the principal.[59] Whoever pledges the principal pledges also the accessories. The same is true in the case of judicial execution over the principal.[60]

THE LEGAL REGIME OF PROPERTY RIGHTS OTHER THAN OWNERSHIP

In the civil law tradition, the already-mentioned principle of the "closed number of property rights" has an important implication: Property rights other than those expressly recognized as such by the law can neither be created by private individuals, nor can they be transferred privately.[61] Because the transfer of immovable property is based on the registration of the owner in some form of public registry, the *numerus clausus* principle means that only entries of property rights recognized by law are those accepted by the keeper of such instruments. The same principle does not exist in common law, where parties, by means of the creation of a trust instrument, can create property rights with a large degree of autonomy.[62] From these antithetic principles of the civil law and common law traditions stems a common implication. Property rights other than ownership share the legal regime of the object on which they insist unless special provisions are dictated by their particular nature. In other words, the rules and principles that we see at play for immovable and movable property are extended to different property rights on such objects. This is true in particular for the regime of pledging, where the movable or immovable nature of property has crucial consequences on the form of this transaction and on its validity against third parties. While the pledging of movables is not usually possible without transferring possession of them, pledges of immovables must be registered but possession may remain with the pledging party.[63]

As already mentioned, the owner's freedom of decision making over the legal regime of the property should be safeguarded until the social signals that he or she conveys to the market are not ambiguous and capable of misleading the reliance of third parties. This means that, in theory, if a legal system is capable of organizing a public registry reliable enough to keep track of limited property rights, there are no reasons in principle to limit their number.[64]

Even those systems that do not share the view that property rights should be freely created by the owner agree in recognizing that whenever limited property rights exist over a given immovable property there is at play a form of "immaterial property" sharing the regime of immovables.[65] Of course, this is not only an interesting taxonomic observation. It carries important implications. For example, "development rights" created by zoning ordinances or similar urban-development instruments should be considered immovable property and be governed by its legal regime. For the sake of a rational urban regime, they should be freely transferable and third parties should be put in a condition to rely on them. If, for example, a zoning ordinance allows a total of 1,000 cubic meters of building opportunities in a given area where two owners, A and B, have equally extended land, and if A only needs 300 cubic meters, A should be able to sell the remaining 200 cubic meters to B, who may need 700 cubic meters. This is an efficient transaction. Of course, if C comes later and is interested in buying land from A, C should know that he or she can only build on 300 cubic meters and not on 500 cubic meters as he or she might gather by simply consulting the zoning ordinance. Treating the development rights as immovable property (allowing registration of the transactions related to them) may solve this crucial problem of social signaling that cannot be resolved by mere possession.[66] Of course, this observation raises provocative implications in the area of environmental law, where we may be in need of private law alternatives to centralized command and control regulations.[67]

PUBLIC LAW OWNERSHIP

Development rights as a kind of special property rights created by the complexities of public law (such as urban law) outside the codes in civil law and the body of the general common law in common law countries is not the only situation in which the complexity of the regulatory needs of the modern state create special proprietary regimes. Occasionally, the state removes certain things from the market and keeps the ownership for itself. In socialist law, this was the rule, and the "ownership of the state" was clearly the most important kind of ownership within the socialist law taxonomy.[68]

Even within the legal systems of capitalistic economies, not all of the property is on the market. Certain movable property is removed from the market for a variety of reasons.[69] For example, parts of the human body are removed from the market for fear of "commodification." Things of particular strategic value, such as uranium, are removed from the market for fear of the rise of strong counterpowers to the state. Some strong sources of unproductive pleasure, such as heroin, morphine, or other drugs, are removed from the market for fear of extensive addiction within the population. In all these cases, the state or other specialized administrative, technical, or political bodies within the state enjoy a position of monopoly. Not only do they have the possibility of being owners of these things, but they also exert the power to decide who their trading partners can be. The choice to remove an object of economic value from the market is usually inefficient and it has to be justified on policy grounds. The "public good" nature of some property might also justify state ownership on efficiency grounds.[70] The French and Italian traditions distinguish some kinds of immovable property that can only be owned by the state (necessary *demanial* property, such as the seashore or military property) from other kinds of property that is subject to the public law regime if it is the property of the state (e.g., freeways).[71]

The large variety of legal regimes and the staggering variety of different immovables that may fall under the notion of public ownership make it difficult to say much as a matter of principle about the choice to remove certain immovables from the market. These are typically political choices and many legal systems (such as the Anglo-American tradition) do not even attempt to develop a taxonomy to handle this complexity. Even within the category of property that can only be owned by the state it is difficult to find structural analogies. In the case of seashore property, the state can neither sell it nor exclude the public from it. Indeed, the choice of withdrawing such immovable property from the market is to guarantee the public enjoyment of natural beauty. In the case of property such as a military base, the state can sell it after changing its status and excluding the public from it. While there are no legal systems so far that have privatized the military, many legal systems (most notably the American) allow private seashore property.

Some legal systems exclude private property from water basins, either because of their importance or because of their natural beauty. Most legal systems exclude private ownership of objects of archeological value. Some of them exclude it even from the natural resources of the subsoil. The principles described in this book may not apply either completely or in part to these kinds of objects.

Finally, it must be said that, depending on the different ideas and notions of public law within different legal systems, certain kinds of property, either movable or immovable, can be withdrawn from the ordinary private law regime. In a number of civilian systems, the very fact that an object belongs to the state or to another public administration is sufficient to remove it from the normal private law regime. Following this rationale, certain objects, such as school buildings, furniture and other equipment of public offices, official cars, and so on, may be the objects of special rules of use and transfer. These rules are usually complex and create inefficiencies and waste. A typical example is the complex procedures of control to which the transfers of such property are subject. By enormously raising transaction costs of replacement (sometimes even making replacement impossible) in a world of rapidly evolving technology, these special public law regimes are possibly the main reason why technology in government offices tends to be obsolete.

NOTES

1. *Structural Variations in Property Law* 6 *Int. Enc. Comp. Law* (1975) offers good evidence. See also A. Candian et al., *Proprieté, Property, Eigentum* (1991).

2. The broader French approach is discussed in J. Carbonnier, *Droit Civil, Les Biens* 397 (14th ed., 1991). See also M. Recht, *Le Droit d'Auteur: Une nouvelle forme de propriété* (1969). For the Italian and a comparative perspective, see V. Zeno Zencovich, *Cosa*, in 3 *Digesto Discipline Privatistiche. Sez. Civile* 438 (1989).

3. For a comparative law and economic discussion of functional divergencies, see H. Hansmann & M. Santilli, *Authors' and Artists' Moral Rights: A Comparative Legal and Economic Analysis*, 26 *J. Legal Stud.* 95 (1997).

4. See H. Hansmann, *The Economics and Ethics of Markets for Human Organs*, 14 *J. Health Pol'y, Pol. & L.* 57 (1989), reprinted in *Organ Transplantation Policy: Issues and Prospects* (J. Blumstein & F. Sloan eds., 1989).

5. See C. A. Reich, *The New Property*, 73 *Yale L.J.* 733 (1964).

6. For the evolution of the proprietary terminology in a common law environment, see P. Butt, *Reforming the Language of Property Law*, in *The Reform of Property Law* 3–26 (P. Jackson & D. C. Wilde eds., 1997).

7. For an overall view on the concept of ownership, see the famous essay by A. M. Honoré, *Ownership*, in *Oxford Essays on Jurisprudence* 107 (A. G. Guest ed., 1981).

8. See W. Blackstone, 2 *Commentaries on the Law of England* 2 (1766).

9. See discussion and references *supra* Chapter 1.

10. See *infra* Chapter 7.

11. See A. Gambaro, *Il diritto di proprietà* 211 (1995); see also, applying a similar idea to land, R. Ellickson, *Property in Land*, 102 *Yale L.J.* 1315, 1362–1353 (1993), for "a Blackstonian bundle of land entitlement." For the definition of the fee simple, the traditional Anglo-American notion of ownership, see A.W.B. Simpson, *A History of the Land Law* (2d ed., 1986). As to the German idea, see N. Horn et al., *German Private and Commercial Law* 172 (1982) (citing Blackstone!); for France, see Carbonnier, *supra* note 2, at 124.

12. See Honoré, *supra* note 7, at 127.

13. See Carbonnier, *supra* note 2, at 66.

14. For a recent, fascinating discussion of this issue, see K.G.C. Reid, *Obligations and Property: Exploring the Border*, 225 *Acta Iuridica* 237 (1997).

15. See Horn et al., *supra* note 11, at 170.

16. See J. E. Cribbet & C. W. Johnson, *Principles of the Law of Property* 380–389 (3d ed., 1989); Carbonnier, *supra* note 2, at 249.

17. See C. Clark, *Covenants and Other Interests which "Run with Land"* (2d ed., 1947).

18. The area of law covered by the law of obligations vis-à-vis the law of property in the Western tradition is well illustrated by P. Birks, *Definition and Division: A Meditation on Institutes 3.13*, in *The Classification of Obligations* 1–35 (P. Birks ed., 1997).

19. The (old-fashioned) English work most traditionally associated with the idea of possession is probably the essay by Sir Frederick Pollock & R. S. Wright, *An Essay on Possession in the Common Law* (1888).

20. Under English law, the notion of possession of personal property is extensively dealt with by A. P. Bell, *Modern Law of Personal Property in England and Ireland* 33–65 (1989). As for the possession of land, see P. Walter & J. Harris, *Claims to the Possession of Land: The Law and Practice* (4th ed., 1998). A comparative discussion can be found in R. Sacco, *Il possesso* (1988).

21. See J. Gordley & U. Mattei, *Protecting Possession*, 44 *Am. J. Comp. L.* 243 (1996).

22. For a "classic" comment on the requisites of possession in a common law perspective, see D. R. Harris, *The Concept of Possession in English Law*, in *Oxford Essays on Jurisprudence* 74 (S. G. Guest ed., 1968).

23. See *supra* Chapter 3.

24. See *infra* Chapter 5. See also U. Mattei, *La Proprietà Immobiliare* (1993).

25. Under English law, the term "interest" is employed extensively, both with reference to real and personal property. For the latter, see A. P. Bell, *Modern Law of Personal Property in England and Ireland* 31–218 (1989). For an overview of interests in personal property, see also the older work by R. H. Kersley, *Goodeve's Modern Law of Personal Property* 1–20 (1949).

26. See R. Cooter & T. Ulen, *Law and Economics* (2d ed., 1997).

27. See discussion and references in U. Mattei, *Comparative Law and Economics* 59 (1997). See also U. Mattei, *Dissimilar Form Similar Substance? An Economic Framework for Western Property Law*, in *European Legal Tradition and Israel* (A. M. Rabello ed., 1994).

28. See G. Calabresi & D. Melamed, *Property Rules, Liability Rules, Inalienability: One View of the Cathedral*, 85 *Harv. L. Rev.* 1089 (1972).

29. Traditionally, the key distinction in common law between real property and personal property could not be considered the same as the distinction between immovable and movable property. The distinction and the terminology stemmed from the kind of legal remedies that it was possible to use to defend the property right. In modern law, however, the distinction between the two taxonomies can fairly be described as irrelevant. See F. Lawson, *Structural Variations in Property Law: Common Law*, in 6 *International Encyclopedia of Comparative Law, Property and Trust* 22 (1975).

30. For the requirements of different types of leases in land, see R. J. Smith, *Property Law* 337–441 (2d ed., 1998). See also S. Bright & G. Gilbert, *Landlord and Tenant Law* (1995).

31. See the comparative discussion in A. Guarneri, *Diritti reali e riritti di credito: valore attuale di una distinzione* (1979). Actually, several attempts have been made by scholars of the civil law systems to overcome the traditional idea that the lease is a mere contract; see R. T. Troplong, *Le droit civil expliqué suivant l'ordre des articles du Code-De l'echange et du louage-Du contrat de louage* n. 4 (1851); for a recent Italian example, see M. Comporti, *Contributo allo studio del diritto reale* 327 (1977).

32. See, for a controversial nonutilitarian argument in favor of such restrictions, M. J. Radin, *Residential Rent Control*, 15 *Philosophy and Public Affairs* 350 (1986).

33. See 5 *Encyclopedie juridique de l' Afrique: droit des biens* (G. A. Kouassigan ed., 1982).

34. See R. Ellickson, *Property in Land*, 102 *Yale L.J.* 1315 (1993).

35. J. Stevens & R. A. Pearce, *Land Law* 6 (1998), agree that "despite the more recent objective of harmonising unnecessary distinctions between the two types of property the difference between land and personal property is still important, especially as legislation has introduced a statutory framework governing many of the important property issues which is exclusive to land." For an overview of statutory sources of property law, see M. Thomas, *Blackstone's Statutes on Property Law* (6th ed., 1998/1999).

36. Carbonnier, *supra* note 2, at 353, for example, devotes a chapter of his leading book to "Le droit publique de l' immeuble."

37. See, for example, *id.* 88– 89.

38. See *supra* Chapter 3.

39. For recent general work on English law, see K. Gray, *Elements of Land Law* (2d ed., 1993); E. T. Burn, *Maudsley and Burn's Land Law: Cases and Materials* (2d ed., 1998). See also S. Bright & G. Gilbert, *Landlord and Tenant Law* (1995).

40. For a recent, theoretical treatment, see Ellickson, *supra* note 34.

41. See U. Mattei, *Socialist and Non Socialist Approaches to Land Law: Continuity and Change in Somalia and Other African States*, 16 *Rev. Soc. L.* 17 (1990).

42. For an economic analysis, see H. Hansmann, *Condominium and Cooperative Housing: Transactional Efficiency, Tax Subsidies, and Tenure Choice*, 20 *J. Legal Stud.* 25 (1991). One of the most important innovations of the 1942 Italian Civil Code was the discipline of condominiums contained in Articles 1117–1139. In Germany, the "Law on Home Ownership" was enacted in March 15, 1951, BGBl I, 341. The possibility of condominium ownership was rejected expressly by the BGB. See Horn et al., *supra* note 11, at 178. For a thorough comparative discussion, see *Ownership, 6 Int. Enc. Comp. Law* 3–535 (A. N. Yannopoulos ed., 1994).

43. See, for critical discussion, Mattei, *supra* note 24, at 75.

44. Indeed, according to some scholars, the insufficient abstraction of the chapters related to property rights is one of the worst defects of the Italian Civil Code.

45. English law deals with movable property in the context of personal property law. The literature on the topic is certainly not immense: On the contrary, personal property is somewhat neglected in academic research. Alongside the old work by R. H. Kersley, *Goodeve's Modern Law of Personal Property* (1949), the most popular recent books on the topic are A. P. Bell, *Modern Law of Personal Property in England and Ireland* (1989), and M. Bridge, *Personal Property Law* (2d ed., 1996).

46. Carbonnier, *supra* note 2, at 96, for example, distinguishes primary from secondary distinctions between objects of property. See the general comparative discussion in Zencovich, *supra* note 2, at 451.

47. See *infra* Chapter 5.

48. See G. Pugliese, *Property* (tentative manuscript prepared for the *International Encyclopedia of Comparative Law*).

49. See Article 2279, C. Civ.: "En fait de meubles la possession vaut titre."

50. See D. North, *Institutions, Institutional Change and Economic Performance* (1991).

51. See, for a classic historical and comparative discussion, L. Mengoni, *L' acquisto a non domino* (3d ed., 1975). See also, for an introductory discussion, R. Schlesinger et al., *Comparative Law* 253 (4th ed., 1998).

52. See Schlesinger et al., *supra* note 51, at 615, focusing on Germany and France.

53. See Article 517, C. Civ.; see also Carbonnier, *supra* note 2, at 111.

54. See A. Gambaro, *La Proprietà* 25 (1990).

55. See Cooter & Ulen, *supra* note 26, at 182.

56. Article 818, C. Civ.

57. See, in a broad comparative framework, Gambaro, *supra* note 11.

58. See, generally, U. Mattei, *A Transaction Cost Approach to the European Code*, 5 *Eur. Rev. Private L.* 537 (1997); A. Gambaro, *Perspectives on the Codification of the Law of Property: An Overview*, *id.* at 497.

59. Article 926, BGB; Article 819, C. Civ.

60. For mortgages in land under English law, see R. J. Smith, *Property Law* 538–581 (2d ed., 1998).

61. See B. Rudden, *Economic Theory versus Property Law: The Numerus clausus Problem*, in *Oxford Essays on Jurisprudence* (J. Eckelaar & J. Bell, eds., 1987), 239.

62. See R. A. Cunningham et al., *The Law of Property* 711 (1984).

63. See U. Drobnig, *Security Rights in Movables*, in *Toward a European Civil Code* 511 (A. Hartkamp et al. eds., 2d ed., 1998).

64. See, however, on the risks of "extreme decomposition" of property rights, M. A. Heller, *The Tragedy of the Anticommons* 111 *Harv. L. Rev.* 664 (1998).

65. See, for an example, Article 952, C.C.

66. See *supra* Chapter 3.

67. See R. Ellickson, *Alternatives to Zoning: Covenants, Nuisance Rules and Fines as Land Use Controls*, 40 *Un. Chi. L. Rev.* 68 (1973).

68. See G. M. Armstrong, *The Soviet Law of Property* (1983); Heller, *supra* note 64, at 627.

69. See S. R. Ackerman, *Inalienability and the Theory of Property Rights*, 85 *Colum. L. Rev.* 931 (1985); M. J. Radin, *Market Inalienability*, 100 *Harv. L. R.* 1849 (1987).

70. See *supra* Chapter 3..

71. See Article 823, C.C.; see also A. De Laubadère, 2 *Traité Elementaire de Droit Administratif* § 205 (8th ed., 1986); S. Cassese, Le basi del diritto amministratives (3d ed., 1996).

CHAPTER 5

Transfer of Ownership

A COMPLEX LEGAL PROBLEM

One of the major economic advantages of owning property is the possibility of appropriating the profit from its circulation on the market.[1] Although a lot of benefit from ownership may come from property's use rather than from its transfer, the easiest way to know the "objective" value of my property is to know for how much I can sell it. Transfers of property do not happen only by sale. I can donate an object to someone I love, or I can bequeath my property to that person after my death. Although these important economic transactions are motivated socially in a very different way from sales, lawyers tend to classify all of them within the common label of transfers of property. Consequently, in most legal systems property law deals with two main categories of transactions related to property: its use and its transfer. While use has to do with the utility that one receives from keeping property (e.g., dwelling in a house, reading a book, etc.), transfer has to do with the utility that one obtains from relinquishing the right to be the owner of a given property, and transferring it, either for profit or for liberality to someone else who hence becomes the new owner. From a property-rights perspective, property use can be considered a static activity which in its physiology is completely within the sphere of an individual. The legal system is consequently involved in a merely negative role to make sure that the use is not socially unacceptable. To the contrary, property transfer is a dynamic transaction that involves the legal system in creating a framework for the market. While use justifies the economic value of a given property (e.g., houses have a market value because people like to live in them, books have a market value because people like to read them), transfer is the mechanism through which the value (both individual and social) of property becomes concrete. Consequently, an efficient and secure system of transfer of ownership is crucial for the development of a market.[2]

From the perspective of the legal system, the reason why property is transferred is less significant than the fact that the transfer has occurred. Whether I transfer my car for money or for free, the legally important fact is that the car now has a new owner. Once a transfer of ownership occurs, most of the social transactions related to that particular property must be conducted with a different person. The property, along with all its positive or negative consequences, belongs to someone else. A new owner is in charge of that property.

As we will see, transfers of ownership can be rather complex social transactions and their structure can vary significantly according to the nature of the property involved. They range from the rather simple physical delivery of a newspaper to the rather complex mechanism of an apartment's transfer of ownership. Moreover, particularly in more complex transfers such as those of immovable property, it is often the case that not all of the attributes of the right of ownership are transferred at the same moment. Consequently, the transfer of ownership cannot accurately be described as a simple, one shot, black-and-white happening after which owner B substitutes for owner A. Legal systems approach the problem of transfer of ownership by trying to balance two opposite and extremely important interests. On the one hand, there is the need to make transfers of ownership as simple, cheap, and easy as possible in order to stimulate transfers and the consequent flourishing of markets. On the other hand, there are different reasons to monitor the transfer: (1) to make sure that people transfer their property rights only if they really wish to do so, (2) to ensure that the social signals after the transfer are correct so that third parties can rely on the effective owner of property, and (3) to make sure that the seller actually has good title.

In striking a balance between these different interests, legal systems depart significantly from one another. The aim of this chapter is to identify common principles, as well as to provide a relatively simple framework to approach a complex problem.

VOLUNTARY AND INVOLUNTARY TRANSFERS *MORTIS CAUSA* (AFTER DEATH)

Within the broad idea of transfer of ownership, a dichotomy exists between transfers *inter vivos* and transfers *mortis causa*. The former are transfers between individuals who are alive, while the latter involve the transgenerational transfer of wealth. The Western legal tradition is split along this distinction. While common law systems consider the law of succession as part of the domain of real property, civil law systems have developed the law of succession as an independent body of law.[3] The common law approach seems more rational because, as we have seen, one of the major reasons why land has economic value is its capability to absorb intergenerational accumulation of wealth. While in this book I will not probe deeply into the law of succession, considering it here as an important part of property law is a convenient way to cut through the details and to shed light on the two patterns of ownership transfer that distinguish legal systems.[4] Namely, the patterns are seen in the distinction between voluntary and nonvoluntary transfers of property rights. The first pattern is based on the will of the owner expressed within due forms. The second pattern operates by law and is independent from the will of the owner.

If we focus on transfers *mortis causa*, it is even more clear that the law of property is always the outcome of the interplay between individual decision making and rules dictated by the legal system. The rules established by the legal system may work as default rules and operate in the absence of the contrary will of individuals. Often, however, they may be considered mandatory and they may disregard the contrary will of individuals. In the domain of transfers *mortis causa*, a larger number of issues related to legitimacy may emerge to limit the will of individuals.

While it is widely accepted that an individual should be able to appropriate the profits of his or her labor and skills, it is more disputed that his or her fortune should depend only on the wealth of the family in which he or she was born. Consequently, most legal systems introduce very high taxes on succession to redistribute socially a slice of the "undeserved" wealth. Such taxes have their share of distortive effects. For example, a father knowing that his daughter will have to pay a very high tax on succession at his death will be encouraged to give property to her while he is alive.[5] In order to discourage such "fraudulent" gifts, legal systems tend to tax gifts at high rates comparable to those of succession taxes. All of this creates inefficiencies and transaction costs, since the same rationale does not generally hold for gifts and succession.

Everywhere in the Western legal tradition voluntary transfers *mortis causa* are made by means of a formal instrument, the will.[6] Involuntary transfers are accomplished by a number of default rules when there is no will or the will is invalid for any reason.[7]

Certain legal systems, particularly within the civil law tradition, feel that individuals should face a degree of obligation toward their close relatives who have relied on receiving property after death. Such systems do not have the nature of default rules, but instead work to limit individual decision making.[8] In many civil law countries, for example, the husband cannot disinherit his wife or his children in favor of a lover or any other third party. A share of his estate is reserved for them by law, regardless of the will of the deceased.

Interestingly, in the domain of the law of succession the difference between movable and immovable property tends to blur. While in modern common law the law of succession can be considered part of the law of real property (although traditionally the possibility of disposing of real property by will was severely limited while personal property could be freely disposed of), the civil law tradition makes use of a supercategory, that of *estate*, that comprises all of the assets and liabilities of the deceased.

VOLUNTARY *INTER VIVOS* TRANSFERS OF IMMOVABLES

We proceed now to focus on *inter vivos* transfers. We need to keep separate the analysis of immovable and movable property, since in this area the two branches of property law show most of their crucial structural differences.

Any transfer of immovable property, be it a house, a piece of land, or a factory, appears as a complex procedure spread over time and organized in different phases. This complex legal transaction is handled by legal systems in different ways by means of different areas of the law. In Anglo-American legal systems, for example, transfers of real property have traditionally been a central part of the law of property. Such transactions are handled by a specialized activity, known as "conveyancing," which in England is a traditional monopoly of one branch of the legal profession, that of solicitors.[9]

For historical reasons, mostly due to a more limited reception of Roman law, common law countries have approached and solved a number of problems within the law of property that their civilian colleagues have solved within the law of obligations.[10] Consequently, many rights that in civil law are seen as merely personal (i.e., as part of the law of obligation), in common law countries are considered real and can be claimed against the whole world because they are property rights.

While in civil law countries the topic of transfer of property was traditionally outside property law and was handled within the law of contracts, such exclusion does not make sense in a book that aims to discuss fundamental principles. Indeed, given the recent reception of the trust in many civil law jurisdictions, we observe a phenomenon of convergence between the common law and the civil law when we consider as property rights a number of rights previously considered merely contractual.[11] Leaving aside a number of other important implications, we may observe here that this convergence highlights a phenomenon already observed by the best comparative law scholarship: In the course of transfer, the different attributions of property rights tend to circulate disjointly by being allocated to different individuals. This is why it is difficult to focus on a single moment in which ownership is actually transferred. The transfer of the attributions of ownership (all of which are property rights) may be seen as a continuum from the moment of the contractual agreement to that of the actual registration of the buyer as the new owner. Asking at which point of this continuum ownership actually "passes" may be a merely formalistic exercise.[12]

Let us consider a simple transaction to buy a house. Even leaving aside the phase of precontractual bargaining, Abraham, who wishes to buy a home from Jacob, will be featured in at least three different phases of the ownership transfer process.[13] In a first phase, Abraham and Jacob will sign a paper which summarily describes the piece of property and the price. Typically, this paper, which may or may not be considered a contract according to different legal systems, will be a standard form offered by a middleman, if one is involved, or simply purchased by the seller or the buyer. In this phase, the buyer will usually tender some money to the seller. The money can be transferred or kept in escrow.

A second phase will typically take place before a legal officer, either a notary in the civil law or a conveyancer in the common law. In this phase there is a search for the title. The mentioned legal official will require and examine all the documents that are necessary to ensure that Jacob is the actual owner, or at least that he has the power to sell the property. In this phase the description of the property is more accurate and the existence of other property rights belonging to someone else (such as servitudes, mortgages, etc.) becomes officially known to Abraham, the buyer. Usually in this phase the balance of the price is paid and the physical delivery of the immovable occurs, either by passing over the key or by a formal declaration that the previous owner renounces any further physical or legal interference with the property.

In the third phase, which usually falls under the care of the legal official, the new title is registered and recorded according to the system of registration established in the place where the immovable is located.[14]

There may be many intermediate phases, such as if Abraham and Jacob were to agree on making intermediate payments. There may be other institutions involved, such as when, due to the shortcomings of the public registration system (as in most American states), Abraham has to purchase title insurance.[15] He may also have to borrow the money from a bank that will claim a mortgage on the property and may require that he purchase some other insurance. Usually, the state has a stake in transfers of immovable property, since this is an easily taxable transaction. In most systems, all tax liabilities are cleared at the moment of ownership transfer.

As this rough description shows, the process is complex and usually diluted over time, and can be better represented by a continuum in which different attributes of ownership are transferred to the buyer (or to other subjects, such as when Abraham borrows money pledging the house in mortgage). Despite this nature of a continuum process, legal systems nevertheless determine a precise moment at which ownership is transferred. In France, the fundamental assumption of the Civil Code is that ownership is transferred in phase one by the contractual agreement. Under French law, preliminary contracts are equated to definitive contracts from this perspective. The French code so favors transfers of ownership by contract that all contract law is contained in the book of the code devoted to "different ways in which property is acquired."[16]

Italian law follows the approach of the French Napoleonic Code but lacks the French unity of approach. The Codice Civile establishes two main phases in the transfer of immovable property. In one, ownership is transferred between the parties (usually in phase two before the notary), and in the other the ownership transfer can be claimed against the whole world (in phase three after registration). For Italian law, phase one does not affect the transfer of ownership but creates only an obligation to proceed to phase two.[17] The same approach of considering phase two crucial for the transfer is followed by English law, which considers ownership transferred at the moment of the conveyance. In Germany, ownership is transferred only in phase three, at the moment at which the contract is registered in the official book.[18]

Such emphasis on different phases of a very similar, continuous process overemphasizes differences among legal systems that in practice are not that important. Whether the preliminary contract has actually transferred ownership (as in France) or whether it has only created a specifically enforced obligation to transfer it (as in Italy), the practical difference is minimal. Of course, when the process gets interrupted (e.g., if Abraham and Jacob have not negotiated in advance what happens in such cases), the different rules of different legal systems may work as different defaults producing different behavioral incentives. If, for example, Abraham knows that ownership is not transferred in phase one, he may be encouraged to keep shopping around for a different piece of property that he might like better. Indeed, if the obligation of the seller is specifically enforceable while that of the buyer is not, the latter is receiving an incentive to behave opportunistically.[19]

On a normative ground, we may say that the most efficient default rules are those which do not separate the costs and benefits of being the owner but try to keep both for the same individual. This is the only way to avoid encouraging opportunistic action in the course of transfers of ownership. In practice, because the title to ownership comes with liability, we should prefer those rules that approach the ideal of the owner–decision maker who is also responsible for the consequences of his or her decision. In the majority of cases the decision-making power related to a given property comes from the physical control thereof; usually, the transfer of physical possession of the property occurs at the conclusion of the complex process that we have described. Therefore, the German solution of waiting until phase three before actually transferring ownership seems to be preferable. However, until that very last moment the parties are given an incentive to keep their eyes open for alternatives. Thus, the German solution carries less of an incentive to actual transfers. Nevertheless, knowing that whoever is actually registered in the official land register is actually the owner and has therefore the full set of powers and liabilities stemming from ownership introduces a higher degree of security of property rights. This has a beneficial impact on the overall efficiency of the system. Of course, the more one relies on official registration, the greater the potential disruption caused by corrupt practices and inefficient bookkeeping. The German model, with its highly reliable bureaucracy, may not be the easiest to reproduce in transitional economies, such as Russia or Hungary, or in countries less endowed with organizational skills, such as Italy.

Moreover, maintaining leeway for prospective buyers or sellers to find better deals in the course of transacting may favor efficient breaches and the consequent better allocation of property.[20] Interestingly, most legal systems exercise some caution before binding the parties to an immovable transaction. While in general contracts do not require a particular form to be binding, developed legal systems agree that when it comes to transfers of immovables a mere handshake is not enough. The importance of these kinds of transactions, third parties' needs to rely on transfers, and the need for protection of the parties involved in the transaction compel the use of a form for contracts that transfer property. While the written form may not be enough to protect these interests, it may well be the way to move in that direction at minimal transaction costs. This is the reason why modern legal systems, in the common law as well as in the civil law, share the requirement of written forms in contracts aimed at transferring immovable property.[21]

TRANSFERS OF MOVABLES

In the case of movable property, the transfer is much less complex and usually happens in one step. However, this general statement is subject to some qualifications. I have already mentioned that transfers of movable property *mortis causa* follow the legal regime of immovables. Also, it should be mentioned that when a transfer of an immovable is a gift, more restrictions may apply if the movable property has a substantial value. Moreover some special property rights such as copyrights or some kind of negotiable instruments (e.g., stocks or bonds), which some legal systems do consider as movable property, have special rules for transfer usually requiring some kind of written form.[22] In general, however, one can observe that in practically all modern legal systems there is no need of a written or other special form in order to transfer movable property. Moreover, no professional is involved in the process.

Despite these favorable premises for describing a common core, transfers of movables is an area of the law in which legal systems follow remarkably different paths, at least in theory. Some of these differences originate in and can be explained by different conceptions of the formation of contracts, as legal systems significantly diverge on whether a contract actually transfers property (as in the Franco-Italian model) or whether contracts are only sources of obligations to transfer property (as in the German model). As has been demonstrated, however, such divergencies are more formal than substantial, so that at our level of abstraction they should not be dramatized.[23]

In general, legal systems wrestle with the problem within three different models. For a number of legal systems, in order to transfer ownership of movable property, a contractual agreement is a necessary and sufficient condition (e.g., France, Italy, Great Britain).[24] For another group, the necessary and sufficient condition is not the contract but the actual delivery of the thing (e.g., Germany, Poland). Finally, for a third group, both the contract and the delivery are necessary but not sufficient elements. The ownership is transferred only when both occur (e.g., Austria, Holland, Switzerland, Turkey). Interestingly, despite the rather different general propositions, the law in practice converges at various degrees. No system adheres coherently to these rules. If we follow the law in the complex interplay of its different components, we will see that all legal systems qualify the general proposition in the more problematic moments of its application to concrete facts.[25] Thus, for movable property, as with immovable property, we could see a continuum transfer of its attributes. By contrast, such a continuum is completed in a much shorter time than where immovable property is concerned.

An important problem—possibly the most important that is faced by legal systems in the domain of the transfers of ownership of movable property—is that of the so-called transfers *a non domino* (i.e., those transfers from someone who is not the actual owner of the movable but who has physical possession of it to a third party who in good faith relies on him or her being the owner). As the careful reader of the previous chapters will already know, this problem is particularly critical because of the very important role that is played by possession as a social signal of ownership in the domain of movable property. Indeed, the need to protect the reliance on possession as a social signal of ownership has framed this complex area of the law as briefly summarized here.[26]

Let us call Anatoli the owner, Attila the thief or unfaithful trustee who as a possessor transfers the chattel, and Zita the third person who acquires possession of the object from Attila *non domino*. What we are here describing is a classic conflict between two innocent parties (Anatoli and Zita) who claim ownership over the same piece of movable property (say a copy of this book). Two competing paradigms developed at the origins of the Western legal tradition.[27] Under Roman law, Anatoli as an owner would prevail. No matter whether Zita acted in good or bad faith or whether she had or had not purchased the book for money, ownership would be protected. The good faith of Zita only mattered in the unlikely possibility that she was able to claim *usuacapio* (i.e., adverse possession for a long time), but the circumstances in which this defense would apply were very narrow.

Under Germanic customary law, the rule would be quite the opposite. According to this rule, the issue would be whether Anatoli had voluntarily or involuntarily relinquished the property. In other words, it depends on whether Attila was an unfaithful trustee or a thief. In the first case, Zita would prevail under the rationale that Anatoli had voluntarily departed from the book and therefore should not be able to recover from anyone other than the person in whom he had put his trust. Zita would keep ownership no matter whether she acted in good or bad faith. Anatoli would only able to recover damages against Attila, even if he had sued Zita on the same day she acquired possession. But Anatoli would prevail under Germanic customary law when he lost the property against his will.

Between the fifteenth and nineteenth centuries, the two rules competed all through Europe. There were occasional attempts to work out compromise solutions, such as the common law rule, developed by the law merchants, of protecting Zita if she had acquired possession in an open market (market overt rule).[28]

During the ages of codification, the codifiers, who were familiar with both rules and with compromise solutions, tried to capture the best of the both worlds. A few countries, in particular Spain and some Latin American jurisdictions, followed the Roman law. They protect Anatoli, the true "owner." However, they introduce some limited, important qualifications, such as the one contained in Article 85 of the Spanish Commercial Code, under which Zita would prevail if she had bought the goods in good faith in a shop or a department store. A similar rule is contained in paragraph 2-403 of the Uniform Commercial Code in America. At the other end of the spectrum, Italy always protects Zita if she acquired the goods in good faith.[29]

In a majority of civil law countries, including France, Germany, and Switzerland, however, the solution seems more of a compromise between the old Roman law and the Germanic approach. Its common core is concisely described by Professor Schlesinger:[30]

1. In accordance with the Germanic approach, a basic distinction is drawn depending on whether A (Anatoli) voluntarily departed with possession. If he did not (i.e., if the chattel was stolen from him or lost by him), then Anatoli prevails over Zita. On the other hand, if Anatoli entrusted his chattel to Attila and the latter without authority transferred and delivered it to Zita, in that event Anatoli normally cannot recover the chattel from her. Thus, in essence, the old Germanic rule is followed.
2. Invariably, however, the qualification is added that even in the case where Anatoli has entrusted the chattel to Attila, no protection is granted to Zita if she acted in bad faith.

One can observe that, on one hand, the more Anatoli is protected the less he will have to invest in precautions to keep control of his property. The burden of searching the title to know whether Attila is the true owner is therefore placed on Zita. On the other hand, the more Zita is protected, the more Anatoli will receive an incentive to take good care of his property and not to lose control over it. Consequently, Zita will be able to rely on the social signal as evidence that Attila has possession and will not have to invest in searching the title. From the perspective of economic efficiency, the latter solution is to be preferred because it reduces the transaction costs that hinder the circulation of movable property and therefore favors Pareto improvements. Ultimately, the potential Zitas will receive an incentive to buy the property, and Anatoli has a more valuable piece of property, since the market will react by enhancing the value of property.[31]

Consequently, one can say that in the case of movable property possession is a cheap and effective way to create social signals and it should therefore be backed by the legal system. The general principle contained in the text of the famous Article 2279 of the Napoleonic Code (but not the exceptions introduced by the details of French law) seem therefore to capture the best alternative in this domain: "In the case of movable property, possession equals ownership."[32]

INVOLUNTARY TRANSFERS OF IMMOVABLE PROPERTY

Some involuntary transfers are governed by public law, while others are governed by private law. Of course, as already mentioned, the very notion of public versus private law is not ontological and varies from legal system to legal system. However, practically everywhere there are involuntary transfers that follow a complex procedure carried on by the state, possibly expressing the notion of a public interest in conflict with individual rights of ownership. Other types of such involuntary transfers are the final incident of other kinds of procedures, such as a criminal trial or a bankruptcy.[33] In these, some property is forcibly transferred against the will of the owner, to someone else, either to the state itself within a punishing function or to creditors of the previous owner. In the first of these cases, lawyers immediately think of the so-called "taking" or expropriation in the public interest. Both these cases of "public law" involuntary transfers of ownership are extremely important in modern law and are usually neglected, particularly in the civil law tradition, in legal treatises related to property law.[34] It seems to me, however, that while it is a mistake to avoid discussion of the negative aspects of ownership (such as being the possible object of involuntary public law transfers), this typology is better captured by the idea of loss of ownership (usually in favor of the state) rather than the idea of transfer. Accordingly, Chapter 9 of this book is devoted to the loss of property.[35] Here I will focus only on transfers from one party to another that are governed by traditional rules and principles of private law carried on within ordinary adjudicatory procedures.

Protection of Possession

The concept of possession is not only important for the transfer of movables. It also is a crucial idea for understanding yet another typology of immovable transfers: nonvoluntary transfers. Individuals may find themselves in a de facto relationship with an immovable over which they have no title. Edith and Iuri, homeless people in the streets of Moscow, may find an abandoned dachia on the outskirts of Moscow and move to live there. In so doing, they do not acquire a property right in the dachia; nevertheless, they acquire a de facto power over it that can be described as a privileged position in defending the dachia against homeless Csaba and Valentina who may later spot it and desire to move there. Given the principle, shared by all of the developed legal systems in the world, that ownership of an immovable cannot be acquired merely by occupying it, if Edith and Iuri are not authorized by whoever the formal owner is, they are violating the former owner's property right. But everywhere the law protects, in a rather substantial way, possessors Edith and Iuri for at least three reasons.[36] First, the law tries to avoid physical conflicts between the members of the polity. Csaba and Valentina (and everybody else including the absent owner Anatoli) must be discouraged from trying to acquire possession by violence. Second, the possessor is usually also the owner. This is not the case in our example, but the law claims the monopoly to determine who the owner is through the judicial process. In the meantime, Edith and Iuri are protected also against Anatoli. Third, the possessor ends up protecting the economic value of the immovable ultimately in favor of the very owner who is absent.[37]

The prima facie protection of possession as a signal of ownership is much more efficient than the continuous search for proof of title and the continuous fight for the physical control of the immovable. Consequently, protecting possession increases the value of ownership because it lowers the costs of its protection.

Within the Western legal tradition, all legal systems protect the de facto relationship between an individual and the immovable and construct in different ways a legal notion able to capture this idea. In the taxonomy used in this book, I simply call it "possession."[38] In a later discussion we will see the very important role that possession plays in the protection of ownership. However, in this section we are interested in a different relationship between possession and ownership: a conflictual relationship. As already mentioned, there are behaviors that even the legitimate owner cannot engage in against the possessor. If Anatoli violently tries to evict them from the dachia, Edith and Iuri are protected by the French action of *reintegrade* (now contained in a special statute of 1971), by the German *Besitzentziengsanspruch* (paragraph 861 BGB), by the Italian *reintegrazione* (Article 1168 Codice Civile), and by the common law action of *ejectment*. Here, the law reacts against violent behaviors that threaten the peaceful organization of society. The state cannot afford to allow individuals to protect their rights by themselves. As already mentioned, the state claims a monopoly over the use of force and consequently the legal system discourages private attempts to use it even to protect one's rights. The rationale behind the principle that protects the bad faith possessor (such as that of a thief) is usually described by lawyers with the Latin maxim "*ne cives ad arma veniant*." This literally means that the state protects the bad faith possessor to avoid (*ne*) the citizens (*cives*) using weapons (*arma*) against each other. Of course, an exception to this ban on self-help can be found in extreme cases of necessity and in the immediacy of the aggression.[39] Also, in the domain of property law Anatoli will be allowed to self-protect his land from aggression if he reacts proportionally and on the spot to an aggression by Edith and Iuri. If he dwells in the dachia, for example, he will be allowed to unleash the dog against them when they try to trespass. In some legal systems, such as in California, which is keen to cultivate the myth of the Far West, he is even allowed to protect it with guns (although not in theory to the point of shooting to kill). While Anatoli may be allowed to fight in the immediate protection of his property, once he has lost control thereof (i.e., once Edith and Iuri have acquired possession), he is not entitled to get his big friends from the gym to come back and physically kick Edith and Iuri out of the property. He will have to resort to the legal system to regain possession. Of course, he can physically kick Edith and Iuri out anyway, but in that case the police will help the possessors rather than the owner (at least in legal theory).

If these cases are a little bit extreme, on other occasions possession can still prevail over ownership even if there is no violent or other unlawful behavior on the side of the owner. There also is substantial unanimity throughout the Western legal tradition under this different hypothesis. This is evidence that allocation of property rights between members of the polity, although tendentially formalized and stable, is not perpetual and immutable, even as far as immovables are concerned. Obviously, there are many nuances between legal systems. However, we can claim to describe the common core of Western law when we say that in order to be protected against the innocent owner (Anatoli), possession must be qualified both from the perspective of the subjective, mental element of the possessor, and from the objective characteristic of the physical relationship itself.[40]

From the first point of view, possession of immovables must be in good faith. From the second point of view, possession should be characterized by a particular intensity (in the common law terminology, it must be "open, adverse, and notorious") as well as, like in the old Roman law, by the elapsing of time.[41] When possession is so characterized, it can defeat ownership and ground a number of involuntary transfers of ownership among members of the community.

Protection of Good Faith

The first characteristic of possession, that I will call subjective, is referred to by the law as the principle of good faith.[42] In general, a possessor can be considered as acting in good faith when he or she does not know he or she is violating someone else's property right.[43] Edith and Iuri may be considered as acting in good faith if they do not know that the dachia is still in the actual ownership of someone. They may think from its appearance that it is abandoned forever. Consequently, they will start behaving as owners, not appreciating that there is someone else out there that is the real owner with intention to exercise his rights. Of course, their ignorance will not help if it is due to gross negligence, as when they behave as owners even though in front of the dachia there are clearly interpretable signals of Anatoli's ownership (such as his name on the mailbox). In contrast, legal systems, either under the code (as in Article 1147 of the Italian Codice Civile) or by case law developments, converge on the point that it suffices that Edith and Iuri be in good faith at the moment in which they acquire possession.[44] Although Edith and Iuri may suspect that someone is the legitimate owner of the property (a likely fact in modern legal systems given the organization of the law of succession; namely, it is unlikely that there is not a heir somewhere in the world), they can still act in good faith if they honestly do not know, at the moment in which they enter the objectively abandoned dachia, that the owner may actually be interested in exercising his right. Their good faith is still considered and protected even when Anatoli actually shows up claiming his ownership. A different solution would strip the good faith test of any meaning, since Anatoli would only have to let them know in order to make them in bad faith and claim his property rights. The principle is that good faith is protected if it exists at the moment possession is acquired.

Another important principle that completes the scheme of the protection of good faith in possession is that good faith is presumed.[45] This means that Anatoli has the burden to show that Edith and Anatoli were acting in bad faith if he wishes to negate the special protection that the law is offering to them. In an example like the one we are discussing, it may be difficult for the good faith principle to survive unless there are very special circumstances; for example, the state of complete abandonment of the dachia. Think, however, of an unclear neighboring limit, or the case in which Irina buys an underground cellar along with an apartment and because of a mistake in the numeration, the apartment is attached to a cellar that actually belongs to Rebecca. The innocent mistake that sets the presumption for good faith may be both of law, such as in the cellar case, or of fact, such as when one mistakenly believes that his or her disappeared landlord is dead (without heirs) and stops paying the rent, later to discover that the landlord was only in mystical crisis in an Indian monastery.

In many cases, the owner is likely to lose his or her property rights against the good-faith possessor even without the further qualification (that we will discuss later) of the elapsing of time. To see concrete examples in a number of legal systems, it is sufficient to refer the reader to where I discussed the various reactions of the law to the problem of erecting in good faith a building on someone else's land. Indeed, all of the many exceptions to the principle of accession (*superficies solo caedit*), according to which whatever is built on the land belongs to the owner of it, find in the principle of protection of good-faith possession a powerful contradictory principle. If Edith and Iuri in good faith have modified Anatoli's dachia by adding rooms to it, although Anatoli might be able finally to evict them (if he does not allow much time to elapse), he certainly in most legal systems will be denied the right to compel them to take away the building. In addition, he will not be able to profit from the improvements given the principles of unjust enrichment at play in different ways in all developed legal systems. Consequently, Anatoli will have to negotiate with Edith and Iuri a way out within a system of default rules that (1) do not allow much time to do so and (2) introduce different forms of economic compensation as a safety net for the good-faith possessor in the case in which ownership is protected. It is difficult here to be more precise, because the law in different legal systems varies in details, such as the length of the time that the parties have for negotiating and the compensatory system for the loser. However, some broad principles and rules are at play.

To begin with, the owner's action in ejectment against the good-faith possessor are subject to rather short terms of limitation. In the case of conflicts between ownership and possession, nobody is allowed to sleep on their rights. If my neighbor builds on my land, I should confront him or her within a short period of time after learning of the illegal construction. The same is true for the good-faith possessor of the land and the owner of the building materials who wants them back. In this hypothesis, either he or she acts promptly or incorporation may happen and the owner of the land can keep the building. In general, this decision to allow a short time for negotiation is efficient. The two parties, both innocent and deserving legal protection, need to bargain promptly to work out a solution. If one of the two sleeps on his or her rights, he or she might later regret it. The law is efficient when it tries to collapse property and possession within one individual. In all of the cases in which the law actually collapses property and possession, it is easy to spot an involuntary transfer of ownership.

Whether the solution is to allow the owner to keep the materials or (more exceptionally) to allow the possessor to acquire ownership of the land on which the building is constructed, the law may use a complex system of liability rules to solve this difficult conflict. Once again, good-faith possession makes the difference.[46] Legal systems may diverge more among each other according to the higher or lower protection they feel possession should be given. A coherent and efficient system, similar to that introduced in the Italian Civil Code of 1942 after extensive comparative work, looks as follows: Because externalities should be avoided, no matter which party is recognized as the owner (i.e., whoever benefits from the involuntary transfer), costs should be allocated to whomever gets the benefits. The builder, who being in good faith has not violated any behavioral rule, should not suffer an externality (by having enriched the owner at his or her expense). The owner should not be liable for the bad investments of the possessor. Thus, Anatoli, who keeps the building created by good-faith possessors Edith and Iuri (he cannot compel Edith and Iuri to remove them), should pay either the value of the materials and the labor or the increase in value of the dachia. In case of bad-faith possession, the owner should be allowed to choose whether to keep the improvement or to compel the bad-faith possessor to remove it.

Finally, it should be noted that good-faith possession grounds yet another involuntary transfer of ownership: that of the fruits of labor. While as a general principle (that I will discuss later) whatever is produced by an immovable belongs to its owner, the principle is subverted in the case of good-faith possession. Our evicted good-faith actors Edith and Iuri not only receive compensation for the improvements they made, but should also be able to retain all of the profits that they have made from the dachia during their good-faith tenure. Bad-faith possessors, to the contrary, should make complete restitution. One can find these general principles at play in all legal systems concerned with fair and efficient solutions.[47]

Adverse Possession

The good-faith possessor receives further advantages if the "subjective" qualification of his or her possession is accompanied by the objective element of the elapsing of time. Adverse possession, as this hypothesis is known in the Anglo-American world, indeed is the most important case of outright involuntary transfer of immovable property.[48] According to this fundamental principle, ownership can be acquired by the long-term possessor.

Let me say first that adverse possession, known in the civil law tradition as *usuacapio,* is not limited to immovable property. As the reader should recall from our discussion on the transfer of movables, Zita, the third party who acts in good faith when acquiring possession from nonowner Attila, could be recognized as the owner in Roman law if she had kept possession for one year and she was in good faith (this is probably the first appearance of the good-faith principle in Western law). Of course, the more systems of movable property recognize the principle "in the case of movables possession equals ownership," the less the adverse possession rule for movables is important or relevant. So, while this hypothesis is still discussed, its importance today is mainly academic, at least in the majority of legal systems belonging to the civil law tradition.[49] In the common law, the overt market principle, which was never as extended as the protection of the good-faith purchaser in the civil law, is now abolished in England by a recent statute without creating much of a stir. Thus, adverse possession of movables is probably still more important in the common law. On normative grounds, however, given the advantages of linking ownership to possession, the possibility of avoiding the measurement costs of the elapsing of time in adverse possession can be considered another good reason to prefer the "possession equals ownership" solution.

In the case of immovable property, the principle of adverse possession is still very important everywhere. However, the problem is more complex.[50] To begin with, the reasons that we were able to detect in favor of the possession equals ownership principle are not at play for immovables. The mere physical location of an individual on a piece of the earth's surface is not enough to create a reasonable prima facie signal that he or she is the owner. Moreover, the costs of avoiding the principle of adverse possession possibly are much higher than the measuring costs created by it.[51] A necessary but not sufficient thing to do in order to eliminate the principle would be to organize a completely reliable land register that conclusively proves that whoever appears listed therein is the owner. Indeed, the adverse possession principle is not abolished even in German law, where a similar kind of land register exists. However, the importance of the principle appears reduced by paragraph 927 of the BGB, under which a thirty-year adverse possession is required to acquire ownership. A similar term of thirty years is required by Article 2262 of the French Napoleonic Code, whereas Italian law (Article 1165 of the Codice Civile) and the basic rule in common law countries reduce the adverse possession period to twenty years. In these legal systems (perhaps the English Land Registration Act creates a major exception within the common law), where the organization of immovable transfer cannot rely on principles of registration of title as secure as in Germany and Austria, adverse possession is a much more lively area of property law.

Certainly, a common core principle is that, in the case of good-faith possession, the time requirement is substantially reduced at a rate that varies among legal systems between one-third and one-half. The time requirement is also substantially shortened for movables.[52]

In order for the principle of adverse possession to work, possession also should be qualified in terms of its intensity. The common law description is that possession must be "open, notorious, and hostile," in the sense that the possessor should behave socially as the owner of the immovable.[53] This intensity requirement, shared by all of the legal systems, simply means that possession should not be hidden or ambiguous in order for time to elapse. Moreover, possession should not be derivative, as in the case of a lease or other title coming from the owner.[54] The hostility requirement specifies that there should not even be an informal understanding by which Anatoli tolerates Edith and Iuri in the possession of his dachia. In other words, the average owner should be perceived socially as unfriendly toward the possession (and vice versa) because the possessor is actually threatening his or her right. There should be a potential conflict between the owner and the possessor over the immovable property, a conflict similar in structure to the one I have described in the previous section.

A number of technical doctrines give content to these principles. If, for example, possession has been acquired by violence or by a hidden strategy (such as breaking into a cellar during the absence of its owner), violence or clandestinity should cease before time starts to elapse.[55] The rationale is that even though the owner is challenged by a hostile possession, it should not be physically impossible for the owner to claim his or her right. Not claiming the right should be socially qualified as a lack of actual (although not potential) interest on the side of the owner toward his or her property.[56]

On theoretical grounds, it is not difficult to reconstruct the reason why all legal systems recognize adverse possession or similar doctrines as the most important involuntary transfer from the owner to the possessor. The law prefers to grant possession to the individual who is actually using the immovable property against the absent, uninterested owner. The former is actually economically exploiting the immovable, while the latter is keeping it idle. In economic terms, this justification is obvious as a way to avoid economic waste.[57] The justification is also reinforced by the fact that the absence of the owner makes impossible the transfer of the piece of immovable property from whoever values it less to whoever values it more within a voluntary transaction. The prolonged absence, whatever its reason, shows that the owner appreciates his or her property very little, or at least less than the possessor. While the owner is doing nothing in terms of investments to improve the property, the possessor invests, at a minimum, in occupying the property by periodically policing to eject other possible claimants of it. Most probably, the possessor is actually economically exploiting the property by putting labor into the maintenance of the immovable in proper conditions.[58] Once the problem of adverse possession is framed in such a way, it becomes clearly justifiable within a theory of just dessert. At this point, one could argue, on a normative ground, that by having such long terms, legal systems are possibly overprotective of the absent owner. The needs of stability of ownership that counterbalance the principle of adverse possession would possibly be served also by shorter terms, such as, for example, five years. This is particularly true because a variety of devices (like suspension of the terms in given circumstances, or maintaining long terms for bad-faith possession) are available to protect the absent but "deserving" owners, such as those whose emigration has been forced by dramatic events or similar occurrences.

A shorter term would give an incentive to put labor into abandoned immovable property, something very much needed in transitional economies. Moreover, the security and reliability of signals coming from property rights would not be impaired, but generally would be promoted by shorter terms that merge ownership and possession in the same person. Among other things, long terms make the proof of title to land extremely difficult, and increase what in economic terms are known as "measuring costs."[59] Moreover, such a reform would be extremely cheap in terms of administrative costs, due to the structure of this area of the law. In few areas would a simple legislative fiat be as effective as one which shortens the time requirement in adverse possession. Indeed, there is no room for interpretation (five years means five years), which makes it impossible for an incremental case law development to follow the needs of justice and efficiency. Finally, there is no reliance to protect.

In this area of property law, one wonders if the convergence of legal systems on very long terms, short of being a proxy for efficiency, is not the product of inefficient, path-dependent tradition.

RIPARIAN PROPERTY RIGHTS

If one considers ownership as a bundle of property rights, the number of involuntary transfers to be described could still be very numerous.[60] For example, as we will see in the chapter related to conflicts between neighbors, sometimes the law allows an industrial activity on one property that makes it completely impossible to dwell on neighboring land. In this case, a servitude is created, and consequently a property right is involuntarily transferred. This hypothesis has such a theoretical importance that it needs special treatment in a separate chapter. In this chapter, we have been concerned primarily with final transfers of full ownership and only incidentally with transfers of some of its aspects.

Historically, the Roman law and the civil law traditions have considered the case of physical detachment of a piece of riparian property as a case of accession similar to the rule *superficies solo caedit* and to its exceptions already discussed in a previous section. In the Italian and French competing solutions to this problem, functionally there are two alternatives that can be easily compared from the comparative efficiency perspective.[61] In the hypothetical case, a river suddenly takes away a piece of riparian land belonging to Claudia and attaches it to the downstream land belonging to Martina. According to Article 559 of the French Napoleonic Code, Claudia is still the owner if she claims the ownership of the piece of land within one year after the moment of detachment. According to Article 944 of the Italian Codice Civile, Martina immediately becomes the owner but has to pay an indemnity to impoverished Claudia in a maximum amount that equals the increased value of the enriched land. To avoid externalities, the increased value should not be the maximum amount but should be the actual amount of the compensation. In practice, the Italian and French solution should not differ substantially because the two parties will probably negotiate among themselves similar efficient solutions. One could observe that effectively protecting Claudia's ownership by reproducing the ex ante conditions before a natural event of this kind would be very costly. The costs of reproducing the ex ante situation are usually higher than both the increase in value of the downstream land and the decrease in value of the upstream land. Those costs are high if the option would be the actual reproduction of the ex ante situation, and, if Claudia would keep the property downstream (augmented costs of cultivation and/or enjoyment and tension between new neighbors). By bargaining between themselves, Claudia and Martina would probably reach the Italian code solution. The exception would be the unlikely case in which the subjective value of the detached piece of upstream property is higher than the sum of the transaction costs of its protection and the increased value of downstream property. Hence, because efficient default rules should reproduce what parties would have negotiated among themselves, the Italian solution proves to be an improvement when compared to the Napoleonic one.

NOTES

1. Among the incidents of Honoré there is "the right to capital value, including alienation." See A. M. Honoré, *Ownership*, in *Oxford Essays on Jurisprudence* (A. G. Guest ed., 1961).

2. Its implications might go beyond efficiency. See R. Craswell, *Passing on the Costs of Legal Rules: Efficiency and Distribution in Buyer Seller Relationship*, 43 *Stan. L. Rev.* 361 (1991).

3. See A. F. Topham, *Real Property* (10th ed., 1947).

4. It is namely for more specific textbooks to deal with this matter in detail. As for English literature on the topic, see R. Kerridge, *Parry and Clark on the Law of Succession* (10th ed., 1996).

5. For an illustration of the aspects concerning taxation and the inheritance tax under English law, see C. V. Margrave-Jones, *Mellows: The Law of Succession* 539–574 (1993).

6. J. B. Clark & J. G. Ross Martyn, *Theobald on Wills* (15th ed., 1993).

7. English law on this topic is illustrated by C. H. Sherrin & R. C. Bonehill, *The Law and Practice of Intestate Succession* (2d ed., 1994).

8. See the classic, E. Pacifici Mazzoni, *Studio storico sulla successione legittima: dalle XII tavole al Codice Italiano* (1870).

9. Things changed after the Court and Legal Service Act of 1990. English solicitors were thereafter deprived of their traditional monopoly. For the mechanisms of registered conveyancing in England, see D. J. Hayton, *Registered Land* (3d ed., 1981); K. J. Gray & P. D. Symes, *Real Property and Real People: Principles of Land Law* 319–352 (1981). A vast literature has always been available on the topic of conveyancing in general. For a classic, see H. Potter, *The Principles and Practice of Conveyancing under the Land Registration Act 1925* (1934); for an updated view of the matter, see D. G. Barnsley, *Conveyancing Law and Practice* (4th ed., 1996). As for U.S. law, see R. A. Cunningham et al., *The Law of Property* 711 (1984).

10. See *supra* Chapter 1.

11. A recent collection of evidence for this statement can be found in *Principles of European Trust Law* (D. J. Hayton et al. eds., 1999).

12. See the classic study, R. Sacco & G. De Nova, 1 *Il Contratto* 739 (1993).

13. For a thorough comparative discussion, see A. Chianale, *Obbligazione di dare e trasferimento della proprietà* (1992).

14. For a short description in English of the German System, see Horn et al., *German Private and Commercial Law* 180 (1982).

15. See T. J. Miceli & C. F. Sirmans, *The Economics of Land Transfers and Title Insurance*, 10 *Real Estate Fin. & Econ.* 81 (1995).

16. Book 3 of the Napoleonic Code.

17. A recent reform made it possible to register the preliminary contract after phase one. See A. Chianale, *Registrazione del preliminare e trasferimento della proprietà* (1999).

18. See Sec. 873, BGB.

19. See R. Cooter & T. Ulen, *Law and Economics* 215–221 (2d ed., 1997).

20. See R. Posner, *Economic Analysis of Law* 131 (5th ed., 1998).

21. German law requires full notarization (in the civilian sense). See Sec. 313, BGB.

22. For the acquisition and disposal of shares and company securities under English law, see P. L. Davies, *Gower's Principles of Modern Company Law* 328–356 (6th ed., 1997).

23. In the Cornell Project carried on by the late Professor Schlesinger in the 1960s. See R. B. Schlesinger, ed., *Formation of Contracts* (1968).

24. For consensual transfers of movables (both sales and gratuitous transfers) under English law, see M. Bridge, *Personal Property Law* 69–89 (2d ed., 1996). Transfers of interests in personal property are also dealt with by A. P. Bell, *Modern Law of Personal Property in England and Ireland* 219–404 (transfers inter vivos), 405–456 (other transfers) (1989).

25. See R. Sacco, *Legal Formants: A Dynamic Approach to Comparative Law*, 39 *Am. J. Comp. L.* 1 (1991). Here, one can find a comparative discussion and references to the legal systems mentioned in the text. This part of Sacco's article is based on his general report on transfer of property delivered at the International Academy of Comparative Law in Budapest. The full report is published in French in *Le transfert de la propriété des choses mobilières déterminées par acte entre vifs en droit comparé, Rivista di Diritto Civile* 1 (1979) 442.

26. Classic in-depth discussion can be found in L. Mengoni, *Gli acquisti a non domino* (3d ed., 1975).

27. See J. G.Sauveplanne, *The Protection of Bona Fide Purchaser of Corporeal Movables in Comparative Law*, 29 *Rabels* Z 651 (1965).

28. The market overt rule has been abolished in England and Wales by the Sale of Goods (Amendment) Act 1994.

29. Article 1153, C.C.

30. See R. B. Schelsinger et al., *Comparative Law* 255–256 (6th ed., 1998).

31. See A. Gambaro, *Il diritto di proprietà* (1995).

32. See J. Carbonnier, *Droit civil, les biens* 366 (14th ed., 1991).

33. See J. E. Cribbet & C. W. Johnson, *Principles of the Law of Property* (1989).

34. The same may not be stated as far as English law is concerned, where vast works on the topic were written as early as decades ago. See, for instance, H. Parrish, *Cripps on Compulsory Acquisition of Land-Powers, Procedure and Compensation* (1962).

35. See *infra* Chapter 9.

36. In Italy, Article 1168, C.C. grants an action called *Reintegrazione*. In France, a Law of 1971 offers a similar action called *Reinegrade*. In Germany, Sect. 861 offers the equivalent *Besitzentziehungsanspruch*. In the common law, where the difference between possessory and proprietary action is absent, the action of ejectment would be available. For a comparative discussion, see A. Gambaro, *La legittimazione passiva alle azioni possessorie* (1979).

37. See J. Gordley & U. Mattei, *Protecting Possession*, 44 *Am. J. Comp. L.* 293 (1996).

38. See *supra* Chapter 4.

39. An interesting collection of material mostly focused on criminal law can be found in A. Eser & G. Fletcher, *Justification and Excuse: Comparative Perspectives* (1987).

40. See R. Sacco, *Il possesso* (1988).

41. See D. R. Harris, *The Concept of Possession in English Law*, in *Oxford Essays on Jurisprudence* 75 (A.W.B. Simpson ed., 1967).

42. See R. H. Helmholz, *Adverse Possession and Subjective Intent*, 61 *Wash. U. L.Q.* 331 (1983).

43. Paradigmatic can be considered Article 1147, C.C.: "Good faith possessor is the person who possesses ignoring to be violating someone else's rights."

44. On the influence of continental thinking on the common law in matters of possession, see M. Graziadei, *Changing Images of the Law in XIX Century English Legal Thought (The Continental Impulse)*, in *The Reception of Continental Ideas in the Common Law World 1820–1920* 115 (Mathias Reimann ed., 1993).

45. See Sacco, *supra* note 40.

46. See Carbonnier, *supra* note 32, at 203.

47. See Sacco, *supra* note 40.

48. See the classic rationale discussed by O. W. Holmes, *The Path of the Law*, 10 *Harv. L. Rev.* 457, 477 (1897).

49. For the requirements of adverse possession under English law, see C. Sara, *Boundaries and Easements* 69–90 (1996). More oriented toward the practical aspects of conveyancing is A. J. Pain, *Adverse Possession: A Conveyancer's Guide* (1992).

50. See J. Miceli & C. F. Sirmans, *An Economic Theory of Adverse Possession*, 15 *Int'l Rev. L. & Econ.* 161 (1995).

51. For a discussion from the perspective of law and economics, see Posner, *supra* note 20, at 89–90.

52. Thirty years is the term for German Law (par. 927, BGB) and French law (Article 2262 of the Napoleonic Code) reduced to twenty. Twenty years reduced to a half for Italian law (Article 1165, C.C.). Twenty years is also the basic rule for American law. There are, however, a number of further reductions at play. See J. M. Netter et al., *An Economic Analysis of Adverse Possession Statutes*, 6 *Int'l Rev. L. & Econ.* 217 (1986).

53. See J. G. Riddall, *Introduction to Land Law* 413 (4th ed., 1988).

54. See Carbonnier, *supra* note 32, at 208. As to German law, see Sec. 868, BGB "It must be said that this extension to the mediate or indirect possessor has destroyed the usefulness of possession as publicity." Se Horn et al., *supra* note 14, at 171.

55. See Sacco, *supra* note 40.

56. See Holmes, *supra* note 48.

57. See Posner, *supra* note 20, at 90.

58. Comparative details can be found in Gordley & Mattei, *supra* note 37.

59. D. C. North, *Institutions, Institutional Change, and Economic Performance* (1990).

60. See, on the issue of transfer of riparian rights and its potential externalities, Posner, *supra* note 20, at 87.

61. As to French law, see Article 559 of the Napoleonic Code and A. Weill et al., *Droit civil, les biens* 214 (3d ed., 1985). As to Italian law, see Article 944, C.C. and U. Mattei, *La proprietà immobiliare* 107 (1995); for English law, see A. S. Wisdom, *Water Rights* 37–62 (1969).

CHAPTER 6

The Power to Use Ownership

OWNERSHIP AS AN AGGREGATE OF POSITIVE AND NEGATIVE CHARACTERISTICS

The French Revolution, which was mostly concerned with relationships of power related to land, has lent to posterity a formidable rhetoric celebrating the relationship between property and freedom in general and the freedom of land law against the feudal structure of the ancien régime in particular.[1] Because feudalism as a sociopolitical structure was by Napoleon's time abolished in most of the West, the already-described natural law tradition has captured the rhetoric around ownership used by judges, legislators, and professors throughout the Western legal tradition (although, as we know, more in civil law than in common law, where the language and the taxonomy of the law is still not understandable without a grasp of its feudal origins). The equation between ownership and freedom became commonplace in legal, economic, and social theory.

Even in Germany, where lawyers are more controlled than in Italy and France when engaging in emphatically rhetorical exercises, the antifeudal polemic inherited by the French Revolution has left its mark. The taxonomy requiring the object of ownership to be a tangible material thing can be explained as an expulsion from the domain of property law of those powers not related to a physical relationship with land, as used to be the case with most feudal property rights.[2]

Only in the common law world did no technical gap between pre–French Revolution and post–French Revolution property law occur. This different historical evolution has captured the scholarly imagination of much of the comparative law tradition.[3] The emphasis has been on the distinction between the absolute notion of ownership, typical of the civil law, and the relative notion of ownership, shared within the common law tradition.[4] Of course, these blunt oppositions have very limited, general explanatory power. However, in the domain of land use an interesting phenomenon can be observed. For the common law tradition, a number of the most important issues related to land use are addressed within the tort of nuisance; it is the dimension of liability (or of the duty toward neighbors) that is central to the analysis of land use. To the contrary, in the civil law the central feature is the power of the owner, and the limits thereto are still perceived as exceptions to be interpreted restrictively.

The subsequent ideological evolution has also compelled legal scholars to rethink critically the equation between ownership and freedom.[5] The focus has been on the limits to the owner's power, which one might call the most visible refutation of the equation. This phenomenon can be seen in France in the work of Duguit and Josserand, in Germany in sociological jurisprudence, and in the United States in the realist movement. Interestingly, the analysis of the technical structure of property as a legal institution is largely unaffected by the political rhetoric surrounding it. It is therefore no surprise that the only technical analysis of property going beyond the old paradigm is owed to a common lawyer, Yale professor Wesley Newcomb Hohfeld, in the early part of our century.[6] Only his technical taxonomy, in which the dimension of the duty is as important as that of the power, seems able today to capture the complex nature of modern property rights. The content of property rights can be captured only by deconstructing it into a bundle of powers, liabilities, immunities, duties, and so on that the law allocates in various way between individuals competing over scarce resources.[7]

Obviously, any realistic analysis of property law must also take into account the dimension of duties. Despite the rhetoric of jurists and other social scientists, duties are part of the very structure of property rights. A self-interested individual will want to become the owner of a given scarce resource only if the difference between the advantages deriving from the power dimension of property rights and the disadvantages deriving from the dimension of duties and liabilities is positive. The competitive mechanism of ownership acquisition that enables a market to work will engage only if ownership is positive in this sense.

POWER IN GENERAL

Immovable property is, from the point of view of its use, much more complex than movable property. As a rule, the typical use of movable property (with the exception of some very dangerous products, such as explosives or cars) has no external effect and both its costs and benefits remain within the owner's sphere.[8] Therefore, the use of most movables may be considered structurally absolute in the sense that the typical limits that the law imposes on use can fairly be described as external to the structure of ownership. Liability may be an important aspect of property rights over dangerous things (e.g., the ownership of a gun does not include the power to use it against another person), but as a rule the description of an absolute power to use a piece of movable property will capture the essence of the legal relationship. My ownership of a book is unrestricted. If I am its owner, I can read it as much as I like; I can use it to decorate my living room without ever reading it; I can use it to start a fire; I can doodle on it and print my *ex libris* on its first page. But I cannot do many of these things if the book belongs to my university library. The fact that even as its owner I cannot throw the book at someone's head cannot be considered a structural limit on my right of ownership. I cannot use the book in that way whether I own it or borrow it from the library. These are limits external to the structure of ownership.[9]

Immovable property is much more complex from this perspective, so most of our discussion in this chapter will focus on it. In the domain of immovables, the law generally enumerates the owner's powers in very general terms. But in practice, the law limits these powers by employing a number of notions, captured by the idea of reasonable use. Consequently, it is crucial to capture the dimension of duties.[10]

A number of civilian codes codify the owner's power to fence property as the most important symbol of the owner's sovereignty. Paragraph 903 of the BGB grants to the owner the power of *Einwirkung*. The same power is codified by Article 840 of the Italian Codice Civile, and is recognized unanimously by French courts and commentators in the silence of the French Civil Code.[11] In the common law, the owner can fence his or her property and the action of trespass will protect it.[12] As to vertical limits, the principle grasped from the same sources of law is the following: Ownership includes the power to use the airspace over land. It does not include the power to exclude activities that are so high as not to impair the value of the property (e.g., airplane flights). The same can be said in principle about the vertical extension into the ground. Of course, the details of the rules vary extensively between systems and deserve some special attention. However, something can already be learned at this level of generality.

As I hinted by calling it "symbolic," the power of the owner within the boundaries of his or her property can be limited (and usually is limited) by a number of exceptions.[13] However, these principles maintain some interpretive meaning as well as meaning from the point of view of the theory of sources of law. From the first point of view, the relationship between the owner's powers and their limits is confirmed.

This was emphatically recognized by the famous definition of Article 544 of the Napoleonic Code, under which the owner can do whatever he or she likes if there are no legal limits. Even in codes (like the Italian one) that were enacted at a time when the rhetoric of the free market and of absolute property rights was already in decline, the burden of proof is carried by whomever wishes to see a limit to ownership recognized.[14] The default rule in all private law systems is still proprietary freedom. Possibly this relationship between the rule (freedom) and the exception (limits) is the most crucial aspect of ownership viewed as a legal institution able to support the development of a market economy. Obviously, any attempt to describe specifically what the owner will actually do with his or her property would not make sense in the analysis of a legal institution.

Generally, this structure of the power of the property owner (and this is true both for movables and immovables) allows him or her to be considered what economists would call the "residual claimant." By this I mean that ownership absorbs all the surpluses that are left after accounting for the social duties attached to it.[15] This capacity to absorb the residual share of social wealth in the long run is possibly the most important, positive aspect of immovable ownership as compared to any other legal institution that appears functionally equivalent in the short run but not in the long run (e.g., a lease). This is the reason why the market for immovable property cannot easily be destroyed by regulatory intervention, and consequently the reason why immovable property tends to be extensively taxed. Its immobility makes it more difficult to conceal; its demand appears rather inelastic for risk-averse investors interested in long-term tranquility. Ownership absorbs positive externalities that are produced by private as well as by public activities. The building of infrastructures, parks, schools, and so on in a given area increases the market value of property therein. For the same reason, the building of a courthouse in a given area of a town makes the value of office space there increase, given the increased demand for law offices.[16]

Usually, property law that actively protects the owner against negative externalities such as nuisances does not deal with positive externalities. An owner is not supposed to compensate his or her neighbor if by creating an attractive garden he or she has increased the value of nearby properties (hence making a positive externality). The obvious consequences of this are double: On one hand, a lower quantity of attractive gardens will be developed. On the other hand, it is exactly the possibility to capture positive externalities that introduces one of the more valuable aspect of ownership and consequently introduces incentives to acquire it.

THE POWER TO FENCE THE LAND

At the top of the list of enumerated powers that different legal systems grant to the owner is the power to fence the land.[17] Such power is the paradigm of the right to exclude that, according to a number of theories, is the essence of a property right. The power to fence was an important conquest of the French Revolution. During the ancien régime, the nobles had maintained the right to enter any land to hunt, and by so doing had created a serious prejudice to agriculture.[18] Hunters have lost such privileges everywhere in the civilized world, with the exception of Italy, where Article 842 of the Codice Civile resurrects this premodern conception of hunting rights. In the Italian legal system, the power to fence is hence transformed into a heavy burden for the owner who wishes to protect his or her land against unauthorized entries to kill animals. To exclude hunters, the Italian owner must fence, and the fencing must have certain characteristics. It is almost superfluous to observe that the inefficient nature of this approach forces the owner to pay the costs of risks created by others.

Despite its clear introduction in modern codes and its recognition as a principle by the common law, the power to fence is still limited by a number of traditional customs, such as rights of grazing, rights of acquiring wood from bushes, public rights of way, and so on. These rights are of very ancient origin, and stem from a different conception of the relationship between the individual and the land.[19] Such traditional limits to the power to fence are particularly alive, even today, in England.

The owner can give up his power to fence by creating a servitude in favor of a neighboring land. The creation of a servitude can be forced on the owner when its absence would completely seal another land from access to the public highway.

The power to fence cannot be lost by the non-use of it. French law emphasizes the ban on a spiteful or abusive use that damages the neighbor without benefit to the owner.[20] Such an approach may be useful against the owners of mountain land who fence it for the sole purpose of avoiding the entrance of skiers during the winter months. Usually, however, such rights of entry are recognized by municipal and other collective-entity regulations. The forced imposition on owners of this kind of innocuous and environmental-friendly access (such as that of mushroom hunters) may be justified because of the high transaction costs that are involved in trying to obtain ex ante permission from each owner whose property is potentially part of a ski resort or of a recreation area. Interestingly, the exceptions to the rule that the owner has the power to fence and by so doing to exclude others shows how the official hierarchy between the sources of law is an empty box in matters of land law.[21] Not only the private agreement of the individuals involved but also customary law and sublegal regulations which are closer to the property involved end up prevailing over emphatic dispositions of codes and of common law principles. Hence, the default nature of property law rules contained in codes is fully confirmed.

THE POWER TO USE THE SUBSOIL

The use of underground soil may confer important utilities on its owner. Leaving aside for the moment the possibility to exploit mines and other resources, it is obvious that, due to modern techniques of digging, waterproof sealing, illumination, and the like, the area under someone's land may have important value. It is sufficient to think about the possibility of building underground parking lots in our modern towns overcrowded by cars.

In principle, the owner of land also owns the underground.[22] He or she may use it directly or may transfer the ownership to someone else. The principles are contained in paragraph 905 of the BGB, in Articles 940 and 955 of the Italian Codice Civile, in Article 552 of the Napoleonic Code, and in common law principles.[23] While the general principle is common across legal systems, we may find some differences in the details.

Legal systems agree in expressly attributing to the owner the right to dig in his or her soil. To avoid externalities on a neighbor's land, such as those due to destabilization that may come from digging the ground, the general power to dig is usually limited by law. The general principle followed by the common law and the BGB is that the owner's power to dig can only be exercised if it does not adversely affect a neighbor's right.[24] The Franco-Italian tradition does not adopt the attitude of this general principle. In the Franco-Italian tradition, digging is permitted, provided that a certain distance from the neighbor's land is respected. Consequently, digging at a smaller distance than that prescribed by law is allowed only if the neighbor agrees to it. Absent this agreement, proof that digging does not create any prejudice is considered irrelevant. Conversely, if the digging respects the required distances, it cannot be challenged by the neighbor on the ground that it creates a prejudice. Such an approach of distances prescribed ex ante seems efficient, since its certainty stimulates the negotiation between the parties without giving the judge the power to rediscuss *ex post facto* the limits between property rights.[25] Some codes, such as the Italian one (Articles 889 and 891), allow local customs or administrative regulations to introduce distances different from those prescribed by the code.

Italian and German law, due to the lack of a full-fledged theory of abuse of right (or of reasonable use of land, as in common law), expressly denies the owner the right to exclude from his or her underground such activities that may be performed so deeply therein that he or she would have no interest to exclude.[26] Moreover, all civilian systems expressly mention in their codes that special limits to the powers of the owner on his or her underground may derive from the public law. Particularly interesting from this perspective is the legal regime of successful digging; namely, when something of value is found in the ground. In France, the Napoleonic Code (Article 552) emphatically states that the owner of land can dig and build whatever he or she likes in the underground and can extract from his or her underground all materials he or she can find. The *Code Minière* of 1956, however, says that mines can be exploited only subject to the grant of a state concession that creates a new right of ownership of the underground different from that on the surface, even if the concession is granted to the owner of the land. However, the owner of the land must grant permission to test the soil for minerals, but his or her right can be expropriated for a compensation that includes at least in part the value of the minerals contained therein.[27] Similarly, in Germany, while the letter of the BGB (paragraph 905) grants in-principle ownership of the underground to the land owner, the *Bundesberg Gesetz* grants a right on minerals only to whomever has a public law concession to extract them. In applying for a concession, one needs to be the owner or to have a contract in which the owner transfers the right to the use of the subsoil. The owner is severely limited in his or her powers to avoid exploration by the possibility of expropriation in favor of the prospective holder of a public concession.[28] Italian law is even less generous to the owner. While the letter of the Italian code emphatically states the right of the owner to whatever is contained in the underground (Article 840), when it comes to minerals, the public law regime harshly intervenes. The minerals do not belong to the land owner, whose permission is not even required to enter the land for experimental excavation purposes once such experiments are authorized by public law. The compensation for the expropriation of the subsoil does not include the value of the minerals.[29] Only in the American common law does the owner of land have a property right that includes the minerals in the underground.[30] In the case of oil, some rules may require particular distances between wells.

A similar attitude, and a similar system of stating the rule and circumscribing it with public law exceptions, is shown in the civil law in the case where the subsoil contains a treasure (i.e., something of value lost or hidden long ago whose owner is impossible to locate). In theory, the owner of land in which the treasure is located can keep it but has to pay half of its value to the finder (Article 716 of the Napoleonic Code; paragraph 984 of the BGB; Article 840 of the Codice Civile). But because the treasure almost always is in the public interest (being an object of art or of historical importance), its ownership shifts to the state. In the common law, there is a large difference between the United Kingdom, where the treasure belongs to the crown, and the United States, where there is a split between states, some giving the treasure to the owner of land, some to the finder, and some sharing it between the owner and the finder.[31] Objects of archeological value usually follow the regime of the treasure trove, so, once again, only in the United States may they be considered private property.[32]

With the exception of U.S. law, one could say that in the Western legal tradition ownership of land does not include what we can consider the exceptional value of the subsoil. Ownership extends only to grant the value that was predictable. The appropriation of the valuable "secrets" that a land may contain are excluded from ownership. These principles seem wise and efficient. By limiting the surprise factor, the law enhances the certainty of the extension of property rights so that the correct allocation of costs and benefits should follow.

THE POWER TO USE WATER

The efficient allocation of water rights is a crucial aspect of property law. Different problems must be faced, depending on whether we have to allocate static water (e.g., a pond) or running water (e.g., a river). In the latter case, property law has to make a choice dictated by the fugitive nature of its object.[33] It will be possible either to allocate it in connection with the land (e.g., water belongs to the owner of land in which it runs) or disconnected from the land (e.g., the river is considered public water subtracted from the property-rights regime). In most legal systems, both options are followed and the comparative efficiency of one over the other depends on the importance of the watercourse as well as on the local conditions. A large part of water law in modern legal systems is now separated from private law and is regulated at different levels by different administrative authorities. Property law, however, plays an important background role, mainly because the land owners close to watercourses are affected by water policy and are therefore encouraged to play an important role in this complex decision-making process. Moreover, frequently a course of water runs between a number of riparian properties belonging to different owners, creating an interdependence effect of the water use (what one riparian owner does will inevitably affect an owner downstream) that calls for a decision in terms of property rights.

To begin with, it is interesting to observe a substantial change of perspective from the French model to the Italian one. In this area of law, the remarkable theoretical independence of Italian law from French law can without hesitation be considered the result of particular developments in legal scholarship. At the beginning of our century, for reasons related to the need to organize an efficient water law system in the Northern plains, some Italian legal scholars became recognized leaders in the world as water law experts. The so-called school of the Italian hydraulic jurists was even called upon to advise the Russian Czar, and the water law model proposed by these jurists was admired and became influential in England, Germany, and France.[34] By focusing on the incentive structure that should determine a system of riparian water rights in order to allow the best exploitation of water, Italian law abandoned the French taxonomy based on servitudes (Article 640 of the Napoleon Code) to emphasize the aspect of the power of the riparian owner (Article 910 of the Codice Civile). Despite the different taxonomies, however, the law in practice in the two countries appears substantially similar.

In Italy, the civil code is very liberal in granting powers to the riparian owner. He or she may use the water to irrigate his or her land and to carry on his or her business, but must allow the remains to revert to the principal course. If a conflict arises, Article 911 of the code expressly empowers the judge to balance the interests of the different riparian owners by allowing the more efficient use of water to prevail.[35]

In France, the riparian owner upstream can use the water and must allow the remainder to run back into the ordinary course. The upstream owner cannot make things worse than necessary for the one downstream and must use water within the limits of his or her need. The downstream owner cannot refuse to receive the watercourse (Articles 642, 643, and 644).

In Germany, the approach is even more restrictive. Significantly, the doctrine is not located in the BGB but in the *Wasserhaushaltsgesetz*. As a rule, the use of water is not a prerogative of the land owner (i.e., water does not belong to him or her). State authorization is always needed. The riparian owner only has the power to use water for basic needs, such as drinking or washing (paragraphs 23 and 33 of the *Gemeingebrauch*). Possible water use is therefore limited to circumstances where no disadvantage occurs in its characteristics and there is no essential diminution in the course.

In the United States, one finds both regimes (the liberal and the restrictive in granting the use) at play in different states as a consequence of geographical differences. In drier states, the so-called "riparian rights system" severely precludes upstream owners' use of water in the interest of downstream owners' rights. The natural flux of water cannot be disrupted. In states with more water, the reasonable-use doctrine closely resembles the Italian model. In these states, water can be used beyond basic necessities, but the use should be reasonable (and of course, as we will see, reasonableness introduces the balancing doctrine). Finally, a third model can be found in some U.S. jurisdictions. Under this model, a "scaled appropriation system" allocates the property right to water independent from the ownership of riparian land to whomever is first able to establish an efficient use of the water.[36]

Generally, one can observe that a water law regime can be organized around the notion of power of the owner over water only in those geographical situations where water is not dramatically scarce. In such cases, upstream owners' power is limited by the balancing test (the most efficient use prevails), and this is likely to introduce the correct incentive structure. When extreme scarcity occurs, a full protection of downstream property rights (such as in the German model) is more likely to guarantee a subsistence use that may be the only possibility given the conditions. Generally, however, whenever a course of water is of substantial importance (e.g., is potentially a "public water," as the French would put it), legal systems in the civil law tradition tend to rely on administrative decision making. Consequently, courts and secure property rights are marginalized in this area.[37]

THE POWER TO PLANT AND ACQUIRE FRUITS

Planting is a traditional activity exercised over land. It is not only an activity conducted by farmers, a fact that is demonstrated by the large number of conflicts between not agrarian but, rather, urban owners, who try to alleviate the sadness of the cement urban jungle by such activity. The civil law tradition tends to follow the example set forth by the Napoleonic Code, which deals in much detail with this particular power by describing the specific distances that one land owner must respect in the exercise of his or her power.

It is not as important to discuss the details of such discipline as it is to observe that this approach constitutes the archetype of the civilian conception of property rights as an entity isolated from all other properties. It is no surprise that such an approach is not followed by the common law tradition, which deals with the same problem within the idea of reasonable use. The civilian approach precludes the judge from conducting any case-by-case analysis of the concrete consequences on the neighbor of each specific activity of planting. Once the distance is formally respected, every consequence of the planting activity on the neighbor is considered irrelevant because it is internal to the proprietary sphere. Conversely, if the distance is not respected, the owner will not be allowed to argue that his or her particular activity is harmless to the neighbor. His or her planting will be treated as if it was done outside the boundaries. The planted tree, for example, must be removed.[38]

This rigid regime may be considered efficient as long as it is efficient to specify clear property rights. In order to be able to plant at a distance shorter than that prescribed by the law (or by other sources such as regulations or customs), the owner will have to obtain ex ante his neighbor's agreement. As we have already observed, judges should refrain from tampering with the choice for clear-cut limits to property rights. Such tempering would be particularly inefficient, not only because it would reduce the clear specification of property rights but also because it would increase administrative costs by encouraging litigation. The right to a shorter distance, as any other property right, can be acquired by adverse possession.

Sometimes the law grants owners some particular rights to take measures of self-help. For example, the neighbor is allowed to directly cut a branch or a root of a tree that, despite the formal respect of the distance, directly invades his or her property. While the indirect effect on the neighbor of planting within limits is completely irrelevant (e.g., shadow or leaves blown by the wind), the direct invasion of roots and branches is considered so important as to allow self-help measures.[39] Interestingly, this different regime of direct and indirect invasion is also found in the common law distinction between trespass (actionable per se in case of direct invasion) and nuisance (actionable only when the indirect invasion is unreasonable).[40]

Typically, the owner will plant in order to be able to collect the fruits of his or her planting activity. Nobody would bother to cultivate land if the law would not protect him or her against someone else trying to acquire the fruits of his or her labor. This obvious observation explains why it is a common principle in the legal traditions that the owner acquires the fruits of his or her property.

Part of these fruits come from the transfer for a given amount of time of the benefits of ownership to another individual. Usually, the owner receives by so doing a given amount of money. Jurists throughout the Western legal tradition have described such benefits as "civil fruits" to distinguish them from the "natural fruits" that are the direct product of cultivation. The possibility of obtaining civil fruits from one property is the consequence of the positive value of a given property. If the aggregate of the positive aspects of a given property right is higher than the aggregate of its negative aspects, that property will be the object of a market demand. The owner who decides to satisfy that demand without completely giving up his or her property will be able to capture a rent. Medieval jurists developed the notion of civil fruits as a rhetorical device to describe this economic rent in order to overtake antiusury law that would have banned the loan of any property for an interest.[41] If the interest was characterized as a civil fruit, the rhetoric introduced by so doing would make the transaction acceptable.

On the other hand, natural fruits are either naturally the product of a given piece of property (e.g., the walnuts in a bush) or those that reward the transformation of a piece of land through agrarian labor. In the case of a conflict over natural fruits, the owner is defeated only by the good-faith possessor who has worked to produce them.[42] This principle, expressed by all of the civilian codes and also by the common law tradition, stems from the efficiency of encouraging productive labor over land, which results in also increasing the value of ownership.[43] This very intimate relationship between possession and acquisition of fruits is among other things evinced by the recognition through the civil law tradition of usufruct (possession and taking of fruits), a typical limited property right that survived even the unitary rhetoric of the French Revolution.[44] The particular attention to reward productive labor over land is clearly evinced, for example, by paragraph 102 of the BGB, which states, "Whoever is obliged to return fruits (to the owner) may claim back the expenses he has incurred for their production provided that such expenses are economically reasonable and are not higher than the value of fruits." Similarly, Article 821 of the Italian Codice Civile prescribes, "Whoever acquires the ownership of the fruits must reimburse the expenses which someone else has incurred in producing and acquiring them."

Economic thinking lies behind both categories of fruits. Within the simplified notions such as those used by economists, in which property is a unitary notion independent from the nature of its object, whoever loans money transfers its use for a given consideration. The owner of money thereby enters into an economic transaction that is identical to that involving the owner of land who partially transfers his or her land by creating an usufruct thereof by leasing it. In both cases, the amount of the consideration includes the owner's risk of not recovering the property at the end of the relationship. The owner of money will charge for the risk of not receiving the capital back. However, a similar risk is faced by one who creates a usufruct or a lease over land. It is not rare for political choices in favor of labor over ownership to preclude the owner from reentering into possession of his or her property. This is the reason why urban rents tend to be more expensive in those legal systems where the law limits the powers of the owner to evict the tenant.[45]

THE POWER OVER BUILDINGS (*SUPERFICIES SOLO CAEDIT*)

A direct consequence of the owner's sovereignty over his or her property should be that in case someone builds or encroaches in any other way across the boundaries of the owner's land, the latter has a choice between keeping the encroachment (in case he or she values it) or forcing the former to remove the encroachment. This logical and strict application of the right to exclude others is, however, severely limited by the need to consider the rights of the good-faith possessor as well as the need to avoid the unjustified enrichment of the owner against the builder.

The Napoleonic Code, in principle (Article 555), grants the owner the power to make the choice. As usual, this is followed by a number of legal systems, including the Italian (Article 936). In both the French and the Italian legal systems, if the owner opts to retain the building, he or she will owe the builder an indemnity which is calculated as the lower sum between the cost of the building and the increase in value of the land. If, however, the builder acted in good faith or the owner had knowledge of the building, both legal systems do not allow the owner to force the removal (in technical terms, they deny the *Ius tollendi*).

In Germany, paragraph 946 of the BGB extends the owner's right onto whatever is "essentially incorporated" to the soil. Paragraph 94 considers buildings essential parts of land. Paragraph 951 affords the builder an action of unjust enrichment when the owner retains the building. If, however, the owner makes use of paragraph 1004 to protect the integrity of his or her land and to force the builder to remove the encroachment, nothing is due to the latter. Paragraph 1004 is not available against the good-faith possessor. In sum, German law reaches, albeit through a somewhat complex path, the same results as the Franco-Italian model.

In common law, the property of the building is acquired by the owner of land, and there is no action of unjustified enrichment available in these cases.[46] The doctrine of promissory estoppel, however, which protects reliance, may allow the remedy of reimbursement for the value of the building in the case where the owner has actually or constructively allowed the building.[47] In a number of American jurisdictions, moreover, special "improver statutes" may offer the good-faith builder an action of unjust enrichment.

This brief description shows how we can observe a common core of Western law as far as the problem of the ownership of buildings on someone else's land is concerned.[48] Through a regime that parties are completely free to negotiate away (default rules), legal systems tend to grant the right to the owner of land and at the same time to limit economic imbalance through a system of compensation to the builder. This is captured by the Latin expression *superficies solo caedit*. When it is correctly interpreted as a general principle, it is efficient because it clearly describes property rights and because it encourages the solution of any possible conflicts by means of direct negotiation. The default nature of such a regime introduces another important power of the land owner. He or she can transfer to someone else the right to keep constructions on his or her soil.

In general, the power to create independent property rights within the vertical extension of one's property is a crucially efficient characteristic of modern property law. This power allows property rights, although restricted as in the civil law tradition by the *numerus clausus* principle, to be supplied in a way coherent with the demand. If I need only one story of a multistory building, it would be plainly absurd to force me to acquire the property of the whole building to use just one story. If I need only the trees in order to gather the wood, it makes sense to allow me to buy and for the land owner to sell only the ownership of the trees and not the whole land. A rule that prohibits the transfer of ownership of trees separate from the soil would lack any justification.[49] Interestingly, this fundamental and efficient power to "slice" property rights in a horizontal way (a power that sets the foundation of the modern systems of urban ownership of apartments in multistory buildings) has found formal recognition in systems of property law relatively recently, and still encounters dogmatic resistance to full recognition.

The notion of a special kind of ownership (superficies) as a property right to keep or to build over or under someone else's land was not used by the Napoleonic Code. Despite its early recognition in Roman law, the notion became common in modern civil law thanks to the work of the nineteenth-century Belgian author Laurent.[50] The first extensive use of this legal institution can be traced back to the French and Belgian colonial experience in Africa, where it was crucial to maintain the principle that the state was the owner of all land (to avoid excessive speculation), but at the same time necessary to grant building rights secure enough to stimulate investments. The same option has been followed by a number of socialist countries, which have nationalized all land but have recognized property rights over buildings.[51] The autonomous proprietary nature of this right is confirmed also by the peculiar development of Roman law where, as scholars acknowledge, superficies (and emphitheusis) have a completely different nature from other limited property rights, since they did not develop in connection with the notion of dominium but found their way later and independently into the legal system.[52]

Nowadays it is recognized almost everywhere that the owner can create and transfer a "superficiary right" over and underneath his or her land (e.g., a right to keep an underground garage). Such a right, becoming an autonomous right of ownership, is not lost by the fall or the destruction of the building, which the superficiary owner always has the right to rebuild. Nor is it necessary in theory that the building actually exist. A right of superficiary ownership can well be acquired and then kept idle (i.e., without actually building) for many reasons; for example, because I do not want my neighbor to build and obstruct my view while I decide whether I am interested in enlarging my home to occupy part of my neighbor's garden.

We have therefore been able to identify a certain number of basic principles in this domain: (1) Legal systems agree that if no specific contractual activity to the contrary exists (i.e., if the default rules are not changed), the land and the building should circulate jointly; (2) if there are doubts as to the legal status of buildings, plantations, and other fixtures, one should consider them in the land owner's ownership; and (3) this default regime is fully changeable by agreement and separate ownerships above or below the ground can always be created.[53]

THE POWER OVER BORDERS

Legal systems, while proceeding with relatively common principles in what we have discussed so far, show considerable differences if the analysis is carried on in further detail. An interesting example is offered by the legal regimes of buildings partially encroaching on someone else's land. While according to the principle *superficies solo caedit* the owner of land should acquire property rights to a slice of the building, the number of practical exceptions that different legal systems fashion in response to this problem could well make someone doubt the principle's practical content.

Theoretically, this example acts as a bridge toward the discussion of limits and liabilities of the owner that will be discussed in Chapter 8. Allow me to illustrate. A problem that all legal systems have to face is the following: Albert is the owner of Blackacre and Bianca is the owner of Greenacre, a neighboring lot. Albert builds his home but inadvertently trespasses and builds a few inches of a support wall on Greenacre. Bianca asks Albert to remove its encroachment on her property, but it is impossible to remove it without destroying the building completed.

We find a variety of solutions to this problem. Let us consider five different legal systems: Italy, France, Germany, the United States, and Great Britain.[54] Four legal systems out of five, the sole exception being France, agree that when the builder acted in good faith and the trespass is not substantial, he should be entitled to maintain the building. Therefore, these systems, by using different techniques, give the property right to Albert. Both Italian and German law consider this problem in different articles of their civil codes.[55] American law works out a number of doctrines, the most interesting for our purposes being that of *easement in invitum*.[56] This doctrine is unknown in England where, however, the problem is handled either by means of estoppel or by refusing the injunction despite the fact that good faith does not excuse trespass.[57] French law, on the other hand, considers such an invasion of the property right in contrast with Article 545 of the Civil Code, which provides that takings can only be for public use.[58] As a result, it gives the property right to Bianca.

The default nature of these legal regimes (and the Coase theorem) tells us that, no matter who between Albert and Bianca is entitled to the property right, the parties will bargain the efficient solution provided transaction costs are kept low.[59] In our hypothesis, we do not face problems related to a complex fact situation, such as when a large number of parties are involved. Indeed, Albert and Bianca may bargain over their efficient legal solution just by walking pleasantly to the fence of their respective gardens and talking to each other. In a case like this, we could consider transaction costs low enough to meet the Coase requirement. Law and economics therefore tell us that a French-like solution (property right to Bianca) is as efficient as its alternative (property right to Albert). However, four legal systems sharing with France the same economic background have converged on the opposite allocation of property rights. Thus, one may well wonder if in practice it is true that the outcome does not change.

Indeed, within these four systems, two (Germany and Italy) also share with France the civil law tradition. We should then give this picture a second look. We could proceed by taking account of the advantages of the French rule and then comparing them to those of the alternative rule, applying therefore a cost–benefit analysis.[60] We could thus establish that the major costs of the French solution are to be faced in event of a breakdown of the bargaining process. Indeed, the building must be destroyed to be rebuilt a few inches backward, with all the costs and waste that this entails.[61] To evaluate this hypothesis, we must remember that we are discussing rules by looking backward, since the good faith and the lack of negligence of Albert are prerequisites to our discussion. In other words, the milk is already spilled and the decision about how to clean the table will have no influence on the future occurrence of the same disaster. The shift in property rights involved in the Italian–German–Anglo-American solution is therefore practically costless.

Moreover, in a case like this, problems for negotiations may arise for the very reason that neighbors are involved. The Western legal tradition envisions a world in which neighbors are on bad terms. It is enough to consider how much scholarly effort has been devoted to doctrines such as spite fences, abuse of rights, aemulatio, intentional nuisances, troubles de voisinage, and so forth to illustrate cases in which neighbors deeply dislike each other.[62] What a good occasion for Bianca to compel Albert, whom she hates, to face an economic disaster! Albert and Bianca may not even talk to each other, as is not at all unusual between neighbors. Indeed, we are discussing a rule which a court is called upon to apply in a costly and time-consuming judicial process. The very existence of the judicial process evidences the inability of Albert and Bianca to bargain out a solution to their problem.

The wasteful destruction of the building will end the suit if Albert and Bianca are in France. The same result will not occur if they are in America, Germany, Italy, or even England. In its normative dimension, comparative law and economics will therefore suggest to a new codifier that he or she should not follow the French solution. It will suggest that the French solution is inefficient because it is wasteful.

Indeed, to suggest the efficient solution of the conflict between Albert and Bianca we should also consider liability rules that legal systems always use in mediating conflicts between owners and good-faith possessors. From this point of view, German, Italian, and Anglo-American law lose their previous uniformity. Only Italian, German, and English law protect Bianca with a liability rule. Albert can maintain his building, but will have to pay compensation to Bianca. Italian law does specify that Albert should pay to Bianca twice the market value of the piece of land encroached on by the building (Article 938 of the Codice Civile). German law offers Bianca the choice between receiving a permanent rent from Albert, to be paid annually in consideration for the servitude imposed on Greenacre (paragraph 912 of the BGB), or forcing Albert to buy the invaded land at market value (paragraph 915 of the BGB). When the English court refuses to issue an injunction against Albert, it has already granted damages for trespass or, if not, has opened the possibility to (reluctantly) provide damages in lieu of an injunction under Lord Cairns' Act.[63] American law, on the other hand, refuses, under the doctrine of easement *in invitum*, any serious relief to Bianca, since the damages provided for are nominal.[64]

Allowing Albert to keep his building is per se a redistribution of property rights. It may actually be seen as a private taking:[65] When certain conditions are met, land is transferred from Bianca to Albert in order to favor its more efficient use. Should this transfer take place free of charge? Let us state clearly at the outset that when a resource is used by someone without paying its price, we are facing an externality. No system of law which considers efficiency as a desirable goal should allow externalities. In view of this general assumption, the protection of Bianca by means of a liability rule is more efficient because it internalizes the external costs created by Albert's action. It should be considered that, with the exception of France, Albert has the choice between maintaining his building or removing it. To be efficient, this choice should take account of all the costs involved therein. The negative impact of externalities on the efficient outcome of the confrontation between Albert and Bianca, in other words, remains despite the innocent nature of Albert's encroachment. The American rule on easements *in invito* seems therefore inefficient if compared to the German, Italian, or English alternatives. Finally, there are no efficiency reasons for Albert to pay twice the value of Bianca's land. Indeed, this sort of "punitive element" in an innocent situation seems difficult to explain, even as a matter of equity. As far as efficiency is concerned, it will lead to an inefficient result in all the cases in which the cost of removing the building falls between the market price of the land and twice its value. The German rule, as well as the English one, seem therefore more efficient than the Italian counterpart.[66] At this point in our analysis we may therefore rank, as a matter of comparative efficiency, the legal systems so far analyzed in the following order: (1) German and English rule, (2) Italian rule, (3) United States rule, and (4) French rule.

Something interesting may emerge from a final comparison between France and the United States. Indeed, we may be curious to know why the two systems have followed such inefficient paths. One explanation can be that we are faced with a problem of ignorance due to parochialism. Or, without any problem of ignorance, we may be confronting solutions technically demanded by the internal fabric of French or American law. We may therefore be surprised to know that in the strictly similar economic problem arising when Albert builds a house right in the middle of Greenacre in a good-faith belief that he owns it when instead it belongs to Bianca, both French law and American law abandon their extreme positions and do make use of liability rules. Indeed, Article 555 of the French Civil Code gives to Bianca the property right in the building but gives Albert compensation in the lesser amount of the increased value of the land or of its expenses. An interpretation by analogy of Article 555 could have created an alternative solution that is neutral from the efficiency point of view when contrasted with the German one. By giving Bianca the property right to the slice of the building and a liability rule to protect Albert, French courts could create a legal shadow to the Coasian pursuit of the efficient solution without the big risk of waste in case of a breakdown in the bargaining process.[67]

The same more-flexible attitude is shown by American courts dealing with the case of a finished building on someone else's land. Indeed, Bianca acquires the property right to the building but the doctrine of promissory reliance and a series of so-called improver statutes may protect Albert with a liability rule when, as in the case we are discussing, he acted in good faith.[68] We can see a complete convergence reached by different techniques in the common law, Germany, France, and Italy. Liability rules are used as a watchdog against externalities so as to arrive at an efficient and common result.[69]

Why does the same not happen when the invasion is only partial? It is easy to detect the ideological reason for this odd situation. Ironically, however, the same ideological concerns (the sanctity of property rights) lead French and American law to opposite, but commonly inefficient, results. French lawyers and courts are worried about restrictively interpreting Article 555 because they see the liability rule which protects Albert as a major exception to the sovereignty of Bianca within the physical boundaries of her property. It is very significant that, lacking an ad hoc provision, they rush to apply Article 545, the ideological flag of the sovereignty of the property owner. By so doing, they argue that a different rule would be a private expropriation.

American law, concerned about the waste that would stem from absolutely protecting Bianca in the idiosyncratic sovereignty of her will, does allow Albert to maintain the building. It nevertheless refuses to give Bianca a serious remedy by a liability rule, because this would sound too much like compensation for a taking which American law forbids in the case of private use. Ironically, offering to Bianca a liability rule protection would sound ideologically subversive of the French-like protection of private property which Madison had enshrined in the Fifth Amendment. As a consequence, Bianca is deprived also of this second-best protection.

Both the French and the American solutions are inefficient because they take a black-and-white approach without making use of liability rules. When we compare them, we may say that the prima facie comparative efficiency of the American solution vis-à-vis the French one may prove to be irrelevant because, in the vast majority of the cases, at low transaction costs, Albert and Bianca are likely to arrive at the efficient solution by bargaining. The American rule may still prove better as a default solution, but in a legal system seriously concerned with the protection of property rights, such an abrupt redistribution may lack political and social support, may create tension and uncertainty, and may therefore be an even less efficient solution than the French one. The French and American solutions may therefore prove indistinguishable from the efficiency point of view. It is also important to consider that, when bargaining, the parties will offer money to each other to buy the entitlement. Thus it makes perfect sense for default regimes to mimic what the parties would have done in their bargaining.

Efficient convergences are more likely to occur where ideological problems are less strong, as in the hypothesis of building in the middle of Greenacre. In this case, there is no redistribution of property rights involved. When a redistribution is involved and the lack of information inhibits the development of a competitive market of legal doctrines, ideology is likely to create an irrational constraint on the development of efficient solutions. It is important to note that inefficient results are reached in France and the United States, the two legal cultures which today are more affected by parochialism in the study of law.

NOTES

1. See A. M. Patault, *Introduction historique au droit des biens* 162 (1989).

2. See Paragraph 90, BGB; H. P. Westermann, *BGB Sachenrecht* (8th ed., 1990); *id. Sachenrecht: Ein Lehrbuch* (7th ed., 1998).

3. See J. H. Merryman, *Ownership and Estate: Variations on a Theme by Lawson*, 48 *Tul. L. Rev.* 916 (1974).

4. See F. H. Lawson ed., *Structural Variations in Property Law, 6 International Encyclopedya of Comparative Law* 3–284 (1975).

5. See F. Zenati, *La nature juridique de la propriété: contribution a la theorie du droit subjectif* (1981).

6. See W. N. Hohfeld, *Fundamental Legal Conceptions as Applied in Legal Reasoning and Other Essays* (1919).

7. See J. E. Penner, *The "Bundle of Rights" Picture of Property*, 43 *UCLA L. Rev.* 711 (1996).

8. The particular dangerousness is in fact reflected by the legal regime. See *infra* Chapter 7.

9. J. Waldron, *The Right to Private Property* 49 (1988), keeps liability out of Honoré's incidents of ownership, considering it a more general duty.

10. See R. C. Ellickson, *Property in Land*, 102 *Yale L.J.* 1315; A. Gambaro, *Il diritto di proprietà* 228 (1995).

11. See Weill et al., *Droit civil, les biens* 239 (3d ed., 1985).

12. See R. A. Cunningham et al., *The Law of Property* 410 (1984).

13. Such exceptions are recognized even at the peak of the absolute, individualistic conception. See Patault, *supra* note 1, at 220.

14. See S. Pugliatti, *La proprietà nel nuovo diritto* 123 (1964).

15. See, for a construction of such idea as control, S. J.Grossman & O. D. Hart, *The Costs and Benefits of Ownership: A Theory of Vertical and Lateral Integration*, 94 *J. Pol. Econ.* 691 (1986).

16. See Gambaro, *supra* note 10, at 225.

17. See, for example, Article 647 of the Napoleonic Code; Article 841 of C.C., *The Italian Civil Code* (M. Beltramo et al. trans., 1978).

18. See Patault, *supra* note 1, at 38.

19. See P. Grossi, *An Alternative to Private Property: Collective Property in the Juridical Consciousness of the Nineteenth Century* (L. G. Cochrane trans., 1981).

20. See L. Josserand, *De l'abus du droit* (1905).

21. See the discussion in R. Sacco, *Il sistema delle fonti e il diritto di proprietà*, in *Riv. trim. dir. proc. civ.* 435 (1970); see also R. C. Ellickson, *Order Without Law* (1991).

22. For a broad study, see C. Tenella Sillani, *I limiti "verticali" della proprietà fondiaria* (1994).

23. See J. G. Riddall, *Introduction to Land Law* 50 (4th ed., 1988).

24. On rules related to "support" in common law, see Cunningham et al., *supra* note 12, at 418.

25. See R. Cooter & T. Ulen, *Law and Economics* (2d ed., 1996).

26. The doctrine of abuse of right is a notable rhetorical divergence, both within the civil law tradition and across the civil law–common law dichotomy. Its practical impact is, however, very limited. See A. Gambaro, *The Abuse of*

Right in the Civil Law, in *Aequitas and Equity* (A. Rabello ed., 1994); see, for the lack of English experience, H. C. Gutteridge, *Abuse of Rights*, 5 *Cambridge L. J.* 22 (1933).

27. For an introduction and a bibliography, see J. Carbonnier, *Droit civil, les biens* 234 (14th ed., 1991).

28. See Westermann, *supra* note 2.

29. See U. Mattei, *La proprietà immobiliare* 126 (1993).

30. See *Missouri Pac. R.R. Co. v. Strohaker*, 152 SW 2d 557; *Sheppard v. Stanolid Oil & Gas Co.*, 125 SW 2d 643.

31. See *A-G v. British Museum Trustees* (1903) 2 Ch. 598.

32. See *Schley v. Couch*, 284 SW 2d 333.

33. See Cooter & Ulen, *supra* note 25, at 5.

34. See C. A. Cannata & A. Gambaro, *Lineamenti di storia della giurisprudenza europea* 271 (4th ed., 1989).

35. See Gambaro, *supra* note 10, at 410.

36. See Cunningham et al., *supra* note 12, at 424.

37. See Weill et al., *supra* note 11, at 203.

38. See Carbonnier, *supra* note 27, at 254.

39. See Gambaro, *supra* note 10, at 571.

40. See R. A. Buckley, *Cricket and the Law of Nuisance*, 41 *Mod. L. Rev.* 334 (1978). In general, see W. L. Prosser & W. P. Keeton, *The Law of Torts* 67 (5th ed., 1984).

41. For an in-depth discussion, see C. M. Mazzoni, *Frutti civili e interessi di capitali* (1985).

42. Historical discussion can be found in Patault, *supra* note 1, at 60, 77, 95.

43. See *Key v. Loder*, 182 A 2d 60.

44. See *supra* Chapter 1.

45. General economic issues in landlord–tenant law are discussed in R. Posner, *Economic Analysis of Law* 83 (5th ed., 1998).

46. See Riddall, *supra* note 23, at 51; see also Law of Property Act, 1925, ch. 1, § 205.

47. See *"Moore" Burger Inc. v. Phillips Petroleum Co.*, 492 SW 2d 934.

48. For more details and references, see U. Mattei, *Comparative Law and Economics* 133 (1997).

49. Article 956 of the Italian Civil Code contains such an absurd rule.

50. See F. Laurent, *Principes de droit civil français* 490 (8th ed., 1878).

51. For a discussion in English, see U. Mattei, *Socialist and Non Socialist Approaches to Land Law: Continuity and Change in Somalia and Other African States*, 16 *Rev. Soc. L.* 17 (1990).

52. Cf. P. Grossi, *Le situazioni reali nell' esperienza giuridica medievale* (1968). See also A. Watson, *The Law of Property in the Late Roman Republic* (1968).

53. See A. Gambaro, *La proprietà* (1990).

54. This discussion is already published in Mattei, *supra* note 48, at 133.

55. In Italy, Article 938 of the Codice Civile reads, "Occupation of a portion of adjoining land. If a portion of the adjoining land is occupied in good faith in the construction of a building, and the owner of that land does not object within three months of the day on which construction began, the court, taking account of the circumstances, can attribute the ownership of the building and

the occupied soil to the builder. The builder is required to pay the owner of the soil double the value of the area occupied, as well as compensation for damages." This translation is provided in *The Italian Civil Code, supra* note 17. This article is discussed, along with a short general introduction to the Italian law of property, in A. Candian et al., *Property Law in Italy*, 1 *Italian Studies in Law* (A. Pizzorusso ed., 1992). In Germany, Paragraph 912 of the BGB reads, "If the owner of a soil in the construction of a building has built beyond the border line without intention or gross negligence, the neighbor must suffer the building unless before or right after the overtaking of the borderline he has objected. The neighbor must be compensated with a cash rent." For a short discussion of this article within a detailed introduction to German property law in English, see E. J. Schuster, *The Principles of German Civil Law* 388 (1907). For a shorter introduction, see N. Horn et al., *German Private and Commercial Law: An Introduction* 169 (1982).

56. R. R. Powell & P. J. Rohan, *Powell on Real Property* (abr. ed., 1968).

57. On the way to create easements in England, see R. E. Megarry & H.W.R. Wade, *The Law of Real Property* 855 (5th ed., 1984); G. C. Cheshire & E. H. Burn, *Modern Law of Real Property* 503 (14th ed., 1988). Estoppel, of course, only works, as in America, where Albert can be blamed for having created a reliance on Bianca. As to good faith not excusing trespass, see M. Brazier, *Street on Torts* 69 (8th ed., 1988). Good faith, however, can be considered by the court of equity in exercising its discretion to grant an injunction. See, generally, G. W. Keeton & L. A. Sheridan, *Equity* 19 (3d ed., 1987). See also *infra* note 68.

58. Article 545 reads, "Nobody can be forced to give up his property if not for public use and after a just and previous compensation." Such a strict approach, constantly followed by the Cour de Cassation, is often criticized by French scholars. See Weill et al., *supra* note 11, at 219; C. Atias, 2 *Droit civil, les biens* 333–334 (1982).

59. R. Coase, *The Problem of Social Costs*, 3 *J.L. & Econ.* 1 (1960).

60. See R. Cooter, *The Best Right Laws: Value Foundations of the Economic Analysis of Law*, 64 *Notre Dame L. R.* 817 (1989) at 829.

61. See R. Cooter, *The Cost of Coase*, 11 *J. Legal Stud.* 1 (1982), according to whom the law should be structured to minimize the harm caused by failures in private agreements.

62. See *infra* Chapter 7.

63. See J. A. Jolowicz, *Damages in Equity: A Study of Lord Cairn's Act*, 34 *Cambridge L.J.* 224 (1975); P. H. Pettit, *Lord Cairn's Act in the County Court: A Supplementary Note*, 36 *Cambridge L.J.* 369 (1977); I. Wakefield, *Equitable Damages under Lord Cairn's Act*, 145 *Conv. & Prop. Law* 286 (1981).

64. See *Hahl v. Sugo*, 169 N.Y. 109, 62 N.E. 135 (1901); *Mc Kean v. Alliance Land Co.*, 200 Cal 396, 253 P. 134 (1927).

65. See C. Atias, *Droit Civil, Les Biens* 334, n. 56 (1982).

66. See *Wrothan Park Estate Co., Ltd. v. Parkside Homes Ltd.*, 1 W.L.R. 798, 812–816 (1974); *Bracewell v. Appleby* (1975) Ch. 408 (1975) All ER 993. In these cases, the idea that plaintiffs should get nothing because they have suffered purely nominal damages was rejected. The rule here was laid down that a just substitute for the injunction was such a sum of money as might reasonably

have been demanded by the plaintiff from the defendant as a quid pro quo for relaxing the covenant.

67. Article 555 reads, "If Plantings, constructions and buildings have been made by a third party with materials belonging to him, the owner of the soil has the right . . . either to keep them or to compel who made them to throw them off. ¶ If the owner of the soil wants them to be taken off this is done at the expenses of the maker without any indemnity to him. The maker can also be condemned to pay damages. If the owner of the soil prefers to acquire the ownership he must pay an indemnity. ¶ If plantings and construction have been made in good faith the owner of the soil will be estopped from asking the removal and will have to pay an indemnity . . . (computed as in previous paragraph)." See, arguing for the extension of this article to the hypothesis we are examining, Weill et. al, *supra* note 11, at 220.

68. See American Law Institute, *Restatement of the Law, Property, Servitudes* Tent. Dr. 1 112 (1989); see also C. H. Donahue et al., *Property* 1072 (1974); A. J. Casner (ed.), *American Law of Property: A Treatise on the Law of Property in the United States* 36 (1952).

69. The text of Article 936 of the Codice Civile, as adopted in 1942, is very similar to Article 555 of the Civil Code as amended in 1960 and reproduced *supra* note 67. The same rule is contained in paragraph 946 of the BGB: "If a movable thing is linked to a soil in such a way as to become a constituent essential part thereof, the ownership of the soil is extended to include this thing." The liability rule is offered by extension of the rules on unjust enrichment, which is, by Article 951, limited to a good-faith hypothesis. It is interesting to note that American law excludes the extension of unjust enrichment doctrines in this case and limits itself to the more strict doctrines of promissory reliance or enacting an improvement statute.

CHAPTER 7

Negative Aspects of Ownership: Limits and Liabilities

IN GENERAL

In the civil law rhetoric, a right of ownership is conceptualized as an airtight entity, completely insulated from the outside world. Each entity is delimited by its boundaries. Within the boundaries, the owner is sovereign. In rigorously following this conception, civil law countries did not discriminate between activities carried on outside the boundaries that affect ownership in a positive way (such as making a beautiful garden to the benefit of neighboring land) and activities that affect it in a negative way (such as building a graveyard to the prejudice of the value of a neighbor's land). Both kinds of activities (externalities, in an economist's terminology) were simply ignored as carried on outside of the boundaries.[1] Of course, this tight principle, stemming from an unrealistic conception of ownership and known in the civil law as the ban on *immissio in alienum*, has created a number of problems for civilian property law. To begin with, it has precluded for many years civil lawyers considering the law of nuisance, a very effective institutional solution at common law, as a possible private law device to govern land use at civil law.[2] Moreover, civilian jurists have been wrestling conceptually with the notion of the limits to ownership, without realizing these limits are part of the very structure of property rights. Much more realistic is the perspective of the common lawyer, according to whom the owner is always restricted by a requirement of reasonable use, which, of course, makes the notion of airtight property rights foreign to the common lawyer's way of thinking. In practice, everywhere in Western law the notion of reasonableness in the exercise of ownership rights (and of property rights in general) is recognized by the law. Thus, we may consider it as a basic principle in beginning our discussion of limits to ownership.[3] Nevertheless, this civilian conceptualization, as we will better see, carries with it a wholly different philosophy from that of the common lawyer when questions arise about those incompatible uses of land that do not violate the physical boundaries of property. However, despite the radically different conceptualizations, most of the rules and principles applied by courts to limit property rights can be seen as common, particularly when the level of abstraction is high enough.

A first common principle from this perspective is that, in all legal systems, negative externalities (such as building a graveyard) receive a different treatment from positive ones (such as building a beautiful garden). An example will clarify this point. If Tom builds a nice garden in his courtyard, Eva will be able to rent her apartment with a view on the courtyard for a higher amount. Eva is therefore enriched at the expense of Tom by the difference between the amount she can now charge and what she could have charged if the garden was not there. In no legal system can Tom sue Eva claiming a share of the benefit that he has bestowed upon her by building the garden. Now imagine that Tom decides to establish in the same courtyard a wrecking activity that requires storing in the courtyard a large number of very old and dirty cars. The rental value of Eva's apartment will collapse as a consequence of the discomfort of being a neighbor to such activities. All legal systems will consider granting to Eva a cause of action, and most will probably give her at least a damages remedy if not an injunction.[4]

This example introduces a crucial aspect for the study of property law. There is a general principle common in all of the legal systems (despite their taxonomy and their rhetoric) that introduces a duty to avoid using property in a way that causes substantial and unreasonable prejudice to a third party or to the community. This general duty is not specifically part of property law, but is so much rooted in the organization of private law that it cannot be disregarded in any description of property law. Such a principle is stated in the general law of tort by paragraph 823 of the BGB, by Article 1382 of the Napoleonic Code, by Article 2043 of the Codice Civile, and by the tort of nuisance in common law countries.[5] All these principles have the same meaning when applied to ownership: They introduce a general liability principle that is aimed at all of the members of a community but that nevertheless is particularly stringent for those activities that are part of the typical idea of land use. Such rules also work as a general clause protecting property from negative externalities, so that they clearly show the correlative nature of proprietary powers and duties as discussed by Hohfeld in his foundational taxonomy.[6] It is no surprise that "the duty to refrain from using the object in ways that harm others" is recognized as an incident of ownership in Professor Honoré's seminal analysis.[7]

THE GENERAL BAN ON ABUSE OF PROPERTY RIGHTS

In modern civil law theory, reasonableness of land use is not an explicit general requirement, as it is in the common law and as it used to be in the precodification European Ius Commune. But such a principle can be seen at play in the law in action as a general clause that at the same time presides over the extensions and the limits of the right of ownership.

For reasons that can only be considered historical and contingent, neither German law nor Italian law has followed the French notion of abuse of right, the closest civilian counterpart of the reasonableness requirement.[8] The idea of abusing a right is considered logically contradictory in legal systems refusing the doctrine. It may appear odd to first grant a property right and afterward refuse its protection on the theory that the use has been abusive of the right.[9] Where is the limit between a free, subjectively apreciated use whose protection is the essence of ownership and an abuse?[10] For example, while the typical use of a book is reading it and that is why people usually buy them, someone may like to buy books to start fires or, even if illiterate, to show off fancy libraries. No legal system can deny protection to this idiosyncratic book owner, claiming that he or she was abusing the right of ownership.

Consequently, the doctrine of abuse of right has been defined as the notion according to which no right can be exercised for the sole purpose of damaging someone else.[11] The doctrine of abuse of right as such is absent in the common law, where it is perfectly well substituted for by the reasonableness limit.[12] On the other hand, the unrealistic civilian conceptualization of ownership makes this notion particularly crucial. Without abuse of right or some substitute for it, every owner who insists on using his or her property just to spite his or her neighbor could claim to be protected by the legal system. And, indeed, there are more important things for the law to do than protect such spiteful behaviors. Consequently, civil law systems that do not accept the concept of abuse of rights can be expected to use some different, more specific notions, usually limited under land law to prohibit spite fences or similar behaviors. One notion used for this purpose and codified in a plurality of systems is that of *aemulatio* (Article 833 of the Italian Civil Code).

RULES AND STANDARDS TO LIMIT PROPERTY RIGHTS

The tension between the definition of ownership as absolute power over an airtight space and the reality of conflicting neighboring property rights has created a number of technical problems and has produced a variety of functionally equivalent doctrines to solve them. As the reader will recall, the notion of "social function" of property rights can be conceptualized in a similar way in the constitutional domain.[13]

All this can be interpreted for our purpose as reinforcing and giving technical content to the idea of a general duty not to produce externalities. Of course, interpreted in this way, the principle of reasonableness that apparently limits ownership in its active dimension (on what the owner can do) also means a general immunity of property in the face of negative externalities. Consequently, it not only works as a limit to ownership but also as a defense of it. On the passive dimension (on what the owner can refuse to take), it is no surprise that in all the civilian tort systems (and this is true also in the common law of trespass) ownership is considered the very paradigm of that "absolute subjective right" whose violation is traditionally necessary to recover in tort.[14]

While the substance of the law may be almost unaffected by these formal differences (as usually happens), the tendency of civilians to consider the owner as absolutely free provided he or she does not face an express limit to his or her freedom has some relevant impact on the semantics and taxonomy of the codes. In particular, civilian codes tend to contain a series of specific articles describing the limits of the owner's freedom. Most of these details would be made redundant by the assumption of a general reasonableness principle similar to that of the common law. However, the reality of the different legal processes gives us good reason to spend some time in discussing them. To be sure, one cannot assume, particularly in transitional countries as well as in most of the civil law tradition, a judiciary qualified enough to be trusted in using the tremendous discretion that standards (as opposed to rules) offer to judges. A standard such as reasonable use is more difficult to administer and requires much more lawyering skills than relatively plain and self-evident rules such as the ones we will discuss.[15]

As we will see in our discussion of nuisance law, it is nevertheless important to consider that the administration of some standard is necessary. In other words, while standards administered by a highly qualified judiciary may make rules redundant, rules may never be able by themselves to capture the staggering complexity of the conflicts over property rights.

LIMITS TO THE POWER TO BUILD

A rather typical use that one would expect to be part of ownership is that of transforming land by a development activity. Such a power in modern societies is so restricted, both in the public interest and in the interest of neighbors, that one can better describe it in a chapter devoted to limits and liabilities than in one devoted to the powers of the owner. In general, one could observe that the owner cannot exercise his or her power to develop land by building on it unless (1) he or she obtains some sort of public authorization (usually from the municipality and usually by paying a fee), and (2) he or she remains within limits imposed on his or her property right by the rights of his or her neighbors.

The first limit, imposed everywhere by the public law, may be particularly intrusive and sometimes may frustrate the whole value of a given piece of property. Since, by its nature, public power to allow development of a given area is remarkably discretionary, legal systems may find it difficult to grant the owner appropriate legal remedies (i.e., both affordable and effective) against the arbitrary denial of building permission by the empowered authority.[16] However, the availability of these remedies is a crucial part of a system of private property since their lack may create the institutional framework for very extensive corruption.

This problem is at the core of what we discussed in our first chapter as the dialectic relationship between individual property rights and the state. Such a relationship is probably better mediated by courts that are, on the one hand, organs of the state but that are, on the other hand, aimed at the protection of individual rights. This is why doctrines such as sovereign immunity (protecting the public authority from being sued by private individuals) or separation of powers (granting immunity to the administration as one power of the state against the judiciary as another power) are extremely dangerous in this domain. Consequently, legal systems that strive for efficient developments and that wish to fight against corruption should get rid of these doctrines and allow the ordinary judicial process to review these kinds of limits to property rights. Of course, the standard of review should be reasonableness and due process, since some policy discretion ought to be maintained in administrative decision making on land development.[17] This does not mean that development rights should be granted free to the owner and that they are part of some natural content of property rights. On the contrary, the administrative process is in the best position to take account of the social costs that a given development project may impose on society; such social costs should be reflected in the price that the owner should pay in order to be allowed to carry on his or her development project. For example, if my project is to build a shopping mall on the outskirts of Budapest, I am likely to impose social costs, such as more traffic, more pollution, need of social infrastructures such as parking, and so on. The price of the administrative authorization should reflect these costs, otherwise private development is subsidized by the community.

The power to develop land, known in the civil law tradition as *ius aedificandi* and in common law as the development right, can be considered one of the most important economic incentives to acquire ownership over land. Indeed, land absorbs the intergenerational increase of value which is mostly created by developing activity. Building is the most important permanent transformation of land and of the environment, so it has never been (nor can be) considered an activity whose impact is internal to the owner's sphere. As a consequence, the owner's idiosyncratic decision making cannot be protected, since someone else pays the costs of it. Nor can building and development be considered activities easy to control by the general idea of reasonableness.[18]

Historically, land development has been controlled by a number of different factors: technological factors, to begin with, since building over the soil may require sophisticated technologies; physical-geographic and economic factors secondary, as crucial factors determining the feasibility of a given development project; and legal and institutional factors third, since the problem of regulating land use arises only when such a use is possible in the first place. All modern legal systems use a double set of institutional controls over proposed activities that may permanently modify land. The first institutional control (both historically and structurally) is the use of a decentralized system. The system exploits each owners' self-interested monitoring activity over his or her neighbors' land use that may negatively affect the owner's property value. When this decentralized private law system proves ineffective because neighboring owners strike deals that do not take care of the more general picture (one neighbor may "bribe" the other to tolerate a polluting activity that has a more general impact), legal systems tend to introduce a collective public law system of land use controls.[19] In this case, administrative or political bodies, such as municipalities, decide which developments can be carried on and which cannot.

The two systems of development activity controls, or this double system of limits imposed on the *ius aedificandi* (in the private and in the public interest), are the consequence of the following factors: (1) the scarce and limited nature of resources and (2) the subjection of property rights to the sovereignty of the state. From point 1 it follows that all the powers that are granted to one owner necessarily conflict with those granted to another. From point 2 it follows that the owner, or any other member of society, can carry on only those activities that do not conflict with a politically legitimized rule.[20] Moreover, as a consequence of point 1, it follows that powers stemming from ownership may be correlated to subjections to other owners' powers: Each owner may have to accept consequences of other owners' choices that are symmetrical with his or her power. As a further consequence of point 2, it follows that sometimes the owner's power is reduced to the mere possibility of submitting an application for a given activity (i.e., building), with the further consequence that whenever such application is not filed (or until it is accepted) the activity is considered unlawful per se.

It is important to maintain that these observations apply to the whole Western legal tradition, without structural distinction between common law and civil law. What varies from one legal system to another is the number of choices that are allocated to the decentralized (courts) or to the collective system (administrative agencies).[21] The difference in the scope of respective decision-making power is itself determined by traditional factors that normative policy analysis should critically evaluate.

From this perspective, one should observe that public law decision making by means of collective regulatory tools should approach property rights realistically, as modeled by the conflicting rights of ownership and by the decentralized private law system. Consequently, it would be a mistake—indeed, a mistake all too common in the civil law tradition—for the public law regulator to decide, as if in the absence of its own decision making, that property rights were completely absolute and unrestricted. In order to make this point clear I will first describe the limits to property rights as determined by the existence of conflicting rights of ownership and uses of scarce resources.

LIMITS TO PROPERTY RIGHTS DUE TO INCOMPATIBLE USES IN GENERAL

The fundamental subjection to which property rights are exposed is due to incompatible activities that, while disturbing the owner, are insufficient to obtain for him or her a legal remedy. For example, if my bedroom is open on the main street of a big town, my utility stemming from quiet sleep may be limited. Yet most of the time this limit to my taking full pleasure from the enjoyment of my apartment is not cured by the legal system. The diminution in my utility coming from the incompatible activities of car drivers is not sufficiently serious, most of the time, to provide me with a legal remedy.[22] In general, a judge is called upon to make a decision whenever two property rights conflict because of incompatible desires over land use. Of course, if the conflicting owners have been able to work out a private deal which can solve the problem, the judge is not called upon to decide.[23]

Examples of such incompatible uses are easy to imagine. Avigdor loves to use his apartment to meditate in relaxed peace and Christopher likes to use his neighboring loft to drink vodka and listen to grunge music with fifteen friends (emissions of noise). Avigdor loves to enjoy the scent of the flowers in his garden and Christopher likes to barbecue pork right on the other side of the fence (emissions of smell).

Avigdor hangs his clean laundry outside, while Christopher digs in the ash of his fireplace (emissions of dirt). Avigdor loves to contemplate his collection of very fragile crystals from Samarcanda and Christopher establishes a business involving substantial ground drilling (emissions of shaking). All of the mentioned incompatible activities are traditional examples of emissions in the civil law tradition which can be considered nuisance in the common law. Some other cases, which would still be considered nuisances in the common law, may be not considered emissions in civil law, since they do not match with the idea of an invasion of physical boundaries of the land. The essence of the problem is, however, the same, and the following cases can also be seen as imposing a subjection over a property right. Avigdor may like to invite the members of a traditional kosher group for tea, while Christopher may like to post heavy pornographic materials on his windows visible from Avigdor's front door. Christopher may impair the pleasure that Avigdor takes from his garden by managing a golf club with the correlated risk of destruction due to the poor quality of the members' shots.[24] Some other incompatible uses are recent, such as those between radio frequencies or between orbits of satellites. Others may be very ancient and may have consequently developed a different autonomous taxonomy that keeps them outside of the core of the law of nuisance. Examples may be buildings or plantations that shadow the sun or incompatible uses of water.[25]

MINIMAL DISTANCES AND OTHER EX ANTE RULES

In theory, two models to handle these conflicts are possible. One possibility is to physically separate the domains of the different rights of ownership and then guarantee to each owner full protection within these physical limits. Such a physical separation may be possible in a number of cases (e.g., emissions of noise), but may require a high level of technology and overinvestments in separating property rights. The other model consists of acknowledging the practical impossibility of complete physical separation in our overcrowded world and consequently creating legal tools to monitor reciprocal influences.

Obviously, the first model is coherent with the absolute, airtight conception of property rights typical of the civil law tradition with its roots in Roman law, as received by the natural law model and emphatically codified in the first part of Article 544 of the Napoleonic Code. Concretely, this model is based on a detailed regime on distances among buildings, walls, trees, fences, specified activities, and so on. It is a system of clear rules as opposed to a system of standards, such as that enshrined in notions of reasonable use.[26] It is no surprise, as a consequence, that the Napoleonic Code, heavily incorporating the naturalistic conception, does not contain any general discipline of nuisance (or emissions, as the civilians call them), while containing a staggering number of detailed provisions attempting to physically separate rights of ownership. Obviously, legal scholarship and case law had to take care of the resulting lacunae, so that case law developments have worked out the theories of *troubles de voisinage* and of *abus du droit*. The textual tools used in such developments have been Article 1382 of the Napoleonic Code containing the general tort provision,[27] and Article 1384, which contains a provision of strict liability for custody of one thing. However, the first provision created problems because it is difficult to find fault in most of the incompatible uses that we have described. In other words, Avigdor is a nuisance for Christopher as much as Christopher is a nuisance for Avigdor.[28] Both are exercising their right to take pleasure from property. Both are claiming exclusivity in their domain. The second provision, although taking care of the objective nature of the conflict over scarce resources by using a standard of strict liability rather than of negligence, forced judges to acrobatic interpretations, since it was obviously drafted to take care of different problems. This is why French case law, although developing the idea that each owner is liable only for those emissions which are higher than "normal" neighboring inconveniences, has never identified one, unified textual basis for its decision making.[29]

It is important to observe that the model of physical separation is not as favorable to property rights as it may appear by its coherence with the natural law philosophy. Indeed, in practice such a model cannot be developed outside of a very thick layer of public law regulatory activity, which may end up creating (as it did in France) an alternative public law decision-making process that most of the time undermines the control of the owners involved in the dispute.

Since it is impossible to foresee at the moment of codification all possible conflicts that may arise in real life, the solution must be the development of administrative regulations that will require ex ante authorization of whatever it is possible to do within a given property. At the same time, an immunity for the owner who respects this regulation is created within the sphere so circumscribed. Any violation of conflicting property rights that is created by an activity duly allowed by administrative law becomes legally irrelevant, and forces the affected owner to accept it without any legal remedy.[30] Evidence of the unfriendly attitude toward property rights that this model ends up creating in practice is the reluctance that French courts show to grant the remedy of injunctions, preferring either damages or the coercive imposition of technical devices to solve the problem. This attitude could not be developed if the responsibility of the judge were not weakened by the competing centralized decision making of the public law. As shown by the French evolution (and a similar phenomenon is also apparent in Italy), the theory of absolute, airtight property rights can be sustained only at the price of considering irrelevant from the perspective of the judicial process most negative externalities.

EX POST STANDARDS: REASONABLE USE

At the opposite extreme, one can find a model that approaches the problems of incompatible uses within a conception of property rights as nonairtight entities. This model inverts the perspective and considers emissions, nuisances, and incompatible activities the rule rather than the exception; the physiology rather than the pathology of land use.[31] Within this conception, the legal system does not attempt to separate the domain of each right of ownership, but rather monitors the reasonableness of the reciprocal interference. In other words, the law uses a standard (e.g., buildings must be at reasonable distance from each other) rather than a rule (no building within three meters from the boundary). This model finds its historical appearance in the common law of nuisance. The perspective shifts from the object of the conflict (the owner's sphere) to the behavior creating the conflict; from Avigdor's and Christopher's property rights to the comparative reasonableness of their behavior. The question asked is not whether Christopher has violated Avigdor's sovereignty sphere. The question is, given the circumstances, is it more reasonable to post porn pictures or to invite kosher people? Is it more reasonable to keep exotic flowers or to manage a golf course? It is not by chance that the common law of nuisance is part of the law of tort and not of property.[32] This perspective obviously does not preclude a consideration of the sacrifice imposed on the opposed ownership in evaluating the reasonableness of the behavior. Not only will the court consider what it is reasonable to do in one's apartment, but also what it is reasonable to force your neighbor to take. Possibly both the behavior of meditating in the apartment and that of drinking vodka with fifteen friends listening to good music are reasonable. The difference may be what kind of suffering one activity imposes on the other and whether it is reasonable to insist on imposing it, given the circumstances.[33] In other words, in focusing on liability rather than on property, one gives up the assumption of the existence of a sphere of individual sovereignty to protect. One also gives up the notion of a general ban on *immissio in alienum*. The tort of nuisance is merely one tool that courts can use to offer private law remedies which guarantee the ordered organization of society and limit antisocial behaviors involving and not involving owners.

Such monitoring in terms of reasonableness is carried on within only one circuit of decision making, the ordinary judicial process, and does not defer to different circuits of decision making, such as the public administration.[34] Ex ante authorization by public law does not make a behavior that in fact imposes unreasonable burdens on the neighbors less unreasonable than other behaviors. Public law ordinances, such as zoning, for example, may guide the judge to decide what is reasonable given the circumstances, but do not confer any immunity that may affect the conflicting property rights. Contrary to what may appear, a model which is not based on an absolute, airtight conception of property rights ends up, in practice, to be more respectful of them.

EMISSIONS

An intermediate position between the extremes of (1) attempting to seal up the boundaries or (2) focusing on the reasonableness of the activities is followed by a number of the more modern codifications, notably the German, Swiss, and Italian.[35] Such codes reflect the suggestions of the famous German jurist Rudof Von Jehring, who developed, in the late part of the nineteenth century, the so-called "balancing of interests" approach.[36] Nuisances are approached within the proprietary framework of the emissions. However, the logical conflict created by the absolute conception of ownership, both on the passive side (the airtight conception of ownership as a protected individual sphere) and on the active side (ownership as freedom of enterprise and activity), is resolved by a sort of unifying theory of property and tort. In this approach, not all emissions are banned, only those that are beyond a certain standard of acceptability or reasonableness. The boundaries of property rights, in other words, are made flexible. Modern codes following this approach do maintain specific boundaries measures, but accept the idea that, while it is possible to specify in detail the distance between trees, plantations, and buildings, it is not as easy to specify boundary measures between activities whose impact by nature is variable.[37]

The proprietary framework is not a mere taxonomic choice without practical impact. Decision making within the proprietary framework avoids the analogical extension of the flexible nature of property rights to other rights of a nonproprietary nature (such as health) that the law may want to protect, whatever the balance of interests might be. The relationship between land owners is clearly economic and this should determine the solution of conflict. According to this approach, the conflict between Avigdor and Christopher is not a conflict between two different philosophies of existence that necessarily have to live beside each other. The proprietary framework shows that it is a conflict over scarce resources, a conflict on the boundaries of property, and should be solved as such. The assumption is that the loser of the conflict can always find his or her agency of protection in the market. If he or she does not like the neighborhood and does not accept the boundaries of his or her property rights as determined by bargaining or by the court, he or she can always sell his or her property and move away.[38]

While these implications clearly follow from the proprietary framework, they would not follow from the traditional thinking about tort, where the decision in terms of right and wrong carries different social implications. In the common law, given the tradition of specific different torts and a very different meaning of analogical reasoning, no one would extend the contingencies of nuisance to trespass or negligence. In contrast, in the civil law with the different, "atypical" tradition, classifying nuisances within the tort system could open the risk of extension of the balancing approach beyond patrimonial rights.

If we are interested, as we are, in describing the law in action rather than the form of the law, we should mention that, in practice, the intermediate approach is followed by all modern legal systems, including French law and the common law, despite the extreme taxonomic choices described in the previous sections. Convergence is shown by the following observation. In England and the United States, while the tort of nuisance shows somewhat of an imperialistic nature in conforming property rights, the allocation ex ante of development rights by a zoning ordinance introduces a strong presumption of reasonableness of a building activity which conforms to the ordinance. Even in France, the underlying notion introduced by the fundamental relationship between administrative law and private law makes the concessions of development rights granted, "keeping safe the rights of third parties"; if violations of conflicting property rights turn out to be too macroscopic, the judicial process may end up reviewing the grant. In conclusion, one can observe that, in practice, property rights in all modern legal systems are framed by a number of decision-making agencies. Assuming that these rights are free from liability and obligations if not regulated by public law is a mistake.[39]

INCOMPATIBLE USES: SOME ECONOMIC ANALYSIS AND A THEORETICAL FRAMEWORK

Emissions arise from a problem that has long been studied in economics. This problem is known as the "noncomplete separability" of property rights. When property rights are not clearly separable, externalities arise. As a consequence, efficiency decreases.[40] This is because the utility of one individual (the amount of pleasure that he or she can receive from his or her property) is affected by the behavior of another individual outside of a market transaction. In legal terms, we say that the right of an individual is impaired by the behavior of another member of the society without agreement of the holder of the right.

Economists consider the problem of imperfect separability as a consequence of the public nature of certain goods. Public goods are, for economists, resources whose consumption is not rival, in the sense that one individual using them will not affect a similar use by another individual.[41] While Avigdor's consumption of a dish of spaghetti (a private good) makes it impossible for Christopher to eat the same spaghetti, Avigdor's use of a lighthouse (a public good) while sailing on the high seas will not preclude the same use in the same moment by Christopher. Given the conditions discussed in Chapter 1 devoted to the tragedy of the commons, if everybody can use free a resource because it is impossible to exclude everybody else from its use, nobody will have incentives to pay the cost of it. The result will be that the public good will not be supplied by the market. A similarly structured economic problem arises whenever one individual can use a resource and have the cost of his or her use paid by all the other members of the society. It is easy to spot the similarity with the problem of an industrial activity polluting the environment. Clean air has characteristics of public good.[42]

The problem of emissions is due to the fact that in the real world (the one jurists have to worry about) most things are not perfectly private goods (as the spaghetti of our example) nor perfectly public goods (as the lighthouse or military defense). Most goods fall within intermediate categories. The use of one property right usually does not completely end within the owner's sphere. It usually affects, at least in part, its neighbors. Exclusion is usually only partially possible. It is often impossible to completely exclude rivals. And it is usually impossible to imagine a commodity whose consumption is completely nonrival. Indeed, even clean air shows aspects of rivalry in consumption. It is very difficult to imagine resources that are not at all scarce. Of course, certain goods, such as a pint of milk or a pen, are clearly private in the economic sense. Nevertheless, in the use of land, where the most important human activities are carried on, problems due to the noncomplete separability of property rights continuously happen.

From the economic perspective, it is consequently the goal of property law, and in particular of the discipline of emissions, to create conditions as similar as possible to those of full separability. These are the conditions in which efficiency will be served.[43] The obvious similarity between the problems that the jurist faces when dealing with emissions and those faced by economists in the domain of separability of property rights should be enough to make an interdisciplinary approach unavoidable in this area. This explains why, for more than thirty years on both sides of the Atlantic Ocean, the best scholarly efforts to understand property rights have relied on economic tools. Even outside this scholarly approach, it is important to mention that both the texts of many modern codes, such as the German, the Swiss, and the

Italian, as well as case law in common law countries and in France, expressly require the judge to balance the economic interests of the conflicting parties in dealing with problems of emissions.

THE RELATIVE NATURE OF EMISSIONS

We have already observed that common law countries use the idea of reasonableness in limiting land use. Reasonableness is a very flexible notion, and is concretely applied by both focusing on what it is reasonable to do and what it is reasonable to require your neighbor to suffer. In other words, both the activity of the defendant and the property right of the plaintiff impaired by the activity are considered in deciding on reasonableness. It will not be necessary here to go into much detail to see a similar approach at work in civil law systems. For example, the German Civil Code states, at paragraph 906, "The land owner cannot oppose the emissions of gas, steams, smell, fumes, heat, noise, shakes, or other actions coming from another land if such emissions do not affect or affect only lightly the enjoyment of his land or it is the product of a land use that can be considered normal given the local conditions and the uses of similar land." Similarly, Article 844 of the Italian Civil Code states, "The owner of land cannot preclude emissions of smoke, heat, fumes, noises, shaking or similar nuisances coming from the neighbor's land if they do not overcome normal acceptability, considered the conditions of the place."

The notion of normal emissions shows the break within the civil law tradition of the airtight notion of ownership as a sphere of individual sovereignty. The judge and not the idiosyncratic desire of each owner has the power to establish if a behavior affecting ownership is permitted or not. While usually it is the owner who can say to someone "stay out of my property" without having to provide any reason for his or her desire to exclude (sovereignty of will), in the case of emissions such decision making is taken away from the owner.[44] This discipline establishes an amount of violation of the "sovereignty of will" that is considered legally permissible. The judge's power actually models and determines ex post the boundaries of property rights. The judge decides on the limits, and traces the line between property rights. By his or her drafting of property rights, the judge has the power to solve in principle all externality problems.

The criteria by which the judge is empowered to do so are relative and, by their nature, very flexible. Since the decision is ex post and not ex ante (as when the limits are drafted in meters and centimeters directly in the code or in a regulation), in drafting the limits between property rights the judge can consider all the information that comes from the actual controversy. His or her reasoning does not have to be abstract, but may actually be concrete. The actual conditions of the place are therefore crucial in the decision making. To be sure, what is reasonable in an industrial area of the town or in a red light district may not be acceptable in the quiet atmosphere of a residential neighborhood. Also, what is reasonable at certain hours of the day may be unreasonable at certain hours in the night. In all legal systems, a number of other conditions are also considered: What may be reasonable during winter months when windows are kept closed may not be reasonable during summer months when windows are open. It is amazing how common the law is in this domain.[45]

FIRST COME, FIRST SERVED: COMING TO THE NUISANCE

Another aspect that one would think relevant in deciding on reasonableness is the priority of a given use. This idea can be captured by the maxim "first come, first served," or by the Latin *"prior in tempus potior in ius."* In the common law, the notion is called "coming to the nuisance." Within this notion, no remedy is given if the plaintiff has voluntarily exposed himself or herself to the nuisance. If Avigdor knows that on Christopher's windows there are pornographic pictures or that Christopher's pigs produce smell or noise and nevertheless he moves nearby the property to establish his own incompatible activity (a kosher club or a collection of perfumed flowers), he should probably not receive a protection. Christopher was there earlier and it seems fair that his decision making is respected. Such a rule is coherent with the needs of social stability, and it seems easy to apply it in practice. When Avigdor buys land in order to establish his activity it is likely that he will go around the garden to look at what his neighbors are doing. The existence of Christopher's pig barn as well as all other factors affecting the value of the house (as the location of the home nearby or away from shops) will probably be reflected in the market price of the house or at least will be considered during the bargaining process. It would therefore be reasonable for the judge to use a doctrine such as first come, first served in order to discourage litigation and to stimulate careful bargaining over property rights.[46]

Obviously, such a notion is not itself rigid. Nor can it be the only one that the judge should consider in deciding the boundaries of property rights. This appears also from other areas of the law, where the rule of first come, first served plays a role. For example, while the rule is based on the legal discipline of "original" acquisition of title over treasure or over abandoned objects and some products of nature, it finds a general limit in its nonapplicability to things already belonging to someone else.[47] Similarly, this idea can be used in the decision on reasonableness without making it the only rule of decision. To be sure, if it was the only rule of decision it would protect an absolute monopoly of the first individual who arrives in a given place to decide forever what it is reasonable to do there. The law does not want to protect such a monopoly, since other uses of the land may later be discovered that may be more efficient and that cannot be precluded by the absolute protection of the first use. The fear of such a kind of monopoly may be the reason why despite the language of some code provisions mentioning the priority of a given use (e.g., Article 844 of the Italian Civil Code), and despite the early conceptualization of coming to the nuisance provided by Blackstone in his *Commentaries on the Laws of England*, legal systems seem reluctant to give to the judge the power to consider the priority of a given use in the process of applying the criteria of reasonableness.[48]

At least one significant recent American leading case, however, has revitalized such doctrine. In *Spur v. Del Webb*,[49] coming to the nuisance was used to protect a pig-feeding lot against the harsh consequences of having to close down because of the smell which affected a nearby village that was subsequently developed nearby. The unease that Western law shows about coming to the nuisance can be explained by the plurality of economic rationales that can be found for this rule, and by the difficulty of figuring out which one is to be preferred on policy grounds.

To begin with, first come, first served has a clear function of providing an incentive to invest. The first investor in development receives a sort of insurance that subsequent investors will not affect his or her return by forcing him or her to change activity. Abraham invests to bring infrastructures to a remote mountain village in the Urals. He faces considerable expense in persuading various utility companies to supply clean water, electricity, and phone lines. He does so in order to open a restaurant with an outside patio. Mauro, profiting by the existence of the infrastructures, remodels the nearby abandoned dachia of his grandfather. Shortly after, he sues Abraham, claiming that the noise from the patio disturbs him in his attempts to produce a publishable novel. The example could also be inverted, with Mauro remodeling the dachia first and Abraham building the restaurant later. The rule of first come, first served grants to the investor in infrastructure a right that (within reasonable limits) his or her choice of the standards of a given area will be protected by the law. While in a case such as this the development incentives of the first-come, first-served rule are clear (no one would develop knowing that he or she will not be allowed to do what he or she is developing for), it is also clear that if this monopoly is interpreted in too strict a way it will affect future developments and uses. Again, coming to the nuisance should be one of the aspects that are considered in a sound balancing of interests, but it cannot be the only one.[50]

INDUSTRIAL EMISSIONS

Sometimes an activity is not considered to be unreasonable because it is productive. Indeed, the evolution of nuisance law that has accompanied economic development through the industrial revolution has relied on this idea to shelter industrial production from the need to pay its social costs.[51] Obviously, this political option is open, but it may be questionable whether courts are the better agencies to apply it. It should be clear that if productivity is the only aspect that the judge considers in his or her balancing activity, his or her exercise will be severely biased in favor of industrial production. As has been pointed out by many observers of a number of different legal systems, such decision making will always favor the stronger interest against the weaker and, by so doing, in the long run will destroy any effective protection of property rights. The paradigmatic conflict is that between a large polluting industrial factory which employs hundreds of workers and the residential neighbors that try to protect the enjoyment of their property rights (for example, to hang the laundry outside) against that incompatible activity. Deciding this conflict is very delicate. On one hand, justice will require that the neighbors are protected if the nuisance imposes on them an unreasonable suffering (which seems to be the case). On the other hand, it is hard to consider industrial activity as unreasonable, particularly when one wishes to promote economic development.

From the economic perspective, if residential neighbors are left without a remedy they are put in a situation of subsidizing the factory by giving to it some inputs of its production (clean air and value of land) for free. Indeed, in order for the factory to produce without creating external costs it would be necessary to acquire more land around it and possibly to install some system of pollution control. All of these are inputs of the production process, and if the factory does not have to pay for them, such a factory will produce an inefficiently high output at the expense of its neighbors and of the collectivity in general. Modern legal systems have realized that if such a subsidy is to be granted to industrial production in order, for example, to safeguard the employment rate, it should not be granted randomly by its neighbors but should be granted by the whole collectivity by means of tax exemptions or similar direct devices.

Consequently, in the domain of industrial pollution, modern legal systems have tried to help the judge in this difficult balancing exercise (for which he or she may be ill equipped) by dividing up the decision making into two steps. In step one, the judge, focusing on the plaintiff's property right, will decide whether its violation is reasonable. In the case it is considered unreasonable, instead of enjoining it by granting an injunctive protection to the plaintiff's ownership, the judge will proceed to the following step. The judge will evaluate whether, given the productive nature of the emission, he or she should grant a different remedy that short of enjoining the activity, will only compensate the victims of it for their losses. If the judge decides for the productive nature of the emission, he or she may then grant only a sum of money as damages or impose some sort of technological device to limit emissions: a remedy, in other words, that while maintaining the productive activity does not make the neighbors pay for it.[52] By so doing, the industrial activity is internalizing its externalities. Efficiency and justice are consequently served. One should notice that, within this decision-making process, the private parties to the controversy are effectively representing more general interests than the conflict between incompatible uses of private property. Plaintiffs are acting also as attorneys for the environment (a public good difficult otherwise to represent in court), while the defendant industry is acting also as attorney for capitalistic development and employment. Consequently, it is natural that the second step in the decision making is carried on with only the public interest in mind. Property of the factory's neighbors is expropriated by denying it the property rule protection if the public interest so requires. As always, however, expropriation in the public interest requires just compensation that, in this case, is the function of damages.

More generally, however, one can see a principle at play in all modern legal systems. When the activity disturbing a property right is of a productive nature, protection of ownership may be reduced in favor of the productive activity. Consequently, ownership has to accept a higher degree of invasion.[53]

OTHER LIMITS IN THE INTEREST OF NEIGHBORS

Nuisance law is not the only source of limits and obligations attached to property rights in the interest of neighbors. A number of other traditional limitations are contained in the civil codes and in the common law to limit dangerous activities.[54] Not only does the owner become strictly responsible for damages stemming from the dangerous activities, but the neighbor can insist to have them carried on at a safe distance from his or her land.[55] Moreover, a number of rules are dictated as far as the distance of buildings is concerned. Sometimes the distance is counted from the boundaries of property (as in France), sometimes from building to building (as in Italy).[56] When this is the model, usually the first owner that builds limits the options that are open to the following owner.[57] A number of rules are devoted to making sure that both owners participate in the expenses of the common parts of buildings or are subject to the duty to maintain any common building, such as a wall that divides the properties.[58] Other rules are devoted to safeguarding the privacy in each home by imposing, for example, some restrictions on opening of windows or the like. These rules are intimately local in their nature, are usually customary, and often vary from place to place to a considerable extent. In modern law, moreover, they have been supplanted in various ways by mandatory public law regulations that may establish minimal distances between buildings or other strict requirements for health or security reasons. It would be well beyond our purpose here to offer any detail of this occasionally very complicated legal discipline whose local character makes it difficult to describe, let alone to find common principles. Again, in general, one can only observe that, unless interests of third parties are involved, these rules should be considered default rules that individuals should be able to bargain around. If bargaining fails, probably the only principle that could offer some guidance to the judge is the need to limit externalities in the interest of justice and efficiency. Make everybody pay his or her share. Do not make a neighbor pay the costs of activities whose benefits are enjoyed by another one.

GENERAL LIABILITIES

So far, the limits to property that we have described (except those prescribed by public law) show a clearly reciprocal nature. Owners cannot do something in the interest of each other such that whether the situation actually advantages or disadvantages the particular owner depends only on what he or she actually desires to do with his or her right. In other words, limits in the interest of each other can either be considered an advantage or a disadvantage of ownership according to the concrete fact situations.[59]

However, ownership sometimes carries with it obligations that are not reciprocal but that are just passive. No owner is actually advantaged by them. Every self-interested owner would rather be free from them. These obligations may advantage either the general public or the state. The kind of obligations that I am about to briefly describe affect the very value of property (particularly immovable) as a long-run investment. They can be seen as the most important real-world confutation of the equation that ownership equals freedom. Because of these kinds of obligations, the owner simply cannot acquire the property and then avoid any further expenses related to it, hoping to capitalize on increase of value. These aspects of the structure of ownership impose on owners active duties, usually to pay significant amounts of money, that may effectively preclude them from keeping their property completely idle. In other words there is a constant, although sometimes limited, further investment of resources that are needed to remain the owner. Such investments are not (only) required by the nature of property, but are actually required by the law. The German Constitution, as we have already seen, is the only one between the legal systems analyzed thus far that explicitly states, "ownership obliges." This, of course, does not mean that the following general observations only apply to German law.[60]

To begin with, immovable property as well as vehicle ownership carries with it a large share of liabilities toward the general public or toward the owner's tenants. In most legal systems, there is a quasi-strict liability regime applied to the owner for damages created by the collapse of his or her building. The burden of proof he or she must meet in order to escape liability is so high that it practically coincides with full strict liability.[61] In a number of systems which have followed a traditional, Roman law rule, there is, moreover, a regime of strict liability for damages created by objects falling or thrown out of property, such as plants falling from the windows and similar events.[62] Some systems do require negligence and classify all of this under tort law, but the fact remains that a number of presumptions make it difficult for the owner to escape many liabilities. For example, in a number of systems the owner is liable for damages occurring to people on his or her property. Some systems even extend liability for injury to children trespassers. All of these liabilities affect the prospective value of a piece of property and can be easily quantified in the cost of a homeowner insurance policy.

TAXES

The second most significant source of obligations is also traditionally outside the domain of property law, but it is crucial to mention it here. The "negative" aspects of ownership stemming from liability are indeed minimal if compared with the tax liability that stems from owning property. This important aspect of ownership affects the rational choice of a self-interested individual facing the choice of acquiring property. Traditionally, however, the legal discourse has been fragmented, so tax law is usually not considered a structural part of property law. This specialization may be acceptable, but it would be a mistake of realism not to consider taxes when discussing property rights and privatization on policy grounds. For example, a fiscal system that allows deduction of interest paid on mortgages is used in the United States as a powerful weapon to free up for investments capital that otherwise would be used to buy (without mortgage) unproductive dwelling property. In other systems, the tax pressure on immovable property may be so high that self-interested individuals prefer not to own.

Obviously, immovable property may be easier to tax than movable because it is easier to localize. In 1086, registrars of immovables (known as the Domesday Books) were organized in England. This early function of immovable property as the main fiscal target may have been justified historically by the fact that land used to be the most important source of wealth. Today, the nature of most important wealth may not be land and other kinds of property; particularly, stocks or information may be much more important. Obviously, the fiscal system, aimed as it is to target wealth whatever may be its source, has to be affected by this change in the nature of its most important source. It will not be sufficient to know how land is distributed among individuals to have a fair proxy of how wealth is distributed in society. In other words, the structural connection between land and taxes should become less strict. This does not mean that the fiscal pressure on immovables lessens. It just means that immovable property moves from being itself the taxed estate to become one of the many structurally different assets of which an estate is made. Property, as a consequence, is not thought of by tax scholars as an autonomous notion. Thus it becomes very difficult to map all the different obligations that tax law imposes on property rights, so scholarship on property is usually unrealistic because of an insufficient grasp on the tax aspects of it. Nevertheless, from a tax law perspective, there is a structural difference of immovable property that makes the distinction between immovables and other property rights somewhat confirmed. Immovable property is indeed the asset more difficult to hide. Consequently, it is cheaper for the state to tax immovable property. The more a tax system is unsophisticated, the more it will only be able to tax the more visible aspects of wealth. The more a financial policy is tottering and the political situation of a country is unstable, the more there will be sudden "emergency" financial needs for the state.

Property is usually taxed according to two different schemes. To begin with, any exercise of the powers that are part of the property right may be targeted. The assumption is that each exercise of an owner's power corresponds to an increase of wealth and may be taxed. According to this model, the following are taxed: transfers of property rights (both movables and immovables), transformations of property rights that require an authorization from the state (e.g., building activity), and partial transfers of property rights, such as leases. Of course, on policy grounds one should consider that taxing an activity means reducing its frequency, so that overtaxing may preclude the growth of a thriving market.

Another model of taxation directly hits ownership, independent from its use. Obviously, there are many justifications for taxing property rights in this way, particularly immovable property. The state, by means of the police, sells protection to owners and should be paid for it. Obviously, in modern states such taxes are by no means accounted in connection with state protection but are merely a function of the needs of the state. Moreover, property (particularly immovable and luxury property, such as sports cars, racehorses, etc.) is targeted as a proxy of the wealth of the owner, so that in a progressive fiscal system redistribution can easily occur by taxing it.[63]

NOTES

1. See discussion in U. Mattei, *Comparative Law and Economics* 33 (1997).
2. See R. Ellickson, *Alternatives to Zoning: Covenants, Nuisance Rules and Fines as Land Use Controls*, 40 *U. Chi. L. Rev.* 68 (1973).
3. See the collection of data contained in F. Lawson & B. Markesinis, *Tortious Liability for Unintentional Harm in the Common Law and in the Civil Law* (1982).
4. See U. Mattei, *Immissioni*, in 10 *Digesto Discipline Privatistiche, Sez. Civile* 311 (1993). For a comparative discussion pointing at common principles, see J. Gordley, *Nuisance in Comparative Perspective*, in 1 *Z. Eu. P.* 13 (1998).
5. These provisions are reproduced and discussed in R. B. Schlesinger et al., *Comparative Law* (6th ed., 1998).
6. See W. N. Hohfeld, *Fundamental Legal Conceptions as Applied in Legal Reasoning and Other Legal Essays* (1919).
7. See A. M. Honoré, *Ownership*, in *Oxford Essays on Jurisprudence* (A. G. Guest ed., 1961).
8. See A. Gambaro, *Abuse of Right in Civil Law*, in *Aequitas and Equity* 375 (A. M. Rabello ed., 1994).
9. See M. Planiol, *Traité elementaire de droit civil* 269–271 (2d ed., 1900).
10. See P. G. Monateri, *Abuso del diritto e simmetria della proprietà (un saggio di comparative law and economics)* in 3 *Diritto Privato* 89 (1997).
11. See the leading French case, Clement-Bayard, Cass. Civ. Aug. 3, 1915, D. 1917 I 705 (spiteful fences to endanger take off and landing of flying balloons).
12. See, however, J. B. Ames, *How Far an Act May Be a Tort Because of the Wrongful Motive of the Actor*, 18 *Harv. L. Rev.* 411 (1905).
13. See *supra* Chapter 2.
14. See K. Zweigert & H. Kotz, *Introduction to Comparative Law* 595 (3d ed., 1998).
15. For an introduction to the much discussed issue of the comparative efficiency of rules and standards, see R. A. Posner, *Economic Analysis of Law* 590 (5th ed., 1998). For a perspective specifically devoted to property law, see C. Rose, *Chrystals and Muds in Property Law*, 40 *Stan. L. Rev.* 577 (1988).
16. See, generally, B. A. Ackerman, *Private Property and the Constitution* (1977).
17. See N. K. Komesar, *Imperfect Alternatives* 123 (1995).
18. See A. Gambaro, *Ius aedificandi e nozione civilistica della proprietà* (1976).
19. See Mattei, *supra* note 1, at 58.

20. See F. S. Cohen, *Dialogue on Private Property*, 9 *Rutgers L. Rev.* 357 (1954).
21. See Schlesinger et al., *supra* note 5, at 539.
22. The seminal framework to study incompatible uses is G. Calabresi & D. Melamed, *Property Rules, Liability Rules, Inalienability: One View of the Cathedral*, 85 *Harv. L. Rev.* 1089 (1972).
23. See *supra* Chapter 3.
24. For some conceptual problems created by this kind of exposure to the risk, one can see R. A. Buckley, *Cricket and the Law of Nuisance*, *Mod. L. Rev.* 334 (1978).
25. See S. M. Cherin, *Casting a Shadow on a Solar Collector: A Cause of Action Recognized, An Alternative Resolution Framework Suggested*, 68 *Cornell L. Rev.* 941 (1983).
26. See J. P. Blaise, *Responsabilité et obligations coutumières dans les rapports de voisinage*, in *Rev. Trim. Droit Civ.* 261 (1965).
27. "Any action that by fault creates a damage obliges the tortfeasor to pay them."
28. This is the fundamental contribution of R. Coase, *The Problem of Social Costs*, 3 *J.L. & Econ.* 1 (1960).
29. See A. Weill et al., *Droit civil, les biens* 264 (3d ed., 1985).
30. In France, a law of 1810 regulating the so-called *établissements incommodes ou insalubres* has shielded polluting activities respectful of standards required by law from liability toward neighbors. See Gambaro, *supra* note 18, at 146.
31. See J. Smith, *Reasonable Use as Justification for Damage to a Neighbor*, 17 *Colum. L. Rev.* 383 (1917).
32. See Lawson & Markesinis, *supra* note 3.
33. See W. L. Prosser & P. Keeton, *Prosser and Keeton on the Law of Torts* 616 (1984).
34. See Ellickson, *supra* note 2.
35. Paragraph 906, BGB; Article 648, C. Civ.; Article 844, C.C.
36. See R. Jehring, *Zur Lehre von den Beshränchungen der Grundeigeitumers im Interesse der Nachbarn*, in 2 *Jahr. Für die Dogmatik des heutigen romishen und deutshen Privatrechts* (1892).
37. For example, while paragraph 906, BGB, is devoted to emissions, paragraphs 912–924 introduce specific, ex ante distances.
38. See M. Polinsky, *Resolving Nuisance Disputes: The Simple Economics of Injunctive and Damage Remedies*, 32 *Stan. L. Rev.* 1075 (1980).
39. Convergence is detected also by Gordley, *supra* note 4.
40. See R. Cooter & T. Ulen, *Law and Economics* (2d ed., 1996).
41. See *supra* Chapter 1.
42. See A. Ogus & G. Richardson, *Economics and Environment*, *Cambridge L.J.* 284 (1977).
43. See Posner, *supra* note 15, at 55.
44. This limit to the power to exclude objectively acceptable behavior can be seen as a way to avoid a possible tragedy of the anticommons. See M. A. Heller, *The Tragedy of the Anticommons*, 111 *Harv. L. Rev.* 625 (1998).
45. See, for England and the United States, respectively, Vol. 34 *Halsbury's Laws of England* 315–336 (Lord Hailsham ed., 4th ed., 1980); 66 *Corpus Iuris*

Secundum 546–563 (1998); for German law, see Munchener, *Kommentar BGB IV* 547 (2d ed., 1986). For French law, see cases discussed in M. A. Robert, *Biens et droits réels*, in 6 *Dalloz* 55, 60–62 (1998); for Italian law, see U. Mattei, *Tutela Inibitoria e Tutela Risarcitoria* 345 (1987).

46. See D. Wittman, *First Come First Served: An Economic Analysis of Coming to the Nuisance*, 9 *J. Legal Stud.* 557 (1980).

47. See *supra* Chapter 6.

48. See J. D. Ingram, *Coming to the Nuisance: Nor Shall Private Property Taken Without . . .*, 5 *N. Ill. U. L. Rev.* 181 (1985).

49. 494 P 2d 700.

50. A convergence in denying recognition to the first-come, first-served principle in nuisance law is detected by Gordley, *supra* note 4.

51. See P. M. Kurtz, *Nineteenth Century Antientrepreneurial Nuisance Injunctions: Avoiding the Chancellor*, 17 *Wm. & Mary L. Rev.* 621 (1976); for the English experience, see J.P.S. Mc Laren, *Nuisance Law and the Industrial Revolution: Some Lessons from Social History*, 3 *Oxford J. Legal Stud.* 186 (1983); J. F. Brenner, *Nuisance Law and the Industrial Revolution*, 3 *J. Legal Stud.* 403 (1974).

52. See the leading American case, *Boomer v. Atlantic Cement Co.*, 257 N.E. 2d 870; Italian case law interpreting Article 844 within the same two-step process is discussed in A. Gambaro, *Il diritto di proprietà* 515 (1995).

53. See J. Carbonnier, *Droit Civil, Les Biens* 278 (14th ed., 1991).

54. Article 890, C.C.; Article 674 of the Napoleonic Code.

55. See *Rylands v. Fletcher* 159 Eng. Rep. 737, 3H & C774 (Exch 1865); materials and discussion in Lawson & Markesinis, *supra* note 3.

56. See Article 674 of the Napoleonic Code and the discussion in Weill et al., *supra* note 29, at 246.

57. As to Italian law, within a prisoner's dilemma model, see U. Mattei, *La proprietà immobiliare* 170 (1983).

58. See Article 653 of the Napoleonic Code; Article 874, C. Civ.

59. See Monateri, *supra* note 10.

60. See Horn et al., *German Private and Commercial Law* 172 (1982), discussing "freedom and duty" as the "two poles of ownership."

61. Article 2053, C. Civ.; 1386 Code Nar; 836–838 BGB; In all these legal systems case law is stricter to defendant owner than the text of the codes might allow.

62. See Schlesinger et al., *supra* note 5, at 251, citing relevant sources (including Blackstone).

63. For a general discussion of real estate taxes in a similar perspective, see Posner, *supra* note 15, at 529.

CHAPTER 8

Remedies

Property law, far from being confined to an abstract set of principles and rules, is rooted in institutions that may or may not be able to enforce those rules. These institutions vary greatly between legal systems, both across the common law–civil law dichotomy and within each of the two families. One must concentrate on the concrete set of remedies available in court, because markets are not affected by what is written in the law: What matters is the law as it is applied.[1] From this standpoint, an important difference still exists between common law and civil law, although some convergences are visible.[2] Common law countries, particularly the United States, have developed a system of property law inspired by remedial creativity administered by courts of law concerned with policy issues. Civil law courts, on the other hand, have been less effective. Their legal reasoning tends to be formalistic. Their organization into a double set of courts, administrative as well as ordinary, seems to introduce useless complication and a tendency on the part of ordinary judges to avoid policy-oriented decision making by claiming that such responsibility belongs to the jurisdiction of administrative law. On normative grounds, the common law approach seems preferable.[3]

Remedial devices, such as injunctions (both mandatory and negative), *astreintes* (developed by French case law as a limited civilian counterpart of contempt power), and interlocutory orders are precious devices for the purpose of creating an efficient system of justice. It is certainly more important to develop them than a perfectly worded code which lacks concrete infrastructures. Given the high variety of possible concrete infrastructures, in this section I will proceed at a somewhat higher theoretical level to show some structural aspects of property law enforcement.

GENERAL BACKGROUND

As we have seen, every property right in a modern legal organization is deeply limited, either directly by means of ad hoc regulation (usually in the form of administrative regulation), or indirectly by the need to protect opposing rights and interests. Under the latter, we could clearly observe in the domain of the law of nuisance that an easy way to put the owner down in his or her indifference curve (i.e., making him or her worse off) is simply to deny the owner a remedy against a neighbor whose activity affects the value of his or her property. In such a case, the judge is redistributing wealth from one party to another and in extreme cases such a redistribution is not structurally different from a taking or expropriation. This similarity shows that the value of a property right derives from the concrete availability of remedies to enforce the right against opposing behaviors. A legal right needs to be accompanied by a concrete set of remedies to be effective, regardless of the rhetoric surrounding it or the level of the text in which it is incorporated. For example, a constitutional right to a pure environment is ineffective if devoid of a system to quantify environmental damages or absent standing devices that allow individuals to claim it.[4]

To guarantee individuals the exclusive enjoyment of certain resources, property law has developed and assigned its own enforcement mechanisms to different machineries of justice. Western legal tradition has developed almost entirely around the protection of property rights. For a long time, the only rights that could be claimed in court had a direct or indirect proprietary character. This is true of both the common law and the civil law.[5] Only in a moment relatively close to our days have individual rights without a proprietary nature started to claim legal recognition from the point of view of the remedies available to protect them.[6]

As a consequence of this very old origin, it is precisely within the domain of property law that the Western legal tradition has been able to develop and test the higher variety of remedial devices available against a great variety of aggressions or risks. The result is a rich and complex remedial typology which the owner is always entitled to use but which sometimes is open also to the possessor; namely, a nonowner appearing as an owner. The civil law tradition has consequently developed a dual scheme of possessory and proprietary remedies. The common law, being more pragmatic and less abstract, has not developed proprietary remedies. This is because possessory remedies are perfectly functional substitutes for proprietary remedies if one seeks to effectively protect the distribution of property rights in society.

POSSESSORY AND PROPRIETARY REMEDIES

Within a realistic taxonomy, possession is to be considered a property right. Sometimes, as already discussed, the possessor's right is to be considered antagonistic toward ownership. Possession can win against ownership.[7] Functionally, the possessor is a particularly efficient individual in a scheme of decentralized, proprietary decision making. Indeed, he or she is guided by a double set of incentives in the protection of his or her right against externalities: He or she wishes to enjoy the benefits of his or her property right and wishes to avoid responsibility toward the owner in case the latter should claim his or her right and prevail.

Possession and ownership are typically in the hands of the same individual. In this case, the relationship between possession and ownership no longer is conflicting, but is to be considered as cooperative. Protecting possession is, for the owner in possession of his or her property, a functional equivalent of protecting ownership. This is why common law systems do not distinguish possessory and proprietary remedies. Moreover, in the civil law tradition, usually the protection of possession rather than that of property is easier for the plaintiff. Consequently, in civil law possessory actions also end up being functionally more important than proprietary ones.

All legal systems share the principle of protecting with great generosity the individual who physically controls a piece of property against dispossession, disregarding the legal title that justifies such physical control. As the reader may remember, such protection is also open against the owner. This is an instance in which the same principle works both in favor of ownership to facilitate its protection (in the usual cases in which the owner is also possessor) and against it when the owner tries to protect his or her right by measures of self-help.

In France, although the Napoleonic Code is silent on the point, case law and commentators have always used an action called *reintegrade,* which was statutorily adopted in 1971. In Germany, the so-called *Besitzenziehunganspruch* is contained in the BGB, paragraph 861. In Italy, Article 1168 of the Codice Civile introduces an action called *reintegrazione*. In the common law, one can choose between actions of trespass or ejectment, which are both part of the law of tort and actionable per se without the need to show actual damage. It is interesting to observe that in all legal systems such actions are open not only against violent dispossession but also possibly against any activity that dispossesses against the desire of the possessor. Such protection of possession seems to have a tortious nature (as is explicit in common law), reacting against a questionable behavior of the defendant without much regard to the legal status of the plaintiff.[8] Legal systems introduce relatively short limits within which the dispossessed must claim his or her right in court.[9]

Interestingly, in less urgent and dramatic events than dispossession, legal systems also show remarkably common principles at play. They all agree that the possessor should be protected, not only against dispossession but also against behaviors of the defendant that merely disturb his or her quiet enjoyment of property. They all agree in being less liberal in granting protection to possession in this case. To be protected against mere disturbances of quiet enjoyment, possession should have been peacefully enjoyed for a while. Property should not have been acquired violently or in some other way which could have given rise to an action against dispossession.

In France, the action is called *complainte* and is contained in Article 2282 of the Code Civil. In Germany, paragraph 862 of the BGB offers to the disturbed possessor the *Besitzordnungsanspruch*. In Italy, as in France, where possession should have been enjoyed quietly for one year, Article 1170 of the Codice Civile offers to the plaintiff an action called *manutenzione*. In common law, in the absence of a distinction between actions to protect ownership and possession, it is again the law of tort that contains the action of nuisance.[10]

The burden of proof is easier in possessory actions than in proprietary ones, although the results can be exactly the same, (i.e., the recovery of possession or the quiet enjoyment of property). Thus, the rational owner will use possessory actions whenever possible, rather than the more complicated proprietary ones that we will discuss later. He or she will use proprietary actions only when possessory ones are precluded, as when, for example, he or she has allowed a year to elapse without reacting. Clearly this is more likely to happen in the case of disturbances to quiet enjoyment. Such disturbances could appear bearable to the owner at the beginning, while unbearable at a latter stage when the possessory action has already been precluded.[11]

Another interesting structural observation is that while in the case of immovables both kinds of actions are conceivable and available, in the case of movables both the structure of property and variations in different legal systems conspire to make it more difficult to describe a common core in property law. It may be difficult to conceive of the idea of physically recovering possession of immaterial property, let alone of disturbances to the enjoyment of a piece of movable property not amounting to dispossession. Such problems should not be exaggerated. While an action of nuisance is, for example, conceived and phrased with immovable property in mind, and the same is true as far as the Italian *manutenzione* is concerned, it is unlikely that legal systems would not grant remedies to protect personal property against disturbances if there are damages. A common core can still be found in the law of tort.

Generally, one can observe that while in practice possessory remedies cooperate with proprietary ones in the protection of the owner most of the time, as institutional devices they compete with proprietary remedies. The more that one category of remedies is successful and used by plaintiffs, the more the other one will be depressed. One can therefore end this section by retaining two notions: (1) the existence of legal systems in which the dual set of proprietary versus possessory remedies is absent (common law), and (2) the general principle of rationality by which legal systems should avoid complications created by useless and costly institutional duplications. Both of these notions show the need to keep a unified interpretation of proprietary and possessory actions as remedies to protect property rights.

FORWARD-LOOKING AND BACKWARD-LOOKING REMEDIES

The complex and varied remedies that an individual can use to protect his or her property right can be classified in various ways. To begin with, remedies can be grouped according to the institutional actor that has the power to grant or refuse to grant the remedial device. We may then talk about private law remedies, criminal law remedies, and administrative law remedies to protect property rights. Within the first group we can find damages in their different forms, injunctions, declaratory judgments, and actions to recover possession. In the second group we find criminal prosecution to protect property rights against intentionally inflicted damages, such as theft or embezzlement or forcible entry into someone else's home. Among administrative remedies we can find all those which can be granted by different administrative bodies; for example, administrative sanctions against someone who permits a dog to trespass onto someone else's land or against someone who illegally parks a car in front of a private driveway.[12]

Remedies may alternatively be grouped according to the nature of the behavior or the factual situation that calls on their use. We may talk about civil, criminal, or administrative remedies to recover possession. Such alternatives remedy the physical loss of control of property. We may talk about remedies for quiet enjoyment (again, civil, criminal, or administrative), employed in the case of nuisances. Or we may talk about declaratory remedies reacting against uncertainty.[13] Obviously, the content and even the possibility to use these and other possible classifications (such as the already discussed one between possessory and proprietary remedies) are linked to concrete structural differences between different legal systems. Therefore, we may be better off classifying remedies according to less contingent criteria.

From the functional and economic perspectives, the key distinction is that between forward-looking and backward-looking remedies.[14]

Backward-looking remedies are aimed at reestablishing the holder of the property right on the indifference curve from which the course of action he or she is complaining about has removed him or her. This is achieved by means of a monetary equivalent or by imposing on the defendant a given behavior that directly recreates the ex ante situation. Forward-looking remedies are aimed at avoiding the future occurrence of a given violation of the property right and impose certain duties of abstention or affirmative duties of precaution before the damage occurs. We could say that backward-looking remedies react against a damage, while forward-looking remedies react against a risk. This remedial taxonomy has developed in common law countries and is less familiar to civilian jurists. In common law countries, where the development of the law has been driven by incremental adaptation to evolving economic needs, certain remedies that look at the past allow recovery for damages, while others that look to the future try to avoid damage by imposing certain precautionary burdens on the defendant.[15] In the common law, injunctions have historically been developed as a consequence of the insufficiency of the damage remedy, which was the only available remedy until the development of the Chancery Court in the fifteenth century.[16] This historical evolution evidences an important economic truth. Injunctions as forward-looking remedies offer to the property-right holder something more than remedies that only look to the past. It is common sense to observe that preventing a mischief is better than trying to cure it once it has happened.

PROTECTION OF TITLE AND PROTECTION OF ENJOYMENT

The complex set of remedial devices that the law offers to the owner can be divided into two main categories. The first is when an individual attempts to substitute himself or herself for another in the enjoyment of property. A typical case would be that of a squatter who, profiting by the absence of the owner, occupies the latter's home and behaves as if he or she has title to live there. The intensity of the squatter's claim can change from case to case. Sometimes the squatter may claim to be the owner himself or herself, while at other times he or she may claim to have a different title (e.g., a contractual agreement) that justifies his or her dwelling there. A less extreme example of someone claiming someone else's ownership is that of the neighboring owner who does not accept the present boundaries separating two lots of property. The real owner enjoys a plurality of remedies to protect his or her property. These different remedies may vary in their requirements and may be more or less burdensome, and as a consequence more or less costly, in terms of proof. Some remedies may be contractual in nature (e.g., against the tenant who does not want to vacate the apartment); others may be based on possession. Finally, some may require the claimant to show the actual absolute title to ownership. Usually there is a direct relationship between the impact on third parties of the right that the plaintiff claims and the difficulty of proving such right. From this perspective one can see a continuum between the ease by which contractual remedies can be used and the difficulty in proving outright ownership in those systems that require absolute proof (civil law).[17]

The second set of remedies does not react against an attempted usurpation of the property right but aims at protecting tranquillity of enjoyment. In these cases, the owner is not dispossessed but is the victim of someone else's behavior which affects either the market value or the idiosyncratic value of his or her property right. In the first case, my neighbor may engage in an activity that directly affects my property. He may produce some polluting emissions that affect the objective attractiveness and consequently the market value of my property. In the second case, my neighbor may offend my personal taste by, for example, posting pornographic pictures visible from my property when I invite for tea the members of a "family values" club to which I belong. Such remedies may react against a nuisance in fact or in law. My neighbor can engage in barbecuing that affects my property with smelly fumes, or he may claim the existence of a servitude to ride through my garden on his horse in order to reach the countryside behind it.[18]

Again, these remedies can be based on different substantive prerequisites. Also, in this case it is not always necessary to prove ownership. Possession, and sometimes even a contractual title to enjoy the property, such as a lease, may be enough to grant access to the courts. As we have already discussed, however, possession in these cases needs to be qualified. In civil law systems that do not consider the lease as a property right, the tenant must usually ask his or her landlord to use remedies to grant the tenant indirect protection if the nuisance comes from a third party. This cumbersome solution is faithful to the notion that a contract does not grant rights and obligations external to the parties involved therein. However, it has become increasingly frequent to find in the rules related to residential leases a statutory exception to this principle. In this way, the tenant may have direct action to protect his or her enjoyment of the property.

The remedial typology that I have just discussed can be found in most legal systems, with major variations as far as technicalities and details are concerned. When such technicalities bar access to courts, they may disrupt property rights. The general principle that there are no rights without remedies, or that each right should have a corresponding remedy to make it effective, falls short of being applied in practice in many systems of law. Therefore, it is important to briefly describe an institutional background for the remedial protection of property rights.

EFFECTIVENESS OF REMEDIES

The principle of effectiveness under which each right has its own remedy is common throughout the Western legal tradition, but its concrete meaning changes according to the structure of the legal process.[19] A major difference exists between common law and civil law systems in this respect. While the common law judge, thanks to the high standing of case law between the sources of law, is free to create the remedial devices that he or she thinks more fit for the concrete problem that he or she faces, the judge's civil law colleague does not enjoy a comparable degree of freedom. The civil law judge is constrained by the formal, ex ante provision in a statute (usually one of the codes), of a remedy that fits the situation he or she is facing. If an ex ante formally recognized remedy is not available, as a matter of theory the judge is not entitled to create it. Of course, the gap between jurisprudential theory and practical reality is such that in practice the civilian judge can be remarkably creative in the domain of remedies.[20] Nevertheless, in the everyday working of the law this theoretical limitation is felt, and the average civil law judge always has available the possibility of bureaucratic reasoning to deny the concrete enforcement of a right. On many occasions, given the aging of the codes, he or she can grant efficacy to legal rights only by forcing the interpretation of a statute. It is easy for the judge to refuse to do so. Not rarely may the civil law plaintiff consequently discover after the costs and troubles of litigation that he or she enjoys a legal right only in theory. This is particularly true when the defendant is a public law entity.

The common law is easy and straightforward. A property right has been protected since the fifteenth century by means of an injunction whenever the remedy of damages is considered not enough to guarantee the effectiveness of a property right.[21] An injunction is a so-called equitable remedy and it is in the discretion of the judge not only to grant or refuse it, but also to decide what content to give to his or her injunction. An injunction can be described as a judicial order against the defendant that compels him or her to do or abstain from doing something. In the case of an order to do something (e.g., to give back the property to the plaintiff, destroy the fixture that he or she has unlawfully built, build a device to reduce the emission of fumes in the plaintiff's land, etc.), the injunction is called mandatory. In the case of an order to abstain from doing something (e.g., not emitting fumes in the plaintiff's land, not parking a car in front of plaintiff's driveway, etc.), the injunction is called prohibitory. The injunction may be the ultimate and final remedy that the plaintiff can get after a full trial, or it may be an order to do or not to do something while the trial is pending. In this second case it is called an interlocutory injunction.

The power of injunction gives to the judge a remarkably flexible tool to fulfill any possible remedial need. It is also a very strong and effective tool. Indeed, the injunction is backed by a quasi-criminal sanction known as contempt of court. Should the defendant not obey the order, the judge has the power to send him or her to jail or otherwise to submit him or her to a progressive fine that increases with the passing of time.[22] Many civilian systems, most notably the French and the Italian, have objected to the use of contempt of court on the ground that the criminal law should not contaminate the civil litigation process. This objection is easy to answer, because, as the common lawyers would say, the defendant may go to jail (which almost never happens in practice), but he or she holds the keys in his or her pocket. Indeed, he or she can get out at any moment by obeying the order.

More generally, civil law systems do not have available a single remedy like the injunction to protect the property right. They have to rely on a plurality of different remedies. The structure of the civilian law of remedies is not based on injunction-like *in personam* orders from the court to the defendant. Civilians, acting within a more state-centered mentality, rely on the so-called principle of subrogation.[23] According to this idea, in the case in which a property-right violation is judicially established, it will be the machinery of justice itself that will remedy the violation by means of an ad hoc official procedure of substitution of the uncooperative defendant. Such a system, introduced by Articles 1143 and 1144 of the French Code (and by accompanying provisions of the Civil Procedure Code), is followed both by Articles 2931 and 2933 of the Italian Codice Civile (and accompanying provisions of the Code of Civil Procedure) and by paragraphs 883 to 887 of the German Code of Civil Procedure. Each remedial device in civil law countries is usually described by the codes and takes care of predefined fact situations.[24]

Typically, one would find a distinction between an obligation to do and an obligation not to do. In the case of most violations of property rights, the subrogation system is as effective as the common law system of injunctions. Some comparative law scholars even consider the civilian approach more effective in the case (not very realistic indeed) in which the common law defendant under contempt would rather stay in jail than respect the property right.[25] In any event, in cases such as the construction of a wall on someone else's land that should be removed, or such as the lack of positive action from the defendant (e.g., building a retaining wall to avoid collapses on someone else's land), or in the case in which a movable property should be delivered, or in which a contract for the sale of land should be registered, the subrogation system does not create many problems. The court will respectively encourage a contractor under judicial protection to do the job (build or destroy the wall) at the defendant's expense, or the sheriff will be allowed to dispossess the defendant and to make the delivery, or the contract will be registered or treated as registered. Indeed, since the subrogation procedure is a very costly default rule for the defendant (he or she will have to pay large sums as judicial expenses), chances are that he or she will end up doing the job or negotiating with the plaintiff in order to have the latter do it in a cheaper way. This is an elementary application of the Coase theorem that shows that the parties will negotiate among themselves a more efficient solution should both stand to gain from it (for example, in building or destroying a wall the condemned defendant will pay less and the plaintiff will have the job done sooner if they reach an agreement after the court's decision).[26]

The problems for the civilian model arise in the case in which the defendant is ordered to do something special that he or she is the only one capable of doing (e.g., a painting or a particular architectural project) or when he or she is ordered not to do something (e.g., stop emitting smoke in my property). In this case, the principle of subrogation will not help, and the idea that the civil justice system should be kept clear of intrusion from noncivil measures results in an unfair advantage to the defendant. Indeed, under Article 1142 of the Napoleonic Code all unperformed obligations to do or not to do will be resolved by ordering the payment of damages. This reduces subrogation to an exception and is incompatible with a system of formalized property rights. As we already know, damages are remedial devices that can protect an interest but not a property right.[27] Particularly in the absence of punitive damages, the defendant who is willing and able to pay would be allowed to change his or her trespass (building an unauthorized wall on an owner's land) into a servitude. He or she will be able to keep the fruits of the wrong committed, provided he or she pays for it.

This is the reason why the German Code of Civil Procedure is less friendly to the defendant than the Franco-Italian model. Under Sections 888 and 890 of the German Code of Civil Procedure, a violation of a duty to abstain from doing, or of a duty to do something that cannot be performed by a third party, will have as a consequence either a severe fine or a term of criminal detention (without the keys in one's pocket).[28]

The need for effective protection of property rights in such cases has induced the slow and piecemeal evolution of Italian and French law. For example, the Italian legal system grants the judge a special power of issuing urgent interlocutory orders to avoid irreparable injustice during the long time that is necessary to litigate. By forcing such a device offered by Article 700 of the Code of Civil Procedure, and by exploiting its connection with Article 388 of the Criminal Code, Italian judges have apparently succeeded in sometimes doing surreptitiously what their common law colleagues could have done openly.[29] Similarly, French courts, restrained by the principle that damages cannot exceed the value of the violation (this is the civil law refusal of punitive damages), have created by pure case law a type of contempt power called *astreinte*. *Astreinte* allows damages to grow in amount for each day of delay in reestablishing the situation preceding the violation (e.g., destroying an encroachment). This case law creation, which has now been adopted by statute and is admired by other civil law systems, is possibly the best evidence of how the civilian system's use of a multiple set of special protective remedies rather than a general power of injunction is an irrational device that should be abandoned.[30] There is a need for effectiveness in the protection of property rights so that judges will pursue ways to issue remedies regardless of the wording of the statutes or the structure of the procedure. It is much better to allow them to do it openly, as in common law, and to assume upon themselves the responsibility that this power should carry with it.

PROPERTY RULE

As the reader will recall, a property right must be protected by a property rule; namely, an effective protection against any behavior which is not ex ante authorized by the owner.[31] A different kind of remedy cannot be considered as a protection of a property right but only as the protection of an interest. In common law, injunctions are the paradigm of the property rule. They can be granted under the judge's discretion whenever he or she thinks the particular facts require this degree of protection.

Moreover, the pragmatic nature of the common law judge and the structure of judicial lawmaking both render the judicial decision on the protection of property rights a comparative exercise. The judge will decide who of the two individuals competing over a scarce resource has comparatively better title and will protect him or her accordingly. No statement is entered in an absolute way. It may well be that the winner who has a comparatively better title today will lose tomorrow should his or her property right be challenged by someone else whose title is comparatively better. This relative nature of the protection of property rights gives concrete meaning to the principle that in common law there are no proprietary remedies but only possessory remedies. Remedial creativity and pragmatic decision making are encouraged by the structure of the common law legal process.[32]

In the civil law tradition the whole picture is more complicated, not only because of the disparate and piecemeal variety of remedial devices that I have briefly described in the previous section, but also because of a divorce between substantive and remedial law that has characterized the evolution of a legal system dominated by the abstract reasoning of law professors.[33] In civil law systems, academic lawyers have focused on the definition of ownership as an absolute and abstract category. Under this logic, protection should follow as a matter of course. Furthermore, the concrete problems that arise because of the need of the plaintiff to offer absolute and conclusive evidence of his or her ownership are largely neglected by the traditional disregard of remedial devices. Civilian judges find themselves in the uncomfortable position of having available code provisions and legal treatises that neglect the remedial aspects of rights. The same sources require them not to invent any remedy but only to apply the law. It is paradoxical to observe that the Napoleonic Code, possibly the most influential code in the civil law orbit, has no provision regarding actions to protect ownership, either against dispossession or against nuisances. Following the logic of condescending disregard toward remedial devices, remedies should flow from rights. Unfortunately, this simplistic attitude does not reflect the law in practice. Most of the time the very job of the judge is to create or reframe property rights by granting or denying different kinds of remedies.

For the civilian jurist it is obvious that evidence of an absolute right should not be comparative but, instead, absolute. And an absolute right such as ownership, of course, should receive an absolute and complete protection. Such protection is traditionally organized in two different actions: the so-called "negatory action," open to the owner against whomever is disturbing him or her in the enjoyment of his or her property, and the *rei vindicatio*, an action that allows him or her to recover possession against any nonowner in possession of the property.[34]

Protection of Ownership Against Dispossession

A fundamental aspect of any property right is that the owner should be able to recover the physical control of his or her property if someone takes it away from him or her. As we have already discussed, this proprietary protection coexists with possessory actions and with personal contractual actions to recover a thing, all of which can be seen as its functional equivalents which are simpler and cheaper to use in court.

In the case where the owner acts in his or her proprietary capacity (typically when the other actions are precluded to him or her for different reasons) and not as possessor or as party to a contract (say, against the tenant who does not vacate the property after the expiration of his or her term), the owner must use an action that corresponds to the Roman *rei vindicatio*, literally, "action to claim a thing."[35] Such an action is unknown in the common law tradition that only uses possessory action. The *rei vindicatio* is the paradigm of the absolute nature of ownership and of the general duty to abstain from taking possession of anything without the consent of the owner. Its theoretical interest stems more from this nature than from its practical utility.

The *rei vindicatio* comes directly from the Roman law. However, in the evolution of Western law it has merged in various ways with German customary actions which protected *Gewere* or *saisine* (i.e., the right to possess).[36] Of course, the more the Germanistic possessory protection is equated to the title to ownership (as in French movable property), the less important the *rei vindicatio* becomes. The triumph of the Germanic notion of *saisine* explains at the same time the absence of proprietary actions in the common law world as well as the most significant divergence of rules related to immovable and movable property in the civil law tradition. In the following section we will discuss in some detail the rules related to immovable property, since the discussion of those related to movables has already been offered in a previous chapter.

Among the modern codes, the French one fails to devote a section to the protection of property rights in general, and to the *rei vindicatio* in particular. However, scholars and courts have always acted as if this action was disciplined by considering that it followed as a matter of course from the very definition of ownership, while modeling its details on the German-inspired *coutumes* (the written customary law of Northern France). The consequence of this lack of a specific code provision is that French law converges with the common law in making proof of ownership a comparative exercise of choosing the party that has the better title to possession.[37]

The German BGB codifies at Section 985 the general power of the owner to obtain the property back from the possessor. Modern German law follows the Romanistic tradition and requires absolute proof of ownership.[38] It is not satisfied by the mere showing of a better title to possess. The same is true in Italian law, where Article 948 of the Codice Civile requires the plaintiff to offer full evidence of his or her right to ownership.[39] In the absence of a system of land registration as reliable as the German *Grundbuch*, where in practice each entry is evidence of ownership, this burden of proof is particularly hard to meet. Strictly speaking, evidence of ownership can only be produced by showing an "original" acquisition. Any derivative acquisition (i.e., any title acquired after a transfer from another individual) is not enough to prove ownership. As we already know, the transferor could have been a nonowner incapable of transferring a title that belongs to someone else. Consequently, whoever wants to produce final evidence of ownership must prove a continuous chain of transfers going back to the original acquisition of ownership. Of course, this does not mean going back to Adam and Eve. It will be enough to show a chain of transfers going back far enough to cover the term of adverse possession (as we know, twenty or thirty years, depending on the legal systems). This considerable burden is known among jurists under the Roman expression of *probatio diabolica*. In practice, the possibility of making use of a number of presumptions sometimes makes life easier for the plaintiff.[40]

The general principles governing the *rei vindicatio* can be summarized as follows. If someone substitutes his or her physical control over property to that of the owner, the latter can sue to have his or her ownership recognized and as a consequence to recover possession. In other words, the recovery of possession is only incidental to the judicial recognition of ownership, although it is the result each plaintiff ultimately desires. The burdensome mechanism of the *probatio diabolica* is not introduced only to penalize the plaintiff against a possessor that is already extensively protected by the law. Indeed, the absolute and automatic impact of the judicial recognition of ownership requires a mechanism that ensures that a third party who is neither the plaintiff nor the defendant is not the real owner. There are different means to reach this result (one of which is to organize a reliable land registration system) and the *probatio diabolica* is a way to privatize the costs of such organizational necessity.[41] Of course, judicial interpretation should consider the purpose of such evidentiary requirements. Even in Italy, where the tradition of the *probatio diabolica* is rather pedantically followed, the better-title system appears in the law in practice when both plaintiff and defendant claim to have received their title to ownership from the same individual. On all occasions on which it is certain that either the plaintiff or the defendant is the owner, the strict requirement of the *probatio diabolica* is a pedantic and wasteful exercise of bureaucratic judicial power.

The action to defend his or her title to possession can be exercised by the owner against whomever physically controls the property. If after the beginning of the action the defendant has parted with possession other than by giving back the property, the plaintiff can nonetheless pursue the action to recover possession against whomever is obliged to give the property back. Obviously, we can formulate two different hypotheses here. A first case is that in which the thing has been transferred to a third party. While we have already seen the rules in the case of movables (good faith of the third party, etc.),[42] in the case of immovable property, due to the fixed location of the land (or other immovable), the principle is merely aimed at relieving the plaintiff of the burden of starting a new action all over again against the new possessor. Technically different is the case in which possession cannot be recovered because it has been destroyed. In this case, the law has two possibilities, both of which require keeping the defendant in court. One is to force him or her to restore the ownership. The other is to use damage remedies. We will address the case of damages as a proprietary protection later in this chapter.

Protection of the Quiet Enjoyment of Property Rights

Another action of Roman origins, the *negatoria*, is available to the plaintiff when he or she is challenged in his or her right in a way other than by dispossession. The negatory action was also not codified by the French code, but French commentators and courts allow it as a general protection without spotting any problem.[43] Such an action can be considered the paradigm of the sphere of sovereignty that the law grants to the owner on his or her property. Nowadays the negatory action is codified by all of the more modern codes, including the Austrian, the German, and the Italian.

The negatory action is not only available to protect the owner, but is also available for the protection of other property rights, such as a servitude. Indeed, in the Roman law tradition the negatory action was called *negatoria servitutis* (i.e., an action granted to the owner to deny the existence of a servitude over his or her right). In other words, the civilian tradition introduced early the notion that any activity contrasting the use of ownership is structurally analogous to subjecting that ownership to a servitude, so that the owner who wishes to protect the quiet enjoyment of his or her property right should challenge the existence of the servitude.[44] To give an example, if my neighbor regularly trespasses my driveway with his car in order to park in his garage, his activity that bothers my quiet enjoyment corresponds to the exercise of a servitude. Indeed, should the law recognize his right to do so he would not be committing a trespass but would be exercising his property right (a servitude of passage). Given this structural reciprocity, we may imagine two scenarios. In the first one, I can be plaintiff and sue in order to deny my neighbor's servitude. In the second scenario, my neighbor may be the plaintiff claiming the recognition of his servitude (a property right) to drive on my property with the consequence that, for example, I would be precluded from fencing it. Consequently, the *actio negatoria* has split into two subactions: one for the protection of ownership and the other for the protection of servitudes. The most clear expression of this reciprocal idea can be found in the Austrian Code, where paragraph 523 states, "Regarding servitudes two actions are available, one that can be brought against the owner to claim a servitude, and one that the owner can bring against whomever claims a servitude." German law and Italian law discipline the two kinds of actions in separate code provisions.

As to the broad nature of the negatory action as the paradigm of the property-rule protection in civil law countries, the clearest and simplest provision can be found in German law. According to Section 1004 of the BGB, "If ownership is disturbed otherwise than by dispossession or refusal of restitution, the owner may obtain against the one who bothers his enjoyment the removal of the interference. If future prejudices are to be feared, the owner may obtain an injunction against their occurrence."[45] Italian law, despite the formulation used by Article 949 (and by correlated Article 1079) of the Codice Civile, evidences the broad nature of this action to offer an effective remedy against all sorts of possible aggressions to property rights, both as a matter of fact and as a matter of law.

The following typology of remedies is grounded in the civilian notion of a negatory action. First, the owner is protected not only against actual damages but also against the risk of damages. It is enough to fear a prejudice to the property right in order to claim a remedy. Such protection is granted through the civil law by a number of different special provisions, some of them also of Roman origin, which deserve special attention in a following section. The negatory action, however, can be considered the synthesis of such provisions, since it protects the property right against every kind of relevant risk exposure able to affect the value of the property.

Included in the negatory action is a declaratory action aimed at obtaining a judicial declaration of a given asset of property rights. Such a judicial statement on the boundaries of property rights should be final, valid against the whole world, and aimed at avoiding the prejudice that may stem from an unclear limit between proprietary spheres. The owner may have an interest in knowing whether his or her neighbor can legally cross his or her property with the car before engaging in the expenses of fencing the court. The clarity and certainty of property rights is a value that this action aims to protect.[46] In different legal systems of the civil law tradition this function of the negatory action is accompanied by other kinds of special actions aimed at clarifying the physical boundaries of the property. Again, however, nothing limits the declaratory action to physical extension of property rights; the negatory action is paradigmatic of the power to exclude granted to the owner.

The negatory action also includes injunctive relief against continuing prejudice to the property right. Such relief can be obtained against any kind of disturbance of an enjoyment that has continuous character. I may want to prevent my neighbor from parking on my driveway; I may want him enjoined against introducing smoke on my property. He may want the same against me, given the nature of competition over the scarce resource which is the source of our confrontation. This aspect shows how this action can be understood only in connection with a number of other provisions, the most important being those related to nuisances that introduce important exception to this rule. However, it is important to keep in mind that in the absence of special reasons to limit the protection of property rights, the full protection (negatory action being the paradigm of it) is the rule and the liability rule is only the exception. Of course, the law of nuisance needs special treatment.[47]

Finally, it is important to observe that, in the case where it is not enough to prevent the future course of action that affects the property rights, the negatory action is still effective. Damages and remedies specifically to redress the ex ante situation (e.g., destroying an encroachment) are in fact also included in it. As we have seen, their effectiveness can be impaired by the concrete machinery of justice as well as by a more doctrinal confusion with damages in tort that I will briefly address later. Here, it is necessary to spend more time on the different concrete applications of the general principle of full protection of property rights as contained in the negatory action.

DAMAGES

The remedial protection of the owner is complete.[48] Ownership needs to be protected against exposure to risk (e.g., negatory actions, trespass, other kind of special actions for exposure to risk codified in certain civil law countries, interlocutory injunctions, etc.). Ownership needs to be protected against uncertainty (e.g., declaratory actions, either specially codified as in Italy or France or offered, as in Germany, by interpretation of the negatory action and of the *rei vindicatio*; declaratory judgments in common law). Ownership needs to be returned when dispossession occurs (e.g., *rei vindicatio* in civil law; ejectment, conversion in common law).

At least in theory, if one disregards the costs and the discomfort of the need to use the judicial process to defend one's property right, such protection is able to return things to as they were. The exposure to the risk or the claim of a servitude stops. Possession is returned. The problem is that in real life the discomfort and other transaction costs may be rather substantial. Moreover, there may be cases in which the unlawful activity has created damage that for different reasons cannot be restored. A unique seventeenth-century chapel with paintings by Caravaggio may have been destroyed after dispossession of my country house in Tuscany. A continuous very noisy activity on my neighbor's land may have created cracks in my wall or may have caused the death of my beloved rabbits and chickens. My mother's wedding ring after dispossession may have been sold in the open market to a good-faith purchaser who has acquired ownership and as a consequence the ring cannot be returned to me.[49]

In such cases, the only possibility left for a legal system is to look at the past using its remedial apparatus to reestablish the ex ante situation as much as possible. In certain cases, as discussed in a previous section, it will still be possible to have the defendant act to correct his or her wrong (for example, by destroying an illegal wall or by rebuilding the cracked foundations of my house). In some other cases, however, restoring the ex ante situation is simply impossible (e.g., repainting a Caravaggio), is outside of the power of the defendant itself (the ownership of my mother's ring belongs now to a third party), or is so expensive as to make it unfair to the defendant and socially wasteful (e.g., finding my mother's ring which has been lost in the middle of the ocean after dispossession; restoring through the use of the most sophisticated technologies a painting by my six-year-old daughter Clara, ruined after dispossession, that has no market value but a very high value of affection to me).

In these cases, the law can only use monetary damages to protect property rights. One should observe, before briefly discussing the prerequisites for obtaining such a protection, that the law also uses damages to compensate the loss of a property right in a rather different situation. I am referring here to the situation where there is a perfectly established market of perfect substitutes for my property. This is the opposite of the destruction of my six-year-old daughter's painting example. In this case, the market works to solve any problem.[50] If I am dispossessed of a gallon of milk, a packet of cigarettes, or a currently produced appliance, the fact that a third party has acquired its ownership in good faith on the open market or that it has been lost in the deep ocean does not really matter. I will be exactly as well off if I receive a check for the price of it. Legal systems part company on this point, and the common law systems (and the French code) only allow damages as a remedy in this situation. Although other systems do not openly follow this path (the German and Italian Civil Codes emphatically proclaim the priority of specific remedies over damages), the result is exactly the same: The plaintiff will receive damages. It would be absurd (when not impossible) to waste money to pursue exactly one particular exemplary of a product easily available on the market.[51]

Consequently, damages are a rather important aspect of the protection of property rights. The structure and the requisites of damages as a proprietary remedy is very different from the structure of damages in tort law. Although torts are used to protect property rights when their violation is the consequence of faulty behavior (e.g., a car accident), and this overlap may create some confusion, one should be aware that damages as a proprietary remedy in cases in which no other protection is available (or in the case in which they better satisfy the purpose of specific protection) must be awarded outside of the requirements to recover in tort. If the violation of property rights is relevant and sufficient to allow a negatory action, a *rei vindicatio*, or an injunction to protect property, it must also be sufficient to allow damages in the case in which no other remedy better protects the plaintiff. In the case of the irreparable destruction of a unique thing or of the impossibility of returning a chattel because a third party has acquired it in good faith, or in the case of harm created by an activity that has been enjoined, damages must be awarded on a strictly objective basis, without any regard to the nature of the activity that has created them. Damages in this case supplement proprietary protection. The owner, by obtaining damages in lieu of a better form of proprietary protection (e.g., injunctive relief), is granted an idiosyncratic and purely subjective protection. Indeed, it is very difficult for damages to fully compensate the owner, given the fact that, having been awarded by a court, they will necessarily try to make the harm objective without reflecting the subjective value of the harm.[52]

Of course, it would be absurd to say that any violation of ownership needs to be protected objectively. The different domains of tort law and property law are, however, rather clear. In a case such as a car accident or other accidental destruction of property, there is no increase in one's property right at the expense of another. Hence, it makes common sense to look into the law of torts (with its subjective requirements) to find the solution. In a case where damages are awarded as a substitute for injunctive relief from the activity producing the damages (or a negatory action in civil law), or in cases where damages substitute for the impossibility of recovering possession, there is a clear conflict between proprietary spheres. The defendant has claimed or exercised a property right belonging to the plaintiff. If the owner–plaintiff successfully resists this claim, he or she needs to be protected with the full arsenal of remedies that are available in the legal system. A different solution would give a property right to the defendant. Of course, such cases are not rare in the law, particularly in the already discussed domain of the law of nuisance.[53]

NOTES

1. To be more precise, what matters are credible signals contained in the law. Signals contained in the law, however, only affect market actors if there are reasonable possibilities that they will be applied in practice. See R. Cooter & T. Ulen, *Law and Economics* (2d ed., 1996).

2. See, in general, R. B. Schlesinger et al., *Comparative Law* 379 (4th ed., 1998).

3. A classic comparative discussion is contained in A. H. Pekelis, *Legal Techniques and Legal Ideologies*, 41 *Mich. L. Rev.* 665 (1943). Some of the deep differences that were pointed out by the author are today attenuated because of phenomena of convergence. See, specifically, Schlesinger et al., *supra* note 2, at 743.

4. The most interesting and theoretically challenging study in the field is still B. Ackerman et al., *The Uncertain Search for Environmental Quality* (1974). More recently, stressing the role of courts as policy makers, see S. Rose Ackerman, *Controlling Environmental Policy: The Limits of Public Law in Germany and the United States* (1995).

5. See H. J. Berman, *Law and Revolution* (1983).

6. According to O. Fiss, *Injunctions* 2 (1973), the notion of property right "is so manipulated as to include any interest worthy of judicial protection."

7. See *supra* Chapter 5.

8. See J. Gordley & U. Mattei, *Protecting Possession*, 44 *Am. J. Comp. L.* 293 (1996).

9. The classic comparative work is A. Gambaro, *La legittimazione passiva alle azione possessorie* (1979).

10. See the general discussion *supra* Chapter 7.

11. See R. Sacco, *Il Possesso* (1988).

12. F. H. Lawson, *Remedies of English Law* 257 (2d ed., 1980), groups together criminal and administrative remedies under the label "non judicial remedies."

13. *Id.* at 231.

14. See Cooter & Ulen, *supra* note 1.

15. See D. Dobbs, *Handbook on the Law of Remedies: Damages, Equity, Restitution* (2d ed., 1993).

16. See T.F.T. Plucknett, *A Concise History of the Common Law* 171 (5th ed., 1956).

17. See S. Ferreri, *Le azioni reipersecutorie in diritto comparato* (1989).

18. These are the kind of remedies mostly focused on in the seminal article by G. Calabresi & D. Melamed, *Property Rules, Liability Rules, Inalienability: One View of the Cathedral*, 85 *Harv. L. Rev.* 1089 (1972).

19. See Pekelis, *supra* note 3.

20. A major example can be found in the French law: With the judicial creation of the *astreinte*, a judge made contempt power then recognized by statute. See J. Beardsley, *Compelling Contract Performance in France*, 1 *Hastings Int'l & Comp. L. Rev.* 93 (1977).

21. See Fiss, *supra* note 6.

22. See D. Dobbs, *Contempt of Court: A Survey*, 56 *Cornell L. Rev.* 183 (1971); a classic historical discussion is in J. C. Fox, *The History of Contempt of Court: The Form of Trial and the Mode of Punishment* (1927).

23. See, generally, M. Damaska, *The Faces of Justice and State Authority* (1986).

24. See N. Horn et al., *German Private and Commercial Law* 58 (1982).

25. See C. Cremonini, *An Italian Lawyer Looks at Civil Contempt: From Rome to Glastonbury*, 3 *Civ. Just. Q.* 133 (1984).

26. See R. Coase, *The Problem of Social Cost*, 3 *J.L. & Econ.* 1 (1960).

27. See *supra* Chapter 6.
28. See W. Heyde, *The Administration of Justice in the Federal Republic of Germany* (1971); the relevant provisions are translated and discussed in Schlesinger et al., *supra* note 2, at 741–742.
29. See U. Mattei, *Tutela inibitoria e tutela risarcitoria* 260 (1987).
30. See Beardsley, *supra* note 20.
31. See Calabresi & Melamed, *supra* note 18.
32. See K. Zweigert & H. Kotz, *An Introduction to Comparative Law* 256 (3d ed., 1998).
33. See J. P. Dawson, *The Oracles of the Law* (1968).
34. See G. Hohloch, *Die Negatorishen Ansprüche und ihre Beziehungen zum Schadensersatzrecht* (1976).
35. See A. Watson, *The Law of Property in the Later Roman Republic* (1968).
36. See A. M. Patault, *Introduction historique au droit des biens* 17 (1989).
37. See Ferreri, *supra* note 17.
38. See J. Staudingers, *BGB Kommentar* Sects. 985–1011 (K. H. Grunsky ed., 11th ed., 1993) 9–102.
39. See A. Gambaro, *Il diritto di proprietà* 871 (1995).
40. See Sacco, *supra* note 11.
41. The German registration system is described in Horn et al., *supra* note 24, at 180.
42. See *supra* Chapter 5.
43. See A. Weill et al., *Droit civil, les biens* 433 (3d ed., 1985).
44. See Watson, *supra* note 35.
45. See P. Eltzbacher, *Die Unterlassungsklage* 215 (1906).
46. See Gambaro, *supra* note 39, at 940.
47. See Mattei, *supra* note 29, at 281.
48. See F. Michelman, *Ethics, Economics and the Law of Property*, 24 *Nomos* 3, 5 (1982).
49. See the discussion of money as a "second best" legal protection in Lawson, *supra* note 12, at 173.
50. A. Kronman, *Specific Performance*, 45 *U. Chi. L. Rev.* 351 (1978). From an economic perspective, indeed, every good has a substitute, although occasionally a very poor one.
51. See the different rules stated in Schlesinger et al., *supra* note 2, at 738.
52. See R. Posner, *Economic Analysis of Law* 215 (5th ed., 1998), on the risk of overcompensation that courts must struggle to avoid.
53. See a rather more detailed discussion in U. Mattei, *Comparative Law and Economics* 58 (1997).

CHAPTER 9

Loss of Ownership

In the unfolding of the previous chapters we have encountered many occasions on which concrete decision making about property rights ends up redistributing them. These occasions include when an injunction is denied and the owner is left with a damage remedy, when possession is protected against property, and when a tax makes a proposed use of property uneconomic for the owner. On all these occasions the owner loses some or all of the structural prerogatives of his or her ownership.[1] The concrete meaning of this observation is that in order to keep his or her property, the owner always has to face some costs. There may be monitoring costs to make sure that no one acquires his or her property by adverse possession, or there may be litigation costs or other bargaining costs to face a proposed incompatible use by a neighbor. More simply, these costs might be out-of-pocket expenses to pay a tax liability, or they might be lost opportunities to transfer ownership or other property rights because of the transaction costs imposed by the legal system (e.g., notary fees).[2]

In this chapter I will briefly discuss what can be considered the paradigmatic case of loss of ownership. This loss does not stem from the unwillingness of the owner to face his or her maintenance costs, but from direct intervention of the government over property rights.

THE NATURE OF EXPROPRIATION

Sometimes (and certainly not only in revolutionary periods) a government imposes losses on owners. This, of course, happens every time a government exercises its power to levy taxes. Sometimes, however, the sovereignty of the state over ownership is carried on in practice well beyond the power to impose taxes. This sovereign power, although reaching a maximum level of extension in socialist law, where all private property may be nationalized, is by no means absent in capitalist systems. It is, indeed, one of the most important tools by which the state can perform its duties toward the citizens and consequently legitimize itself. This tool is known with a variety of names: "power of eminent domain," "expropriation in the public utility," or "taking" to mention just a few of the most widely used.

The power of eminent domain is as important as it is dangerous.[3] The Western constitutional experiences, therefore, have worked out a number of techniques to try to limit this power in order to avoid abuses. The power of eminent domain naturally follows from the primacy of politics over law, of force over principles. As a consequence, every limit, in order to be effective, requires a substantial amount of legal ripeness in order to work properly. It requires a strong, independent, and reliable judicial system able to confront the contingent needs of the government. Such conditions are not met in all the Western legal systems today, and even where they are now effectively protecting the individual, they constantly face challenge from governments. Despite this observation, it is often considered crucial for a legal system aiming at economic development to secure property rights in the face of the challenges to them stemming from the government.[4]

To be sure, as we have discussed, a certain amount of security of property rights seems necessary as a framework for the development of a market. Nevertheless, such an observation should not be overemphasized. There are phases or historical circumstances in the legal and institutional development of a society in which flexibility and a certain amount of freedom in reshuffling property rights might themselves be justified from an efficiency perspective, particularly when property is too concentrated. There are examples in the recent history of economic development of major growth outside any such security of property in the face of the government. In Italy, for example, in the last thirty years much insecurity has accompanied property rights in the face of the government as far as legal mechanisms are concerned. Even today, compensation is paid at a fraction of the market value of property and the due process guarantees for the Italian owner are certainly not very strong.[5] The taking of private property from the individual is a crucially political issue, so that not much can be said of principle from the technical point of view. I will nevertheless try to detect some common trends within most advanced economies, and I will try to show some economic reasons behind certain formal guarantees of property rights.

LEGAL AND ECONOMIC PRINCIPLES

Despite its deeply political nature, the legal discipline of expropriation may be seen as the ultimate guarantee of ownership against the state. In modern legal systems, the individual should also be guaranteed against the state, this being one of the most crucial aspects of what we call the rule of law. In other words, the expropriation of property, although inherently political, should not be arbitrary and unprincipled.[6] The law should be in certain ways binding on the government as well as on the individuals. The government should take political responsibility on every occasion on which it decides to tamper with property rights.

The guarantee that the individual owner enjoys against the state might be seen as having a dual nature that makes it structurally similar to the dual set of remedies (property rules and liability rules) that the owner enjoys against another individual. Against the government (or another public authority enjoying the power of eminent domain), the owner will first try to avoid the loss of his or her property right by challenging the whole expropriation or nationalization. If the first full remedy is lost, the owner will at least try to obtain a pecuniary satisfaction for the sacrifice that is imposed on his or her property right. Such pecuniary satisfaction is known as compensation and has the same structural nature of the damage remedy.[7]

The justification and limits of the power of eminent domain and the requisites and amount of compensation—exactly paralleling choice of the remedy to protect property rights that we discussed in the previous chapter—are the fundamental question faced by all modern legal systems.[8] All modern legal systems have organized guarantees for the individual owner against the state along two main directions: the requirement of the public use and the requirement of just compensation. From this general perspective, modern legal systems seem to show a considerable degree of convergence.

In comparative law jargon, a convergence is defined as the phenomenon of similar solutions in different legal systems coming from different points of departure.[9] In France, there is no ex post judicial review of constitutionality.[10] In Germany and Italy, there are special Constitutional Courts.[11] In the United States, any judge may strike down an act or decision as unconstitutional.[12] In the United Kingdom, there is not even a written constitution to apply.[13] Despite these huge divergencies in the relevant institutional background, the law of takings may be considered largely convergent in these systems, as far as the underlying principles are concerned.[14]

The guarantee of private property against the state, theoretically described by the natural law and embodied in the revolutionary Declaration of Human Rights, has been one of the cornerstones of modern political and legal doctrine. From France it has found its way directly to America and Italy, and, more indirectly, to England and Germany.[15] Its content has been clear enough to lay the foundations of a somewhat common law (necessity of public use, compensation). It has been flexible enough to allow historical divergence, particularly as to the amount of compensation, although, in most developed countries, the trend is toward market value.

Legal questions of tremendous importance are faced by any legal system which for the first time has to confront the problem of takings in the light of a guarantee for private property. Is private taking allowed? If not, what are the standards for a public use? Is compensation to be paid? If yes, of what amount? If we examine the problem of takings, there can be no serious doubt that there are strong economic reasons to compensate at market value private property sacrificed for public use. As far as the public-use requirement is concerned, the economic theory of public goods provides both a justification and a limit.[16] The justification is that the government needs to be able to acquire the inputs that are necessary to provide public goods for which the market cannot easily provide. The limit is set by the consideration that any private use of the power of eminent domain will be inefficient, since it produces a result that private parties were not able to reach by bargaining. The forced sale, in other words, would move the property from a higher-valued use to a lower-valued use.

Compensation should be paid for takings to avoid externalities and to foster equality in front of the law. It is irrational to compel a private property owner to pay alone for benefits that are enjoyed by the whole community. Moreover, the costs of government action should be internalized. In a public use of eminent domain, however, it is inefficient to allow the private property owner to force the government to pay the reservation price for his or her property (i.e., the subjective value which he or she could insist on obtaining from a private person) because this would make the government supply of public goods utterly impossible. Every single owner whose property is involved would overestimate the value and, moreover, would have an incentive to be the last person to settle. The efficient outcome is therefore guaranteed by paying the objective market value.

It is not only efficiency which justifies the payment of objective market value for takings in the public interest. The broad principle of equality according to which no single person should bear the complete burden of a course of action whose benefits are common to a large number of people also supports this solution. The one whose property is taken for the public use is already suffering a loss. This loss should be minimized as much as possible by paying a compensation which makes it possible for him or her at least in theory to buy a similar property elsewhere. The amount of this compensation should be paid by the community, which in fact will benefit of the taking according to the old Justinian maxim of justice "*suum cuique tribuere.*"[17]

INFORMAL TAKING AND REGULATION

This brief look at general principles is not sufficient to convey both the complexity and the expansion of takings law in modern legal systems. The crucial issue is how to draw the line between those limitations to the owner's powers that constitute takings and those which do not.[18] As I have already observed, from the point of view of the owner, takings, regulations, and invasions of the private sphere of sovereignty not accompanied by an appropriate remedy are all aspects of a same phenomenon; the difference is only quantitative. They are all limitations on the amount of utility that the owner is able to receive from his or her property right.

Suppose that the value that one owner can get from his shop is 100 if he can keep it open around the clock. Suppose that a municipal regulation is enacted limiting the business hours of shops. Obviously, such a regulation will limit the amount of utility that the owner can receive from his shop. Suppose now that a regulation completely limits certain activities; for example, selling sex toys and other red light appliances in a given sector of the town. Such a regulation also will significantly lower the value of a shop that is engaged in that activity. It would be easy to know objectively the amount of compensation that the owner of such regulated shops should receive in each of the two cases. In the first one, it will be compensated by the prorated decrease of utility from his shop. If he cannot keep it open for 20 percent of the time, then his compensation should be 20. In the second case, he should be compensated with the difference of utility that he would have obtained by selling sex toys and the next best alternative that is open to him, for example, selling blue jeans in the same shop. If he could make 20 percent more with the sex-related activity, this 20 percent is the amount that would compensate him for the loss inflicted by the regulation.

Now, if from the perspective of the owner, takings and regulation have a similar impact, from the perspective of the state, such a similarity is not recognized. Even if a general regulation completely frustrates the economic value of a given property, the law would not compensate it. Everywhere, from Italy to the United States (to mention two systems with radically different attitudes toward private property), if Regina buys a piece of property on the beach in order to develop it and to make a luxury hotel, and then a regulation is passed that prohibits any development of oceanfront property, Regina will not receive any compensation. If a piece of legislation is considered excessively intrusive on property, it might be struck down as unconstitutional, but no compensation is paid. The obvious rationale of this principle is not to impair the regulatory activity of the state by creating the fear of being condemned to compensate the losers.[19]

Therefore, the first problem that is revealed is to distinguish the cases in which we are facing expropriation from those cases in which we are facing regulation. This problem cannot by its nature be solved with the proper wording of a statute or by a code, because there are no technical ways to trace a line whose nature is clearly political. Comparative analysis, however, allows us to detect some common lines of evolution in this attempt. What usually discriminates between regulation and regulatory taking is the general nature of the first and the specific nature of the second. Moreover, whenever private property is physically invaded as a consequence of a regulation, this might be yet another rationale for characterizing the event as taking. Obviously, none of these problems arise when takings are ritually decided and carried on formally. However, the problem is crucial if the legal discourse wishes to capture the substantive nature of the problems and not only their form.

While in the matter of formal takings the paradigmatic experience seems to be the French, in this area some light can be obtained by focusing on two experiences that have faced this problem the most, the American and the German.[20] According to the German Supreme Court, expropriation is a sacrifice that is required not by the generality of individuals but only by a given individual. According to the German Constitutional Court, an expropriation can be distinguished from a regulation because of its regulatory intensity (i.e., the amount of its interference with ownership). On the basis of these principles, it has been considered acceptable to ban the cultivation of grapes because of the lack of individual sacrifice. On the other hand, a regulation forbidding large agrarian owners from dissolving location contracts with their tenants has been considered unconstitutional.[21] In the United States one can find similar broad standards. According to the Americans, there are no problems in considering taking a physical and permanent invasion of property. A statute requiring homeowners to allow cables to pass on their property has been considered taking.[22] American courts also follow an intensity test when there is no physical invasion.[23] On the other hand, certain statutes have not been considered takings because of their general nature, even if they completely annulled the value of certain property.[24]

Even Italian law, although usually possessed by formalism, has shown a tendency in this direction. The Constitutional Court has stated that expropriation does not necessarily require a change in the formal ownership of a piece of property, but it might also be recognized when regulation has a "substantially expropriatory nature." This line of decision developed around the issue of regulations which absolutely ban building in certain areas of towns.[25]

Before moving to briefly discuss the main problems arising from the perspective of the formal requirements of public use and fair compensation, several more observations are necessary on the substantive ground. To begin with, there is a counterprinciple that balances the common idea which considers taking, which requires compensation, the substantial physical invasion of property. This is a remarkably common principle observable only by focusing on the law in action. When an illegitimate physical invasion is carried on by a public authority in the course of a building activity, it is practically impossible for the owner to obtain the removal of the building. Once a public building is built or substantially initiated, it becomes impossible to challenge.[26] While this principle of the "nonremovable nature of a public work" is recognized by the civilian administrative law tradition, it is nevertheless applied also by the Americans.[27] This means, in general, that there is no property rule protection in these cases but only at best a liability rule.

Second, while takings law has substantially developed in the case of expropriation of immovable property, its principles are by no means limited to land law. As a matter of fact, a number of new properties (such as a job) and even of personal rights (such as physical integrity) have been protected, particularly in Germany, by applying takings notions.[28] For example, taking principles have solved the problem of indemnifying victims of diseases following compulsory vaccination programs.[29] These developments are of growing interest with the dematerialization of property rights. As usual in property law, while land law offers the most interesting and sophisticated developments, principles borrowed from it might be applied for approaching different areas and interests analytically as well as normatively.

PUBLIC USE AND DUE PROCESS OF LAW

The notion of public use is the most important guarantee against the unprincipled taking of ownership from the government. It is a typically procedural guarantee (due process of law), in the sense that a project of expropriation that is able to survive a formal scrutiny in which the owner can challenge it is considered of public use. In other words, while the substantive decision of what is of public utility pertains to the government and is typically discretionary, the formal decision making is crucial to guarantee the principled and balanced determination on the side of the government. The moment at which the individual challenges the public utility (trying to avoid the expropriation) and the moment at which he or she tries to obtain as high a compensation as possible are kept separate by most legal systems and the decision on the first is a necessary step before approaching the second.

French law can be considered the prototype of this model. The guarantee of ownership against the government dates back to the aftermath of the Revolution. The language of the Declaration of Human Rights has been codified in Article 545 of the Napoleonic Code and has been incorporated in all of the following constitutions. According to these principles, taking is admitted for the public use in consideration of a fair and previous compensation.[30] Despite the lack of a proper system of constitutional adjudication, French administrative law has always been pretty effective in controlling abuses. Moreover, the French *Cour de Cassation* has gone so far as to consider the "serious impairment of property rights" a good reason to contrast the fundamental principle of its own lack of jurisdiction to control the exercise of administrative discretion.[31] The language of the code allows takings only *"pur cause d' utilité publique,"* and the relationship between administrative judges, ordinary judges, and (in Italy and Germany) constitutional adjudication has been complicated and made the taking process costly and time consuming.

The French expropriation is carried on in three crucial phases. The first phase aims to recognize the public utility of a project. The second phase aims to find out which property rights are involved by such project. The third phase aims to quantify the amount of compensation. While the administrative justice system has jurisdiction for the first two phases, the final phase is the province of the ordinary judge.[32]

Public utility of a project might be declared after an adversary procedure by a number of public authorities. The *Conseil d'Etat* has tried to circumscribe the substantial discretion enjoyed by the government in this domain. Today, public utility not only means the interest of the state but also that of other public bodies and even that of private firms whose activity is considered in the public interest. The decision on public utility as well as the subsequent decision that identifies the object of expropriation may be appealed in front of the *Conseil d'Etat*, the highest administrative court. The final phase ends up with a decision of an ordinary judge who actually transfers the piece of property to the new owner and liquidates the compensation that has to be paid to the previous owner. Against this last decision, the owner can appeal to the *Cour de Cassation*, the highest ordinary court.

Very similar procedures can be found in Italy and in Germany, with the only notable difference of a possible involvement of the Constitutional Court.[33] Occasionally, in a number of systems, the formal procedure has been short-circuited by the procedure of urgency, implicit declarations of public utility, or other devices that undermine the due process guarantee of the owner. The trade-off between a fast and effective determination by the public utility and the guarantees of the owner seems to be inevitable. Both in the civil law and in the common law tradition, it is now recognized by scholars that in this domain there is a substantial amount of arbitrary decision making that formal or formalistic due process attempts to change into principled discretion.

The economic analysis cannot help much from this perspective. Once it is admitted, as happens today everywhere in Western law, that public utility might also support the transfer of a piece of property in favor of another private individual because private activities might carry on the public interest, cost–benefit analysis becomes the only possible recipe. However, there are major problems on normative grounds in applying such an analysis. It is a cornerstone of Western legal thought that an individual right of small economic value also deserves protection against large or very large economic interests. Outside of the jungle's law, no individual interest can be sacrificed by a mere comparison of wealth. This crucial objection to applying cost–benefit analysis in property-rights contexts has been formulated, for example, in the United States, as a reaction to a Supreme Court decision admitting the expropriation of a whole residential neighborhood to offer to General Motors the possibility of building new headquarters.[34] This takings decision followed the threat from this large industrial concern to move its business out of state with consequent social disaster in terms of employment.

Cost–benefit analysis cannot consequently be the only factor to be considered in deciding on the public use. It might, however, be kept present in the exercise of the inevitable amount of discretion that is involved in cases like these. Other principled decision-making devices can be borrowed from the analysis of the choice of remedy that we have discussed previously. For example, if transaction costs are low it might be advisable to be very restrictive in recognizing the public interest, particularly when private activities will benefit from it. If it is really efficient to maintain a certain activity, the private party should be able to purchase on the market the right to perform that activity, rather than resorting to a taking. On the other hand, if transaction costs are high, such as is possible in a case in which a high number of parties are involved, it might be advisable to recognize the public use in a more generous way.

JUST COMPENSATION AND DUE PROCESS OF LAW

Takings, if considered admissible because of public use, should be compensated. But how much compensation should the owner receive? Legal systems use abstract and traditional ideas, dating back to medieval times, such as the notion of just compensation, of fair market value, of fair compensation, and so on.[35]

In the previous pages, I have observed a certain synergy between economic notions and legal principles in this domain. Indeed, the idea conveyed by the notion of just price is that of a price on which the parties would have agreed in a free negotiation between themselves.[36] Since the nature of takings is that of a forced sale of ownership, compensation should correspond to the price at which such a hypothetical sale would have happened. Obviously, this idea is in practice defeated by the unique nature of most kinds of property that might be the object of takings. The dachia in which your great grandfather was born probably has for you a much higher value (the so-called value of affection) than it would cost on the market. Indeed, by definition, the utility that each one of us receives from our home is higher than the market price of the home. Otherwise we would sell it. Our homes would constantly be on the market for sale. Since the market value of a piece of property is given by the meeting of the offer with the acceptance (supply and demand), it is exactly the absence of the consent to sell that makes the notion of fair market value logically impossible. To solve this logical problem and to take care of practical legal needs, we became accustomed to consider as the market price not the value of the particular object of expropriation but the price at which an average buyer and an average seller would agree given the present conditions of the market. Such average sellers and average buyers are assumed to be unwilling to capture the surplus stemming from the knowledge that a very valuable development will take place, thus raising the value of the property. This artificial notion is rendered by economists with the idea of objective market value.[37]

Obviously, even with the limit of the objective market value that does not compensate the value of affection, acquiring immovable property for a project of public utility might be very expensive. Municipalities and other public bodies are usually not very rich. Thus, the link of just compensation to the market value ends up impairing the possibility of developing many public projects that simply become too expensive to be afforded by municipalities.[38] Consequently, although it is true that reducing compensation below the market value creates externalities and might be unfair (to property owners) and inefficient, it is also true that property rights occasionally might be redistributed. This is particularly so when some projects might have the nature of public goods, such as hospitals or schools. Moreover, from a public policy perspective, one should consider that the value of each piece of ownership in a given historical moment and in a given geographical place reflects the long-term development of the society to which everybody, owner and nonowner alike, has contributed. As a consequence, some principled redistribution is not devoid of justification. This seems to confirm, once more, that in this area the problem is political and cannot easily be reduced to formal legal or economic categories.

All we can add at this point is the following. First, the constant redistribution of property rights has itself a cost that is paid by the whole community. Second, in the Western legal tradition the market price is the only parameter principled enough to be used in applying the just compensation idea. Third, political decision making can lower the compensation below market price, but in so doing it should try to maintain a connection with it (e.g., reduced by 20%), otherwise the decision making might become only political with the aforementioned social costs of constant rediscussion of property rights. Fourth, complicated institutional machinery might end up increasing transaction costs (wastes), and by so doing create both unfairness and inefficiency.

Comparative observation of the German, Italian, and American experiences show that the last world in this domain ends up belonging to the constitutional adjudication mechanism, the only mechanism which is sensitive enough to mediate between political needs and principled legal decision making.[39] Interestingly, even in France in the absence of a rigid constitution, the *Conseil d'Etat* and the *Cour de Cassation* exceptionally end up developing, in the area of takings, a constitutional language and a constitutional adjudication approach.

Possibly, the solution to the problem of just compensation is once more not to be taken by working out new substantial concepts. It is to be found in the legal process. An improvement would be to reduce transaction costs due to the complexity of the relationship between different decisional bodies (ministries, administrative courts, ordinary courts, constitutional courts, etc.) by considering that constitutional adjudication anyway ends up having the last word. Some good practical tips might also come from some more details of what should be included in the notion of an objective market value of compensation in the case in which high transaction costs make this solution preferable.[40] Obviously, the notion of what should be compensated to avoid externalities given a certain distribution of property rights does not ban legislators from moving away from it if they are willing and able to take political responsibility for such a decision. Compensation in order to avoid externalities should cover the entirety of the "direct, material and certain" prejudice to the property right. This amount, in order to be fully compensatory (although objectively and not subjectively so), should not be limited to the value of the particular piece of property, but should also cover all prejudicial consequences that can be seen as direct consequence of the taking (fruits, relocation expenses, expenses in improvements not reflected by the market, etc.). In addition, the possible increase in value, due to the public project, of other properties belonging to the same owner should be discounted from the compensation (e.g., the value of a neighboring house that increases because of the building of the park for which the first house was expropriated).

The requisite of materiality shows that the moral aspects (such as reservation price, suffering for relocation, etc.) are not part of the objective market value. These are too speculative to become objective. The requisite that the prejudice should be certain is there to avoid the mere possibility (e.g., the hope that there are minerals in the ground) but not future benefits (e.g., oil in the ground which is certainly there although not yet exploited). A complete internalization should also cover certain accessory sources of prejudice. Some legal systems recognize the indemnity of replacement (money spent to locate a similar property in order to move onto it) or an indemnity for depreciation of other nearby properties in the case in which losing integrity depreciates the part that is not expropriated (e.g., a villa whose attached park is expropriated to build a freeway).[41]

Obviously, the idea of an objective market value should be accompanied by a number of institutional arrangements aimed at avoiding speculation. For example, it is common among legal systems to refuse to indemnify those improvements that have been introduced once the owner could have knowledge of the plan to take his or her property. In the French *Code de l'Expropriation*, as well as in U.S. case law, it is justified by the same rationale of avoiding speculation and corruption. This is evidenced by the requirement that, in order to consider a piece of property as "potentially developed" for the purpose of computing the compensation amount, there should already exist, even if at an embryonic stage, in the land or in the immediate vicinity, necessary infrastructures of development, such as access, electricity, and water. This requirement avoids a rush to fake developments in order to profit from market-value compensation.

NOTES

1. The lack of some incidents in certain legal systems is not incompatible with the existence of "ownership," provided that the right remains the most extensive that that legal system recognizes. According to S. Muntzer, *A Theory of Property* 22 (1990), "Incidents are jointly sufficient though not individually necessary for ownership."

2. See A. Chianale, *L'atto pubblico: contributo allo studio dei costi transattivi* (1993).

3. See, from different political perspectives, two classics in the American literature: F. Michelman, *Property, Utility and Fairness: Comments on the Ethical Foundations of Just Compensation Law*, 80 *Harv. L. Rev.* 1165 (1967); R. Epstein, *Takings: Private Property and the Power of Eminent Domain* (1985).

4. See D. North & R. Thomas, *The Rise of the Western World: A New Economic History* 24 (1973).

5. See A. Gambaro, *Il Diritto di proprietà* 102 (1995).

6. See C. B. Macpherson, *Liberal-Democracy and Property*, in *Property: Mainstream and Critical Positions* (C. B. Macpherson ed., 1978).

7. See J. Coleman & J. Kraus, *Rethinking the Theory of Legal Rights*, 95 *Yale L.J.* 1335 (1986).

8. A convenient collection of data is contained in *Compensation for Expropriation: A Comparative Study* (G. M. Erasmus ed., 1990).

9. For examples in different contexts, see R. Schlesinger et al., *Comparative Law* 390–391, 402–403, 422, 582, 644 (5th ed., 1988). See, generally, C. J. Bennett, *What Is Policy Convergence and What Causes It?* 22 *Brit. J. Pol. Sci.* 215 (1992); C. Kerr, *The Future of Industrial Societies:Convergence or Continuing Diversity?* 3 (1983).

10. Constitutional review is exercised right after the enactment of a statute by a quasi-judicial body called the *Conseil Constitutionel*. Once checked, the statute is unchallengeable as a matter of constitutionality. See *A Source-Book on French Law* 50 (B. Rudden & O. Kahn-Freund eds., 3d ed., 1991); P. Ardant, *Institutions Politiques et Droit Constitutionnel* 130 (2d ed., 1990).

11. For German law, see Article 93, Basic Law; A. T. Von Mehren & J. R. Gordley, *The Civil Law System* 137 (2d ed., 1977). For Italian law, see Article 42 Cost.; M. Cappelletti et al., *The Italian Legal System: An Introduction* (1967).

12. *Marbury v. Madison*, 5 U.S. 137 (1803).

13. A. V. Dicey, *Introduction to the Study of the Law of the Constitution* (8th ed., 1915).

14. For an updated, systematically exposed outline of the law of compensation for expropriation, see *Compensation for Expropriation, supra* note 8.

15. Of the founding fathers, Madison was particulary influenced by French political thought. Until "his" Fifth Amendment, private property was not introduced into the fundamental values of American law. See B. Bailyn, *The Ideological Origins of the American Revolution* 34–93 (1967). Blackstone's scholarship was based on the same natural law literature which was the very cultural asset of the French Revolution. See S.F.C. Milsom, *The Nature of Blackstone's Achievement*, 1 *Oxford J. L. Stud.* 3 (1983). As with all post–World War II constitutions of defeated countries, the German Basic Law is very much influenced by the U.S. Constitution.

16. See, for a discussion, R. Cooter & T. Ulen, *Law and Economics* 191 (2d ed., 1996).

17. According to Michelman, *supra* note 3, the denial of just compensation would have a demoralizing impact on the condemnee. As to the construction of private property as a value in Western society, see P. Stein & J. Shand, *Legal Values in Western Society* 223 (1974).

18. The issue is clearly stated in these terms by B. Ackerman, *Private Property and the Constitution* (1977). See W. A. Fishel, *Regulatory Takings: Law, Economics and Politics* (1995).

19. For different economic rationales, see R. Posner, *Economic Analysis of Law* 64 (5th ed., 1998); L. Blume & D. Rubinfeld, *Compensation for Takings: An Economic Analysis*, 72 *Cal. L. Rev.* 569 (1984).

20. See A. Weill et al., *Droit civil, les biens* 495 (3d ed., 1985). Of course, the most interesting aspect of the French experience has been the law on nationalization. See L. Favoreu, *Les Decisions du Conseil Constitutionelle dans l' affaire des nationalizations, Rev. Droit Publique* 377 (1982).

21. See, for all details, F. Ossenbuhl, *Staatshaftungsrecht* (2d ed., 1978).

22. See *Loretto v. Teleprompter*, 458 U.S. 419 (1982).

23. *Pennsylvania Coal C. v. Mahon*, 26 U.S. 393 (1922).

24. See the classic discussion in J. Sax, *Takings and the Police Power*, 74 *Yale L.J.* 36 (1964); see also the most recent, M. A. Heller & J. E. Krier, *Deterrence and Distribution in the Law of Takings*, 112 *Harv. L.R.* 997 (1999).

25. See D. Sorace, *Gli indennizzi espropriativi nella Costituzione fra tutela dell' affidamento, esigenze risarcitorie e problemi della rendita urbana, Riv. Crit. Dir. Priv.* 405 (1989).

26. See Di Qual, *Le règle "Ouvrage publique mal planté ne se detruit pas,"* 1 *J.C.P.* 1852 (1964).

27. See *Williams v. Parker*, 188 U.S. 491 (1903); *Greatfalls Mfg. Co. v. Attorney General*, 124 U.S. 581 (1888).

28. See C. A. Reich, *The New Property*, 73 *Yale L.J.* 733 (1964).

29. See BGHZ 9, 83; for more decisions on the same principle, see O. Palandt, *BGB Sec 903 Anno* 3b (45th ed., 1986).

30. A special statute, known as "Code de l' expropriation pour cause d' utilité publique," *Décrets* 77–392 and 77–393 of March 28, 1977, J.O. 14–4–1977, contains all the rules of detail. See the annotated edition by R. Hostion (6th ed., 1998).

31. A decision of the French *Cour de Cassation* (January 1, 1975) makes this power clear. See, generally, C. Le Berre, *Les Pouvoirs d' Injunction et d' Astreinte du juge judiciare a l' egard de l' administration, A.J.D.A.* 14 (1979).

32. The process is described in detail in Weill et al., *supra* note 20, at 420.

33. See authorities cited *supra* notes 21 and 25.

34. See *Poletown Neighborhood Council v. City of Detroit*, 304 NW 2d 455 (1981).

35. See Michelman, *supra* note 3. For an historical discussion, see E. E. Meindinger, *The Public Use of Eminent Domain: History and Policy*, 11 *Envtl. L.* 2 (1980). For a survey of recent developments in U.S. law, G. S. Alexander, *Ten Years of Takings*, 46 *J. Leg. Ed.* 568 (1996).

36. See J. Gordley, *Just Price*, in 2 *The New Palgrave: A Dictionary of Economics and the Law* 410 (1998).

37. See Cooter & Ulen, *supra* note 16.

38. See S. Rodotà, Article 42, in *Commentario alla Costituzione* 111 (G. Branca ed., 1982).

39. See M. Cappelletti, *The Judicial Process in Comparative Perspective* (1989).

40. See Posner, *supra* note 19, at 62.

41. For details of various systems, see *Compensation for Expropriation, supra* note 8.

Index

Absolute notion of property, 19, 124, 153
Abuse of right, 149, 150, 155
Accession, 112, 117
Accessory, 90
Administrative law, 17, 31, 41, 61, 130, 151, 155, 171, 172, 175, 199, 200. *See also* Public law
Adverse possession, 66, 107, 114, 115, 116, 133, 184
Aemulatio, 149
Africa, 30, 54, 82, 136
Analytical jurisprudence, 13
A non domino, 106–107
Anticommons, 2, 11, 59
Antiusury laws, 12
Archeological property, 94, 130
Armenia, 81
Astreintes, 171, 181. *See also* Remedies
Austria, 33, 34, 106, 115, 185, 186

Balancing of interests, 18, 157, 163
Bargaining, 6, 54, 66, 135, 138, 158, 161, 165, 193, 196
Battle of Hastings, 13
Belgium, 136
Better title, 181, 183
Black market, 54
Blackstone, Sir William, 14, 20, 77, 162
Buildings, 134–136, 150–151, 179, 188
Bundle of sticks, 18, 20, 33, 124, 148
Burden of proof, 66, 174, 176, 177, 183
Bureaucracy, 43

Central Europe, 44
Chancery, 7, 9, 75, 176, 178, 179
Chose, 13, 75–76
Coase Theorem, 54, 55, 138, 140, 180. *See also* Bargaining
Collective land tenure, 30, 54
Collective versus decentralized decision making, 21, 44, 60–61
Commodification, 32, 53, 93
Common core, 20, 21, 106, 108, 111, 115, 135, 137, 174, 178, 199
Complainte, 174. *See also* Possession
Concession, 129
Condominium, 76, 85
Conseil d'Etat, 200, 203. *See also* Administrative law
Constitutional court, 34, 35, 52, 195, 200. *See also* Judicial review
Contempt of court, 171, 175, 179, 180
Contracts, 8, 9, 13, 14, 38, 57, 78, 104
Convergence, 11, 12, 158, 171, 195

Conversion, 187
Conveyance, 11, 102
Cost–benefit analysis, 201
Cour de Cassation, 200, 203
Coutumes, 183. *See also* Feudalism
Criminal law, 175, 179, 180
Customary law, 5, 107, 127, 130, 165, 183
Czech Republic, 31

Damages, 15, 139, 164, 166, 176, 178, 180, 181, 187. *See also* Liability rules
Declaration of Human Rights, 195–196, 200. *See also* French Revolution
Declaratory remedies, 175, 186
Default rules, 54–55, 126, 165, 180
Development rights, 92, 129, 187, 151–152
Distances, 132–133, 147, 164, 165
Distribution, 29–30
Domesday Books, 167
Dominium, 77–78. *See also* Roman law
Due process of law, 199–204
Duguit, 20, 31, 33, 124

Easement, 137, 139
Eastern Europe, 44
Economic analysis, 51–53
Efficiency, 51–53. *See also* Coase Theorem; Transaction costs
Ejectment, 173, 187
Eminent domain, 42, 194–196. *See also* Expropriation; Takings
Emissions, 153, 154, 157–158. *See also* Nuisance; *Troubles de voisinage*
Enchroachement, 136–137
England, 7, 17, 19, 37, 83, 84, 104, 106, 115, 127, 131, 137, 139, 140, 196
Equity, 7, 75, 178. *See also* Chancery
Escheat, 10, 11
Estate, 9, 10. *See also* Feudalism
Ethology, 5
Expropriation, 164, 172, 194, 195, 198–201. *See also* Eminent domain; Takings

Externalities, 38, 44, 45, 57, 60, 64, 68, 69, 113, 114, 118, 126, 128, 139, 140, 148, 156, 158, 173, 203

Family law, 5, 102
Fee simple, 11
Fee tail, 11
Fencing, 125, 127, 186
Feudalism, 7, 11, 13, 19, 123
First come, first served, 70, 161–162
Fixtures, 84, 112, 117
Formalism, 36
France, 13, 14, 16, 17, 20, 32, 38, 41, 43, 58, 63, 75, 81, 88–90, 104, 106, 108, 110, 115, 117, 118, 123–126, 128–132, 135–141, 158, 160, 164, 173, 174, 179, 180, 182, 183, 185, 188, 195, 196, 198, 200, 203, 204
Freehold, 12. *See also* Feudalism
Free tenure, 10, 12, 83
French Revolution, 14, 15, 16, 123, 134
Fruits, 114, 132–134
Fugitive property, 70

Gaius, 8. *See also* Roman law
Gambaro, 16
Geny, Francois, 15
Germany, 13–15, 17, 18, 20, 32, 34, 38, 41, 58, 75, 85, 86, 89–91, 104–108, 110, 115, 123–125, 128, 129, 131, 132, 134, 135, 137–139, 159, 166, 173, 179, 180, 183, 185, 186, 188, 195, 196, 199, 200, 203
Gewere, 108, 183. *See also* Possession
Gierke, 18, 20
Gift, 101
Good faith, 63, 111–114, 134, 184, 188
Gordley, 79
Gorla, 15

Halter, 89
Hegel, 18
Henry II, 7
Hohfeld, Wesley Newcomb, 18, 20, 124, 148
Holland, 106
Honoré, Professor, 17, 20, 148
Hungary, 1, 2, 31, 79, 105

Immaterial property, 69, 76, 92, 174
Immovables versus movables, 9, 67, 81–82, 124, 167, 174, 183
Improvements, 113, 140
Indemnity, 58, 195, 196. *See also* Liability rules
Indians, 54
Industrial Revolution, 163
Injunction, 7, 62, 171, 176, 178, 179, 181, 186, 189. *See also* Property rules
In personam, 10, 179
Interlocutory orders, 171, 180, 187
Inter vivos, 100, 102
Involuntary transfers, 100, 109, 117
Italy, 14, 20, 32, 34, 43, 58, 63, 75, 81, 86, 89, 90, 104–106, 108, 110, 112, 113, 115, 117, 118, 123, 127–131, 134, 137, 138–140, 160, 162, 164, 173, 174, 179, 180, 183–186, 188, 194–196, 198, 200, 203
Ius aedificandi, 151
Ius cogens, 55
Ius dispositivum, 55. *See also* Default rules

Josserand, 124
Judicial review, 31–32, 34, 35, 42, 52, 195, 200, 203. *See also* Administrative law
Jurisprudence of interestes, 18, 157, 163
Just compensation, 194, 196, 199, 200, 201

Land, 83–84
Land use, 124, 153, 156
Laurent, 136
Law of obligation, 102. *See also* Obligations
Law of Property Act, 9, 10, 12, 37
Lease, 10, 12, 63, 126, 134, 167
Legal pluralism, 5, 6
Legal positivism, 4, 13
Legal process, 21, 44, 61
Liability rules, 89, 150, 165, 173, 187–189, 195, 199. *See also* Damages; Torts
Life estate, 11
Limited property rights, 77. *See also* *Numerus clausus*
Limits, 125, 150, 153–154, 165
Littleton, 12
Lord Keynes, 84
Louis XIV, 17

Madison, James, 141
Manutenzione, 174. *See also* Possession
Marbury v. Madison, 34
Market, as an institution, 3, 14, 31, 38, 45
Market overt rule, 107, 115
Market value, 62, 99, 202, 203, 204
Minerals, 129, 130
Monopoly, 69, 162
Mortgage, 103, 104
Mortis Causa, 100, 101, 106. *See also* Succession
Movable property, 13, 75–76, 87, 106
Movables equated to immovables, 89

Nationalization, 30, 32
Natural law, 4, 5, 13–17, 20, 123, 154
Negatory action, 18, 182, 185, 186, 187, 189
Negligence, 158, 166, 189. *See also* Torts
New properties, 76
Non domino, 106, 107. *See also* Good faith; Possession
Notary, 103, 193
Nuisance, 17, 19, 20, 64, 65, 124, 126, 133, 156, 164, 174, 177, 187, 189
Numerus clausus, 14, 39, 55, 92, 136

Obligations, 9, 13, 78, 166
October Revolution, 30

Pandectist school, 15, 17, 18, 36
Parliements, 17. *See also* Feudalism
Path dependency, 21
Personal rights, 9, 13, 78, 79, 166
Planting rights, 132–134
Pledge, 91
Poland, 106
Police power, 32, 36, 197

Pollution, 60, 64, 163, 172, 177
Positive externalities, 123, 148
Possession, 66–67, 79–80, 107, 108, 109–111, 172, 177, 181, 182, 184
Pound, Roscoe, 18
Principle of specialty, 40
Probatio diabolica, 184. *See also* Burden of proof
Professional knowledge, 6–7, 16, 34, 76
Promissory reliance, 140
Property rules, 62–65, 164, 181–182, 186, 187, 193, 195, 199
Public goods, 59, 93, 159, 196, 202
Public law, 17, 20, 42, 45, 82, 93, 129, 153, 155, 157, 197. *See also* Administrative law
Public use, 139, 140, 195, 196, 197

Quia Emptores, 11. *See also* Estates; Feudalism

Radio frequencies, 154
Real action versus personal action, 9
Real property versus personal property, 8, 13
Real rights versus personal rights, 39, 40
Reasonableness, 125, 132, 147, 150, 160, 161, 163
Redistribution, 37, 40, 61, 66. *See also* Liability rules; Taxes
Registration of title, 67, 68, 105, 183, 184
Regulation, 40, 190, 198. *See also* Public law
Reintegrade, 110, 173. *See also* Possession
Reintegrazione, 110, 173. *See also* Possession
Rei vindicatio, 182–184, 187, 189
Relational idea, 20. *See also* Hohfeld, Wesley Newcomb; Honoré, Professor
Remainder, 11. *See also* Estate
Remedies, 62, 164, 171, 172, 182, 195. *See also* Liability rules; Property rules
Residual claimant, 126
Reversion, 11. *See also* Estate
Revolution. *See* French Revolution; October Revolution
Right to exclude, 14, 80, 127, 134, 166
Right to possess, 183, 184. *See also* *Gewere; Saisine*
Right versus interest, 80, 81
Riparian property rights, 117, 118
Risk, 176, 186, 187
Roman law, 13, 15, 77, 102, 107, 108, 111, 114, 117, 136, 183, 197
Rule against perpetuities, 11, 39
Rule of law, 53, 195
Rules of inalienability, 32, 53
Rules versus standards, 52, 154, 149–150, 156–157
Russia, 31, 105

Saisine, 183. *See also* *Gewere*; Possession
Satellites, 154
Schlesinger, Rudolph, 108
Scialoja, 20
Security of property rights, 65, 116, 194, 203
Servitudes, 77–79, 103, 117, 127, 139, 177, 180, 185, 187. *See also Numerus clausus*
Social function of ownership, 20, 31, 33, 46, 58, 124
Socialist law, 93, 194
Sociological jurisprudence, 18
Sources of law, 29–30
Soviet Union, 59
Spain, 34, 107, 108
Special statutes, 39, 40
Spur v. Del Webb, 162. *See also* First come, first served
Squatter, 109, 110, 176. *See also* Possession
Stare decisis, 66
Stocks, 167
Subjective right, 17, 18, 150
Subrogation, 179–180
Subsoil, 128–129
Succession, 3, 11, 101, 112

Superficiary rights, 136
Switzerland, 157, 159

Takings, 15, 36, 42, 109, 139, 194–202. *See also* Eminent domain; Expropriation
Taxes, 104, 126, 163, 166, 193, 194
Taxonomy, 75–76
Title insurance, 103
Torts, 9, 16, 18, 38, 57, 148, 155, 156, 157, 158, 173, 174, 188, 189
Tragedy of the commons, 1, 2, 11, 58, 59, 70
Transaction costs, 46, 56, 57, 64, 88, 91, 138, 187, 201, 203. *See also* Coase Theorem; Efficiency
Transfer of ownership, 99, 100
Treasure trove, 161, 129, 130
Trees, 133
Trespass, 6, 69, 133, 139, 158, 173, 180, 185, 187
Troubles de voisinage, 17, 33, 155. *See also* Nuisance
Trusts, 8, 10, 12, 14, 92, 102
Turkey, 106

Unfree tenure, 12. *See also* Feudalism
Uniform Commercial Code, 108
Unique goods, 71, 187, 188, 202
Unitary Judiciary, 45
United Kingdom, 130, 195. *See also* England
United States, 20, 32, 70, 89, 94, 108, 124, 129, 130, 131, 140, 141, 158, 171, 195, 196, 198, 199, 201, 203, 204
Use of property, 99
Usuacapio, 107, 114. *See also* Adverse possession
Usufruct, 77, 78, 82, 134

Vehicles, 88–89, 166
Voluntary transfers, 100–105
Von Jehring, Rudolph, 18, 157
Von Savigny, Friedrich Karl, 18

Wall, 179, 188
Water rights, 130–132
Writ system, 8, 9

Zoning, 36, 56, 92, 157, 158

ABOUT THE AUTHOR

Ugo Mattei is Alfred and Hanna Fromm Professor of Law and Economics at the University of California, Hastings, and Professore Ordinario in Turin, Italy. He teaches Civil Law, Comparative Law, and Law and Economics. His English language publications include many articles and one book, *Comparative Law and Economics* (1997).

Lightning Source UK Ltd.
Milton Keynes UK
UKHW022029170920
370034UK00003B/100